High-Energy Dogs

A Practical Guide to
Living With Energetic
and Driven Canines

Tracy Libby

High-Energy Dogs

Project Team
Editor: Heather Russell-Revesz
Copy Editor: Stephanie Fornino
Indexer: Dianne L. Schneider
Design: Mary Ann Kahn

T.F.H. Publications
President/CEO: Glen S. Axelrod
Executive Vice President: Mark E. Johnson
Publisher: Christopher T. Reggio
Production Manager: Kathy Bontz

T.F.H. Publications, Inc.
One TFH Plaza
Third and Union Avenues
Neptune City, NJ 07753

Printed and bound in China
09 10 11 12 13 1 3 5 7 9 8 6 4 2

Library of Congress Cataloging-in-Publication Data
Libby, Tracy, 1958-
    High-energy dogs : a practical guide to living with energetic and driven canines / Tracy Libby.
        p. cm.
    Includes index.
    ISBN 978-0-7938-0670-6 (alk. paper)
    1. Dogs--Behavior. 2. Dogs--Training. I. Title.
    SF433.L53 2009
    636.7--dc22
                                2009005221

This book has been published with the intent to provide accurate and authoritative information in regard to the subject matter within. While every reasonable precaution has been taken in preparation of this book, the author and publisher expressly disclaim responsibility for any errors, omissions, or adverse effects arising from the use or application of the information contained herein. The techniques and suggestions are used at the reader's discretion and are not to be considered a substitute for veterinary care. If you suspect a medical problem consult your veterinarian.

The Leader in Responsible Animal Care for Over 50 Years!®
www.tfh.com

Contents

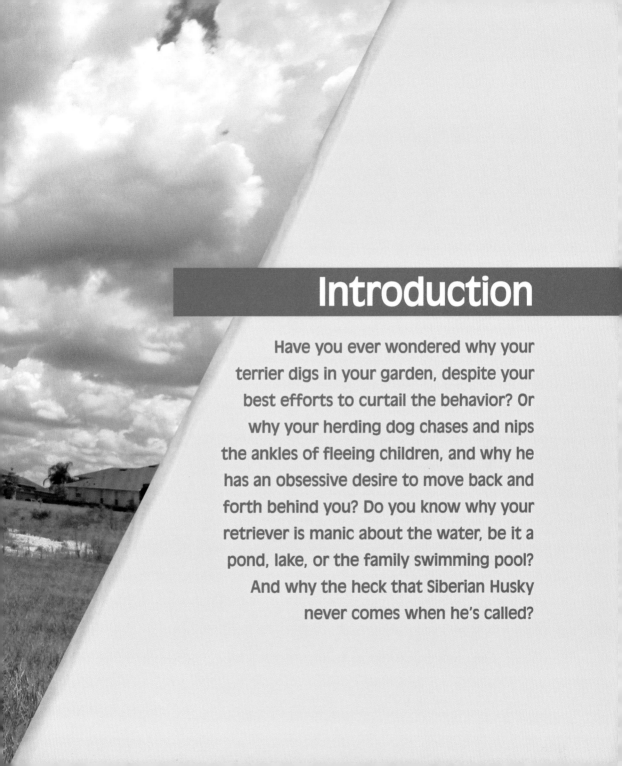

Introduction

Have you ever wondered why your terrier digs in your garden, despite your best efforts to curtail the behavior? Or why your herding dog chases and nips the ankles of fleeing children, and why he has an obsessive desire to move back and forth behind you? Do you know why your retriever is manic about the water, be it a pond, lake, or the family swimming pool? And why the heck that Siberian Husky never comes when he's called?

Would it surprise you to know that these behaviors are normal canine behaviors? Well, it's true. These "normal" behaviors are actually part and parcel of your dog's heritage. They have been bred into a breed for a specific reason and for hundreds of years and are one of the primary reasons that many people have trouble training and living with their dogs. Terriers, for example, were originally bred for ratting out vermin from underground dens, as well as unearthing other animals like foxes and badgers. The instinct to dig is in their genes. It matters not one iota to a terrier that he's digging under your prized flower bed.

The full-time jobs for which dogs were originally bred, be they hunting, herding, retrieving, or guarding, require enormous amounts of energy, drive, stamina, courage, tenacity, and intelligence. The qualities that make them superior working dogs are the very qualities that can make them unsuitable as urban pets. In the absence of adequate physical and mental stimulation, high-octane dogs can quickly become bored and destructive, driving owners to the brink of insanity.

Sadly, behavior and training problems are some of the primary reasons most adolescent dogs between 9 and 18 months of age are relegated to the backyard, given away, or surrendered to the animal shelter. Each year, millions of dogs are destroyed for behavioral problems. That's a sobering fact. These dogs are not inherently bad. They were not born bad puppies. For the most part, problems arise because well-intended owners fail to recognize, understand, and subsequently meet the unique training and energy requirements of high-drive, high-energy dogs. A terrier's fanatical

Why does this terrier love to dig?

behavior of digging in the garden or a Border Collie's obsessive behavior of nipping the legs of fleeing children is not abnormal—these are perfectly normal behaviors for dogs. That said, just because it's normal doesn't mean that it's acceptable. However, by realizing that the behavior is normal canine behavior, you can begin solving the problem by understanding the root cause.

The author and her high-drive Australian Shepherd at an obedience trial.

Apologies not Necessary

The good news is that making apologies for your dog can be a thing of the past. You also can stop thinking "My dog is too difficult to train!"—or too stubborn or too willful or too hyper or too anything. Indeed, the road ahead is bumpy and challenging. Your intestinal fortitude and sanity, not to mention your pocketbook, will occasionally be strained to the breaking point.

But no one said raising and training a dog—especially a turbo-charged dog—was all play and no work.

Once you have a better understanding of why dogs do what they do and how to maximize their drive and energy to your advantage, you can channel all that gusto into productive behaviors and activities, which will make life for you and your dog much easier and more rewarding. Once you learn to see things through the eyes of your dog, which is the key to solving—or better yet, preventing—behavioral problems, you'll be able to let go of the preconceived notion that he is untrainable or too stubborn, or worse yet, misbehaving out of spite.

With a bit of guidance, a dose of common sense, and an unwavering commitment, living harmoniously with a high-octane dog is well within the capabilities of most dog owners. Of course, to do so you will need plenty of energy to keep up with your high-energy dog. If you are a couch potato, life will be miserable for both of you because his triple A-type personality will want to play while you want to nap. An endless reserve of patience, as well as a spirit for adventure and the ability to view problems with a sense of humor, are paramount because living with a turbo-charged dog is a journey that is guaranteed to be simultaneously exhausting and exasperating. A basic understanding of why dogs do what they do, and most importantly, a strong human–canine relationship that is built on a foundation of mutual trust, respect, and love, will help you navigate the delightful but often chaotic world of living with a high-drive, high-energy dog.

Part I

Understanding Your
High-Energy Dog

Chapter 1

The Genetic Lottery: A Blueprint for Your High-Energy Dog

Dogs have been around for thousands of years as hunters, herders, guardians, and trackers. They were even used in military campaigns, including in 2100 BCE, when Hammurabi, the king of Babylon, equipped his warriors with huge dogs. Since domestication, a dog's task or purpose has always been emphasized—protective guardian, fast hunter, agile tracker, fearless fighter, dependable drover, scrupulous herder, and comforting companion.

Long before dogs became pampered pets, early breeders—primarily farmers, ranchers, and hunters—selectively bred dogs based on working ability and physical and mental soundness, rather than the dogs' physical appearance and uniformity, which are more modern-day requirements. Their livelihood and survival depended upon producing dogs who could perform a specific job. A dog used for hunting fast rabbits and gazelles, for instance, required a certain body size for speed, long legs, and a deep chest. Good scenting ability was a prerequisite for tracking dogs who hunted in heavily forested regions. Guarding and fighting dogs needed to be strong, brave, and aggressive, with imposing body structures and powerful jaws to instill intimidation and fear. Retrievers needed a soft mouth to fetch a downed bird without putting a mark on it. Herding dogs had to be powerful enough to move a stubborn bull or cantankerous ewe across a creek bed, fast enough to chase down a 1,000-pound (454-kg) running bull and make him turn the other way, and be physically and mentally capable of doing it all day long.

As a result, farmers and ranchers selected breeding stock based on a dog's most favorable or desirable traits, including instinct, physical agility, stamina, trainability, physical attributes of size and strength, temperament, and so forth. By doing so, the genetic factors responsible for these desired traits tended to become "fixed," or concentrated in succeeding generations—meaning that certain traits could be reproduced with some uniformity. Simply put, good working dogs were bred to other good working dogs, and many of their puppies were found to have good working instincts, too. These dogs were put to the test

Dogs were bred based on certain desirable traits, such as size, strength, and temperament.

Genotype and Phenotype

How a gene is expressed makes up a dog's genotype and phenotype. Genotype is the actual genetic construction or identity of a dog—the type of genes that an individual dog carries but does not show as outward characteristics. Phenotype is the observable or visual expression of the genes—what you actually see, such as a dog's size, eye and coat color, or coat length. These traits can also be influenced by environmental and developmental factors. For example, a Labrador Retriever's size as an adult dog is determined by his genes, but poor health, disease, or an inadequate diet during the formative puppy stage can influence his size.

in a working environment, and the dogs who could not survive the work demands were eliminated from the gene pool. The process (which is slightly more complicated then we have time for here) helped ensure breeders that only the best workers were being bred, thereby increasing their odds of producing puppies with strong traits specific to their purpose or task. After all, what would be the point of a hunter breeding a bird dog who did not flush or retrieve? What good would a retriever be who mangled a downed bird? How useful to the rancher would a herding dog be who did not herd? What about a terrier who couldn't go to ground or a sled dog who wasn't fast and efficient in a harness? Equally inefficient would be a dog with excellent instincts but no get-up-and-go to work long hours through all weather conditions.

The Bare Bones of Genetics

You may think that a dog is a dog is a dog. But in fact, different breeds have different behavioral tendencies. And even within breeds, dogs are individuals, with some puppies from the same litter being as different as night and day. Golden Retriever puppies, for instance, may look identical, but they possess a high degree of variability, meaning that they will possess different temperaments, personalities, and varying degrees of instincts.

How is this possible? The traits a puppy inherits depend upon the gene combinations he inherits from his ancestors, primarily from his parents.

Genetics is too complex and arcane to go into here, and while a number of excellent and comprehensive books devoted entirely to the intricacies of canine genetics are available, that is not the purpose of this book. That said, a few basic points are worth mentioning, because the more you understand about your dog's history, origin, and original function, the easier it will be for you to understand his quirks and idiosyncrasies and why he does what he does.

Genetics in a Nutshell

Genetics is the study of inheritance, with the gene being the basic unit of hereditary expression. Dogs have somewhere around 19,300 genes that are located on chromosomes, which are thread-like molecules of deoxyribonucleic acid (DNA) located in the nucleus of cells. DNA passes along a databank of information from one generation to another, which is stored and replicated in the genes.

Dogs have 78 chromosomes that occur in 39 pairs—38 pairs of autosomal chromosomes (nonsex chromosomes) and 1 pair of sex chromosomes, which determine whether a dog is male or female. Half of each chromosome pair comes from the sire (male parent) and the other from the dam (female parent), with each chromosome having its own content of genes that belong to it and remain with it.

A dog's complete genetic makeup is determined when the sperm of the male parent fertilizes the egg of the female parent. The dog's genetic DNA is inherited equally from each parent (except in cases involving sex linkage and extra chromosomal inheritance, which are topics for an entirely different book). By inheriting 50 percent of his genes from each parent, the dog also inherits genetic information passed on from each parent's ancestors, primarily his grandparents and great grandparents.

Breeders of bird dogs usually select for retrieving instincts, endurance, and intelligence.

It is the intermingling and coupling of the genes from both parents that control hereditary characteristics by encoding a set of instructions as to what the genes are to build, such as size, coat color and length, eye color, metabolic function, the occurrence of genetic disease, temperament, and so forth.

Basic laws of genetics control the inheritance of most, if not all, canine characteristics. The traits a dog inherits, such as retrieving, herding, or guarding instinct; aggression; dominance; independence; tractability; speed; and so forth depend on the trait's mode of inheritance.

Dominant or Recessive

In the simplest form of genetic expression, genes are expressed as either *dominant* or *recessive*. If a gene for a specific trait is dominant, a puppy need inherit only one copy of the gene to express the trait because a dominant gene will be expressed regardless of whether or not it is paired with a recessive gene. For example, the trait of being easily stimulated to bark appears to be dominant and shows an inheritance pattern similar to that of a single gene trait. Therefore, a Cocker Spaniel, a breed noted for barking, would need to inherit only one copy of the gene to inherit the easily stimulated-to-bark trait.

For a recessive trait to show up, a puppy must inherit two copies of the gene—one copy from each parent. For example, studies suggest that "eye"—the style of concentration or the intense gaze that gives a herding dog the power to control and move livestock— might be recessive in its mode of inheritance. This means that a puppy would need to inherit two copies of the eye gene—one from each parent—to possess the trait.

Traits can also be inherited in varying degrees. If, for instance, both parents are strong-eyed dogs, meaning that they both possess strong characteristics associated with eye, chances are good that some, if not most, of the puppies are likely to inherit strong-eye traits as well. However, despite all of our technology, genetics is a game of chance, and some puppies may inherit a medium amount of eye or very little to zero eye.

Unfortunately, not every trait is determined by genes that follow strict dominant–recessive relationships. The mode of inheritance for many characteristics or traits, such as a working retriever diving into icy water and bringing a downed bird to hand, is not yet known. Most likely these traits are genetically determined by multiple factors, with most traits being a result of the action of many genes at many locations on the chromosomes.

Selecting Traits

The traits a breeder selects for depends on her goals. A rancher will most likely select for strong herding instinct, style, power, intelligence, stamina, endurance, speed, and agility. Bird dog breeders generally select for flushing or retrieving instincts, soft mouth, intelligence, endurance, and low aggression tendencies. Terrier breeders customarily select for behavioral traits that include courage, fortitude, tenacity, intelligence, and high-spiritedness.

What's Your Personality Type?

Dog owners should scrutinize their own personality to determine whether a high- or low-drive dog best suits them. If you are a couch potato, you will not have the energy or inclination to keep up with a high-drive Border Collie, Australian Shepherd, Labrador Retriever, Nova Scotia Duck Tolling Retriever, or similar turbo-charged breeds. If you prefer calm and quiet to blast mode, perhaps a slower-paced dog, say, a Saint Bernard or Bulldog, is better suited to your personality.

Depending on where and from whom you acquired your dog, he may possess one or more of these traits in varying degrees. A Border Collie straight off a working ranch, for example, will probably be too intense and energetic for all but the most experienced dog owner. A Belgian Malinois bred for police work may have too much drive to live happily as a companion pet. A Miniature Schnauzer's intense attitude is not for everyone, as he is a lot of dog in a little package.

Once you understand your breed's history, origin, and the function for which it was originally bred, you will have a better understanding of what traits and behaviors your dog is likely to possess. Then you are better equipped to develop a training program that manages these behaviors by working within the confines of your dog's breed.

What's Driving Your Dog?

In the simplest of terms, *drives* are built-in instincts or impulses that make animals (and humans) seek the core necessities of life, such as food, sex, and social interaction. Dogs have all sorts of drives, such as hunting, retrieving, and guarding, to name a few. However, prey, pack, and defense are three primary drives. These are broad concepts

Sighthounds, like this Greyhound, have a strong prey drive, causing them to take off and chase after small animals.

that describe a dog's behavior, but the brain circuits that control these drives are quite specific and complex.

The intensity of these drives contributes to a dog's individual temperament and personality. Understanding or at least recognizing them can help you determine why your dog does what he does, as well as develop the best training techniques and methods for him.

Prey Drive

Prey drive includes the inherited behaviors associated with hunting and foraging behaviors, such as stalking, chasing, grasping, and defeating, subduing, or killing food-related items.

How Prey Drive Affects Your Dog

For the most part, domesticated dogs no longer rely on hunting for their food, so their prey drive normally shows up in the form of chasing anything that moves, stalking cats or other animals, shaking toys, pouncing on toys or other animals, scenting and tracking, shredding, biting, and high-pitched barking. All of these behaviors are usually activated by motion, sound, and smell.

For instance, a Border Collie who stares intently at sheep, herds the vacuum cleaner, or nips and chases fleeing kids is displaying the qualities of an inherited prey drive. When a working retriever enthusiastically dives into icy water and brings a downed bird to hand or a terrier goes to ground, he is utilizing his prey drive. Dogs can have varying degrees of prey drive— from low to very high and anything in between. However, as previously mentioned, working dogs tend to have tons of prey drive, more so than, say, a Japanese Chin, whose primary job was to warm the laps of the Chinese aristocracy.

Pack Drive

Pack drive is a dog's desire for social contact or interaction—being part of a group or pack, be it humans or other dogs or animals. Dogs are pack animals, and dogs who continually seek social contact or group interaction are said to be highly pack driven.

Dogs Are Individuals

While it's tempting to apply generalizations to breeds, it is essential to remember that dogs are first and foremost individuals. Any number of Australian Shepherds and Border Collies, for example, enjoy being with their owners but don't necessarily enjoy cuddling. And while many sighthounds are considered aloof, the Pharaoh Hound is an exception. This breed tends to be more demonstrative than most sighthounds and seeks out human attention.

How Pack Drive Affects Your Dog

These dogs usually want to be with their owner, interacting with the family, and they enjoy being petted and groomed. Most Australian Shepherds, Border Collies, and German Shepherd Dogs, for instance, fall into this category, as do many tough Australian Cattle Dogs and tiny Pomeranians. Many scenthounds who are used to hunt in packs, such as Foxhounds and Harriers, have a strong pack instinct.

Some dogs are more independent and have little need or desire to be part of a team or pack. Basenjis, Siberian Huskies, and Chow Chows have a lot of drive and energy, but they are also bred to be aloof and independent, meaning that they are bred to work on their own—independent of their owners. Salukis tend to be aloof, like many sighthound breeds, and require diligent socialization. Terriers also are bred to be independent and are therefore not always willing or happy do what you want—including cuddling or standing on a grooming table. Although these dogs still make wonderful pets, they can be more challenging in terms of training.

Defense Drive

Defense drive—also known as the *fight or flight mode*—is a survival and self-preservation behavior. The fight mode reflects a dog's self-confidence in stressful situations. Dogs with a strong fight drive tend to stand their ground. Their hackles may go up. They usually stand tall and stare at other dogs. They may posture, such as putting their head or front feet over the shoulders of another dog. They may not start a fight, but they tend not to back down either.

Flight drive is also a defensive mode. The common behavior for wild dogs is to flee unless forced to defend themselves. How close a dog allows you to get to him before he moves away is called the *flight zone*. The more fearful the dog, the larger the flight zone surrounding him tends to be. These dogs tend to be less sure of themselves and will likely flee rather than stand their ground. When cornered, though, they may bite, as will almost any dog who is severely stressed.

How Defense Drives Affect Your Dog

Agonistic behavior, according to John Paul Scott and John L. Fuller, authors of *Genetics and the Social Behavior of the Dog*, "is reduced to a relationship of dominance and subordination." It stands to reason that dogs with a strong fight drive tend to be dominant. Yet dominant dogs can also be quite sensitive. They require a strong owner who is dog savvy and firm but fair. Any number of turbo-charged breeds, including German Shepherd Dogs, Rottweilers, Belgian Sheepdogs, Labrador Retrievers, Border Collies, and American Pit Bull Terriers fit into this category. That said, a dominant dog is not automatically going to fit the "devil's profile." Not all dominant dogs are brawlers. In fact, many dominant dogs do not use aggression to get what they want. Just as some confident people don't feel the need to threaten or intimidate others, some confident or dominant dogs don't always need aggression to get what they want.

High-flight-drive dogs tend to be submissive and may lack self-confidence. They can also become fear biters if not properly trained. They tend to have soft temperaments and frequently lack confidence in stressful situations. They can make wonderful pets, but they require a very gentle touch in terms of training and discipline. They are also more likely to become a "one-person dog." Any number of breeds can fit into this category. You can find some of the toughest breeds—Australian Cattle Dogs, German Shepherd Dogs, and American Pit Bull Terriers—who are soft (or sensitive) in temperament. In most breeds you will find temperaments ranging from sensitive to dominant to middle-of-the-road.

Again, while it is tempting to lump or generalize specific breeds into categories, it is worth noting that many times a dog's temperament can be attributed to owner ignorance, lack of socialization, or poor environmental conditions during the formative socialization period. For example, a dog who lacked adequate or proper socialization may lack self-confidence. He may be shy, sensitive, fearful, and so forth. Whether or not he would have been that way had he been reared properly is the question.

These types of defensive drives and behaviors show up relatively early in a puppy's life. Unfortunately, some owners and a lot of breeders do not recognize these behaviors for what they are. As a result, high-drive or high-energy dogs with dominant or independent personalities frequently end up in the hands of novice owners who lack the qualifications to

Dog Groups

The American Kennel Club (AKC) divides its recognized dogs into seven groups, based on their heritage and working traits:

1. Herding
2. Hound
3. Non-Sporting
4. Sporting
5. Terrier
6. Toy
7. Working

Some Border Collies live to work and think of nothing else.

be strong leaders. Then it is only a matter of time before all heck breaks loose.

Mislabeling Leads to Problems

Unable to decode a puppy's behavior and body language as dominant, submissive, fearful, independent, high drive, or high energy, these natural behaviors get labeled as disobedient or unmanageable. Worse yet, the dog is labeled as bad, stupid, willful, spiteful, untrainable, stubborn, and so forth, which could not be further from the truth.

High Drive, High Energy, or Hyperactive?

Problems often surface for owners of high-drive, high-energy, and hyperactive dogs. (Note: Some animal behaviorists dislike the term *hyperactive*, but for the sake of simplicity, that is the term used for this book.) Although the terms *high drive* and *high energy* are frequently used interchangeably, there is a difference, although both appear to be genetically determined by multiple and complex factors. What are the differences between these dogs, and how can you tell if your dog is one of them?

High Drive

High drive is sometimes referred to as a drive to perform. Most high-drive dogs are imbued with a strong work ethic that is part of their genetic makeup, part of their soul. Some Border Collies, for example, think of nothing else but working. Their work is their sole purpose in life. As long as there is work to be done, they will continue at it until they drop. Genetically driven to herd or retrieve or flush or go to ground, high-drive dogs can do their job for hours on end, which of course requires a tremendous amount of energy. As a result, most but not all high-drive dogs are also high-energy dogs. Yet these dogs can relax (or appear to relax) when energy outbursts are inappropriate. In other words, when they are not working, they are able to lie down until given another job to do. They are not zooming around uncontrollably, getting into trouble.

Is My Dog High Drive?

You may have a high-drive dog if he:

- Was bred to do a specific job that requires a lot of stamina, such as herding, retrieving, going to ground, and so forth.

It Looks Easy on TV

Who can resist a Hollywood canine, be it Lassie, Rin Tin Tin, or Fly (the adorable Border Collie in *Babe*)? From Corgis to Dalmatians to an assortment of lovable terriers, dogs on the big and little screen have charmed us for decades with their shenanigans and irresistible good looks. While those cinematic canine high jinks always end happily in the movies, real life isn't so fortunate for the breeds that are propelled into the national spotlight. It's inevitable that a breed's popularity will increase after a hit movie or television show. After all, look how cute and funny they are, and they're so well behaved! But if you have a high-drive, high-energy dog, you know that living with a Jack Russell Terrier is nothing like living with *Frasier's* Eddie. Hundreds—if not thousands—of hours go into training these high-octane dogs to sit, stay, come, roll over, swim, jump, and bark (and stop barking!) on command. Absent adequate and sufficient training, living with these breeds is a nightmare. Poor or nonexistent training is also the primary reason why dogs are abandoned, surrendered, and euthanized daily.

Studies indicate that the top behavioral reasons that dogs are surrendered to an animal shelter include:

- are aggressive toward people and/or other animals
- chase animals and/or cars
- too active
- need too much attention
- vocalize too much
- escape
- are disobedient
- are destructive inside and outside the house
- jump on people

Interestingly, these "problems" are all normal high-drive, high-energy canine characteristics. And what breeds are popular in the movies and on television? You got it—high-drive, high-energy breeds. The majority of these dogs are relinquished between one and two years of age. That said, owning a blast-mode dog need not be a nightmare—and you don't even need Dr. Dolittle on speed dial. These animals make amazing companions when you understand their history, origin, and the reason for which they were originally bred. You can then temper your training based on those requirements. Of course, you'll need to spend hundreds—if not thousands—of hours training them, but think of the rewards!

- Has a pedigree that includes parents and grandparents from strong working lines.
- Has an infectious enthusiasm for everything, such as tugging, fetching, running, and so forth.
- Is wild, highly frantic, or loses control in dog obedience class—or anywhere in public—during recall or retrieve-type games or while other dogs are playing.
- Is consumed with a particular task, such as retrieving or herding or running for hours on end.
- Engages in blood-curdling or feral-type screams (a cross between barking and crying) when other dogs are running or playing nearby. You may have seen this behavior with dogs at the park or while watching dogs compete in agility.
- Acts as if he is possessed by the devil himself when he sees his favorite toy or other dogs playing.
- Dives back and forth at the end of his leash trying to reach his favorite toy, get to his favorite agility equipment, the swimming pool, and so forth.
- Is more interested in working than food rewards.
- Is frequently referred to as off the wall, over the top, a raving lunatic, or a squealing out-of-control maniac.

It's worth mentioning that while these characteristics are commonplace in many high-prey drive dogs, they can also be common behaviors in untrained dogs. Reading your dog's body language and understanding his history, origin, and original job function will help you decipher between high drive and downright unruly.

A Dalmatian can be just as high energy as a dog from the herding group.

High Energy

A dog's energy level is affected by both internal and external factors. High-energy dogs have the staying power to work all day long, but they may or may not have any natural instinct or drive to perform a specific behavior, such as herding or retrieving. For example, an Australian Shepherd may have tons of energy and want to go, go, go all day long, but he may have little or no herding instinct.

Some high-energy dogs can quickly reach their threshold—that fine line between energetic and overexcited or overstimulated—to the point of being out of control. When high-energy dogs become too pumped up, they cannot think clearly or perform as well. Perhaps you've observed this in your own dog when you're playing a game of fetch or walking him through the neighborhood.

When considering drive and energy, it helps to think in terms of genetics. For instance, consider a litter of puppies where one puppy has a very high drive to perform, while a littermate has a low drive to perform yet a very high energy level. The puppy with the low drive and high energy will most likely grow into an adult dog who wants to do a lot of things—retrieve a ball, catch a Frisbee, jog with his owner, and so forth—but he isn't necessarily driven to perform the particular task for which he was bred. But the high-drive puppy will be genetically compelled to perform that task—his whole life will revolve around it, in fact.

Although any dog can have high-energy-type characteristics, the majority of dogs with seemingly nonstop reserves of energy tend to come from the herding, sporting, hound, and terrier groups. That is not to say that a Dalmatian from the non-sporting group or a Siberian Husky from the working group is not high energy, as he most certainly can be. Similarly, not all hounds or herding dogs will have boundless energy. However, dogs bred for specific tasks tend to be the dogs who are full of energy all of the time.

High-Energy Breeds on the Rise

Dogs who require a high level of activity (lots of physical and mental exercise) make up nearly 50 percent of the American Kennel Club (AKC) registry today versus 35 percent in 1915. Low-activity breeds make up only 7 percent of the AKC registry.

Is My Dog High Energy?

You may have a high-energy dog if he:
- Comes from strong working lines that were bred to do a specific job, such as herding, retrieving, going to ground, guarding, and so forth.
- Is always raring to go, be it working or playing.
- Is constantly up for any activity that involves movement, be it running, playing, tugging, retrieving, swimming, and so forth.
- Requires two or more hours of physical exercise daily to take the edge off but could easily continue for several more hours.
- Is easily overstimulated to the point of losing control.

Many of the characteristics that define high-drive dogs also define high-energy dogs. The primary difference is that high-energy dogs may or may not be genetically compelled to perform a specific task, such as herding, retrieving, guarding, and so forth.

Hyperactive dogs have trouble focusing.

Hyperactive

High energy and *hyperactive* are closely associated and frequently used interchangeably, but they are quite different. Hyperactive dogs seem to have no "off" switch. They tend to zoom around all day long but can rarely focus on a specific task for more than a minute or two. They have tireless energy but no focus. They are so "busy" that they cannot control themselves under any circumstances. These busy dogs are constantly in motion and seldom relax. They often run mindlessly, pace continually, appear restless, and pant frequently. While small-breed dogs tend to come to mind, it's important to remember that—just like high-energy and high-drive dogs—hyperactive dogs can come in all shapes, sizes, and breeds, too.

High-drive or high-energy dogs who are not given enough physical or mental stimulation to burn off their enormous energy reserves are frequently and incorrectly labeled as hyperactive or busy. Interestingly, most pet owners consider the activity level of working dogs to be extremely high. In reality, the energy level for, say, a Border Collie, German Shorthaired Pointer, or Labrador Retriever is well within normal activity levels for those breeds.

Is My Dog Hyperactive?

Your dog may be hyperactive if he:

• Is busy all day long, meaning that he is always on the go or in constant motion—walking, pacing, running, circling, and so forth.

- Has difficulty focusing on any one task, such as retrieving, sitting or quietly lying down at your feet.
- Runs mindlessly, paces continually, appears restless, or pants frequently.

21st-Century Dogs

So what does all of this have to do with your 21st-century urban dog?

The majority of today's retrievers, hounds, terriers, and herding dogs—those breeds that typically fall into the high-drive, high-energy category and now live as companion pets—descended from strong working ancestry. Many of today's breeds retain levels of the inherent characteristics and drives for which they were originally bred, and therein lies an enormous problem: Most of today's working breeds no longer have full-time jobs. Taking the sheepdog off the farm, the retriever from the side of his hunting companion, and the terrier out of a vermin hunting environment does not squelch their desire to work. Moving working dogs from the fields to the suburbs does not eradicate their need for daily physical and mental exercise—quite the opposite, in fact. In the absence of adequate physical and mental stimulation, dogs will come up with all sorts of creative and destructive ways to vent their excess energy. Almost all of these behaviors will be counterproductive to living in a domesticated society, such as chewing, digging, chronic barking, escaping, fighting, and a whole host of obsessive-compulsive behaviors.

Understanding your dog's origin will help you channel his natural instincts.

The majority of canine-related problems—or at least those behaviors that are problematic to owners—can be solved, or better yet prevented, by providing a dog with appropriate and adequate amounts of mental and physical stimulation.

Understanding your dog's history and origin and the purpose for which he was originally bred will help you channel his natural instincts into productive behaviors while simultaneously discouraging unwanted behaviors.

Characteristics of 13 High-Drive, High-Energy Breeds

All dogs have individual personalities and characteristics that are formed at birth and influenced during subsequent weeks and months. While your dog may display some, none, or varying degrees of these characteristics, it is important to remember that these profiles are simply a guideline, and each dog should be taken on his individual merit.

Breed	Originally Bred for	Characteristics	Trainability	Activity Level
American Staffordshire Terrier	Bull-baiting	Powerful Courageous Loyal	Average	High
Australian Shepherd	Herding	Agile Versatile Reserved w/ strangers	High	High to Very High
Australian Cattle Dog	Herding	Trustworthy Courageous Alert	High	High to Very High
Basenji	Hunting	Independent Affectionate Fast moving	High	High to Very High
Border Collie	Herding	Alert Intense Strong work ethic	High	Very High
German Shorthaired Pointer	Hunting	Gentle/Affectionate Loyal Can be aloof w/strangers	High	High

Characteristics of 13 High-Drive, High-Energy Breeds

Breed		Originally Bred for	Characteristics	Trainability	Activity Level
German Shepherd Dog		Herding	Loyal Courageous Versatile	High	High
Golden Retriever		Retrieving water fowl & upland game	Reliable Friendly Trustworthy	High	Moderate to high
Labrador Retriever		Retrieving game	Dependable Eager to please Versatile	High	High
Parson and Jack Russell Terrier		Fox hunting	Determined Relentless Fearless	High	Very high
Schnauzer (miniature)		Ratter	Athletic Intense Spirited	High	High
Shetland Sheepdog		All-purpose dog— driving, protecting, herding	Loyal Sensitive/Responsive Can be noisy	High	High to very high
Siberian Husky		Endurance sled dog	Friendly/gentle Independent Bred to run	Low	Very High

Chapter 2

Why
High-Energy Dogs
Do What
They Do

If you have a high-drive, high-energy dog, you know that he's always raring to go. With endurance and enthusiasm to spare, these dogs are always up for work or play, be it running, jogging, swimming, or power climbing mountain peaks, and that makes them wonderful companions for equally active and energetic owners. They have become increasingly popular in all areas of canine competition, especially the fast-paced sport of agility, because experienced owners make training and showing them look like a stroll in the park. Of course, nothing could be further from the truth.

High-drive, high-energy dogs are frequently misunderstood, and owning, training, and living with one can test the patience of the most experienced dog trainer, let alone the average dog owner. These dogs are highly intelligent and complex, which means that they can be hard to live with and manage. You must stay two steps ahead of them at all times because they also tend to quickly become bored or nervous. Then it's only a matter of time before they get into trouble, leaving a path of destruction in their wake. This can be very distressing to owners, especially when the dog decides to dig up the underground sprinkler system, relocate the patio furniture, or shred the expensive spa cover.

Let's face it, the bottom line is that high-drive, high-energy dogs can be a handful. Despite that minor detail—which is definitely not a canine character flaw—there is nothing wrong with your dog. He is a fabulous dog with a lot of drive and energy who no doubt wants nothing more than to be loved and trained by you. Understanding what makes a dog tick will go a long way in developing a training program that works for your dog and his personality.

Nature or Nurture? The Clashing of Brilliant Minds

Early European ethologists and American comparative psychologists defined early animal behavior, but they asked different questions because the types of behavior they studied differed. Studying animals in a natural habitat, ethologists such as Konrad Lorenz and Nikolaas Tinbergen focused primarily on the function and evolution of a behavior. Believing that a behavior evolved to suit the environment, ethologists asked the fundamental question "*Why* is that animal doing that?"

On the other hand, American psychologists, such as Edward Thorndike, a pioneer of trial-and-error learning (now known as operant conditioning), B.F. Skinner, the "grandfather" of operant conditioning, and Ivan Pavlov, who provided the methodology for classical conditioning, focused on observable, quantifiable patterns of behavior in a laboratory environment. More interested in how an animal's behavior developed rather than explaining its adaptiveness, psychologists asked questions that concerned the development or causation of behavior. For them, instinct and innate tendencies were irrelevant.

A period of extreme divergence and debate over inherited versus acquired behaviors existed—hence the infamous nature versus nurture debate. Over time, the distinction blurred, and today's trainers recognize that most behaviors develop under the combined influences of hereditary and environmental factors. This is a theory that is supported by the work published in John Paul Scott and John L. Fuller's comprehensive book *Genetics and the Social Behavior of the Dog.* Their in-depth study and authoritative work on dog behavior concludes, "Behavior is never wholly inherited or wholly acquired but always *developed* under the combined influences of hereditary and environmental factors."

Bowwowza! Turbo-Charged Presidential Dogs

Did you know that many unruly, mischievous high-drive, high-energy dogs have roamed the grounds and corridors at 1600 Pennsylvania Avenue? Some of the presidents' dogs were involved in typical canine shenanigans that were relatively minor in nature, not unlike behaviors in which any dog might engage. Other transgressions, however, which were more serious, had a major political impact and received international attention.

- Charlie, a Welsh Terrier owned by John F. Kennedy, was known for sneaking up on White House gardeners and nipping their backsides or pant legs, then racing across the lawn in great excitement.

- Millie, George and Barbara Bush's Springer Spaniel, relieved herself in the middle of the Yellow Oval Room of the White House during Mrs. Bush's interview with ABC's Sam Donaldson.

- Yuki, Lyndon Johnson's white terrier, soiled the rug in the Oval Office.

- Richard Nixon's Irish Setter shredded a carpet in the Oval Office.

- Ronald Reagan's Bouvier des Flandres, Lucky, drew blood when he nipped the president's hindquarters while attempting to herd the most powerful man in the world across the lawn.

- Peter Pan, Calvin Coolidge's Wire Fox Terrier, leapt at a visiting woman's skirt, catching the material in his teeth, at which time the skirt "appeared to disintegrate, leaving the poor woman exposed and embarrassed."

- Theodore Roosevelt's Bull Terrier, Pete, nipped at a naval officer, snapped at some cabinet members, and chased the French ambassador, Jules Jusserand, down a White House corridor, eventually catching him and tearing the bottom of his pants.

- Franklin D. Roosevelt's German Shepherd Dog, Major, nipped British Prime Minister Ramsay MacDonald's trousers so vigorously that his pants were "nearly ripped off." Roosevelt's other dog, Winks, a Llewellin Setter, jumped onto a breakfast table set for a diplomatic meeting and gobbled up 18 breakfasts of bacon, eggs, and fried potatoes before the visitors arrived. A hasty and minimal substitution of pastries had to be served instead.

It goes on to state that it is almost always possible to "modify behavior by modifying environment as well as hereditary."

In simple terms, both genetics and the environment play important roles. Genetics predispose much of what a dog will be—his temperament, personality, energy level, size, etc.,—and the rest is created and influenced by your training (or lack of training) and the care you provide. The two appear to be inextricably bound together in the development of behavior, with certain periods in a dog's life greatly influencing his behavior, such as the critical socialization period between 3 and 12 weeks of life. The learning theories forged by early pioneers still govern the scientific practices of learning, with each having its use in a trainer's program. Without delving too deeply into the complexities of genetics and canine behavior, it is safe to say that dogs do what they do for two reasons: inherited behaviors (genetics) and acquired behaviors (environment).

Shetland Sheepdogs display the chasing and nipping behavior common in herding dogs.

Inherited Behaviors

Inherited behaviors, often referred to as animal instincts or genetic predispositions, are hardwired behavior patterns with which a dog is born. These are the traits that Mother Nature genetically programmed and are likely to show up in your dog's life whether you want them to or not. The stalking, chasing, and nipping behavior of herding dogs, the speed and running ability of sighthounds, the pulling and running tendencies of sled dogs, the digging behavior of terriers, and the natural guarding instinct of mastiff-type dogs are examples of specific, identifiable, and inherited characteristics or predispositions.

These natural tendencies are part and parcel of your dog's complete package. They are traits that he inherited from his ancestors, primarily from his parents and grandparents. These natural behaviors tend to annoy the average dog owner because most owners do not want their terrier digging up the garden, their Siberian Husky running for the hills kicking up a cloud of dust behind him, or their herding dog attacking weed whackers, rakes, brooms, vacuum cleaners, or any other moving object.

Managing and controlling these behaviors is possible. Eradicating or suppressing them is difficult, if not impossible. Problems arise when owners acquire a high-drive dog and immediately attempt to suppress his natural instincts. This creates nothing but grief for both dog and owner. Most high-drive dogs have a high sense of self-worth. They show great fortitude and heart in their ability to think and carry out the jobs for which they were bred. As a result, they frequently resent it when you try to dominate them.

Suppressing his natural instincts or punishing a dog for doing what comes naturally will not only stifle his unique personality but may also result in him finding other ways to vent his frustrations. Border Collies, for example, are so intelligent and complex that they frequently develop obsessive-compulsive behaviors. Some become mesmerized by reflective surfaces, such as mirrors, glass, or the stainless steel on refrigerators and dishwashers. Others go berserk at the sight of a fly. Some snap at the rain. Others spin in endless circles, and almost all of them have a propensity for herding small children by biting and nipping at their ankles.

Rather than trying to stifle these natural behaviors, it is up to you to find a way to channel them into enjoyable obedience commands and fun games and tricks. (See Chapters 9 and 10.)

Part of the Golden Retriever's breed type is his infectious joy for life.

Acquired Behaviors

Acquired behaviors are behaviors a dog has acquired from the day he was born. These behaviors are learned, be they good or bad, desired or undesired. Swiping food off the kitchen counter, refusing to come when called, peeing from one end of the house to the other, bolting out doors, and committing heinous crimes against your personal property are all acquired behaviors. An eight-week-old Australian Cattle Dog who learns to have fun chasing young children and nipping their pant legs will see no harm in doing this as a 40-pound (18-kg) adult dog. An adorable Border Terrier who is mollycoddled every time he whines or barks will grow into an adult dog who barks and whines whenever he wants attention. A pushy, bossy Labrador Retriever puppy who is allowed to bully other dogs will grow into an adult dog who wants to dominate other dogs.

This is not to say that all acquired behaviors are negative or bad. Acquired behaviors can be positive. If, for example, when your six-month-old German Shepherd Dog hears "Come!" he tears back to you with his head and ears up, his tail wagging, and a happy attitude that screams "Here I am!", this is an acquired behavior and a good one, too. Sitting while you greet visitors, walking nicely on leash, and not barking incessantly are first-rate acquired behaviors.

Purebred Dogs and Their Genes

As mentioned in Chapter 1, fixed genes are the science and essence behind purebred dogs. One advantage of owning or acquiring a purebred dog is that with purebred puppies, you have a pretty good idea of what they will look like and how they will act as adults. A purebred Golden Retriever, for example, will look and act in a specific way, which, when bred true to the breed, will fall within the attributes and characteristics of the breed—or what is known as *breed type*. Golden Retrievers have fixed genes for medium to large size, water-resistant coat, golden color, head shape, retrieving instinct, and that classic joie de vivre temperament. This is what distinguishes a Golden Retriever from, say, a Labrador Retriever. Breed characteristics help you recognize and identify a Golden Retriever as a Golden Retriever and not a Flat-Coated Retriever, Chesapeake Bay Retriever, or any other type of retriever.

Of course, for every rule there is an exception. A Golden Retriever from a master breeder may look and act differently than a Golden Retriever from a backyard breeder. Golden Retrievers bred on the East Coast may vary slightly in structure and appearance from those bred on the West Coast. Some, although not all, of the sporting and herding breeds bred specifically for working versus the show ring can vary dramatically in both their appearance and energy expenditure. Golden Retrievers specifically bred for fieldwork, for example, tend to have more drive and energy than many of their show dog counterparts. Labrador Retrievers used for working purposes tend to be smaller, lighter, and faster than Labs bred for show.

A dog's natural instincts can also vary dramatically within a breed and within the same litter. A litter of Weimaraners, for example, will look pretty much the same, but one puppy may have an intense desire to track, while his littermates may have zero instinct.

Because purebred dogs have their own fixed genes and identifiable characteristics, experienced dog people can identify predictable breed-specific behaviors. This in turn helps owners understand why their herding dog is obsessed with movement, why their independent terrier digs and digs and digs and may not always be willing to do what his owner wants, or why their Golden Retriever retrieves anything and everything in sight.

Unfortunately, the purebred label does not guarantee quality. Many of today's popular breeds are bred without consideration for optimum temperament or breed-specific characteristics, thereby perpetuating overly shy, aggressive, or neurotic characteristics. That is why, when looking for a purebred dog, finding an ethical breeder is of the utmost importance.

Who's Your Doggy's Daddy?

If your curiosity gets the best of you and money is no option, you might consider DNA analysis for your mix. Genetic identification tests are available and can help people with mixed-breed dogs learn their dog's genetic origins. Two types of tests are available: a cheek swab or a blood sample drawn by a veterinarian. For additional information, contact: Mars Veterinary www.marsveterinary.com Canine Heritage Breed Test www.canineheritage.com 1-800-DNA-DOGG

Mixed-Breed Dogs and Their Genes

Decoding a dog's quirks, idiosyncrasies, and madcap personality may be easier when he is a purebred, but what happens if he is a combination of two or more purebred or mixed-breed dogs? And what if you know nothing of his ancestry?

Often referred to as crossbreeds, mutts, curs, mongrels, all-American, or Heinz 57s, mixed-breed dogs can do pretty much anything and everything their blue-blooded

Mixed-breed dogs can make equally wonderful pets as their purebred counterparts.

cousins do, with the exception of participating in events organized and hosted by the American Kennel Club (AKC) and its member clubs. They make equally wonderful pets as their purebred counterparts, and they are quite adept at stealing your heart with their one-of-a-kind looks and unique personalities.

What separates the purebred dog from the mixed-breed dog is the inheritance of genes. While purebred dogs inherit fixed genes that produce true to type, mixed-breed dogs inherit random, unfixed genes from their parents. Remember, puppies inherit 50 percent of their genes from each parent. Whether or not these genes contain traits that are going to appeal to you is often unknown until the dog is grown because it is difficult, if not impossible, to predict the future size, coat type, or temperament of a puppy from a litter where the sire is unknown, or worse yet, both the sire and dam are unknown. Equally important, because these genes are random, unfixed, and often wildly contrasting, they cannot be passed on predictably to any offspring.

A dog of unknown ancestry and no obvious breed affiliation will have a more diverse set of gene versions than a given purebred, especially for those genes that contribute to physical and behavioral differences. Depending on the particular combination of genes (and breeds), it may be difficult to sort out breed background because almost any shorthaired, muscular dog with a broad muzzle weighing between 30 and 80 pounds (13.5 and 36.5 kg) is labeled a "pit bull mix." However, there are many combinations of breeds that might produce a large, shorthaired dog with a broad muzzle. That said, purebreds are frequently misidentified, too, with many of them being labeled as terrier, shepherd, or collie mixes.

Identifying breed-specific characteristics of purebred dogs, such as size, coat type, ear set, tail set, and behavioral traits, can help shed some light on what breeds might be milling about in your dog's DNA makeup. More often than not, however, these are simply educated guesses because while your dog may look like a Newfoundland, he might just behave like a Border Collie, or vice versa.

Terms for Mixes

For the sake of clarification, distinctions exist between crossbreeds, mixed breeds, and designer or hybrid dogs. Let's sort out the terminology:

- A *crossbred* is an animal that is a blend of two or more pure strains, such as a Labrador Retriever and a Border Collie.

- A *mixed breed* or *mutt* is a largely random combination of breeds and types of dogs. Often the ancestry of such dogs is only partly known, if it is known at all.

Designer or hybrid dogs are deliberate, planned crossbreedings. Labradoodle (Labrador Retriever and Poodle), Goldendoodle (Golden Retriever and Poodle), and Puggle (Pug and Beagle) are some of the more popular designer dogs specifically bred to create these crosses. The deliberate crossing of two breeds has created a designer dog fad. However, regardless of their stylish labels and hefty price tags, these designer dogs are still mixed-breed dogs because a mixed-breed dog by any other name is still a mixed-breed dog. Here's why: A breed is not considered a purebred until the offspring breed true, which means that the offspring are just like the parents. This can take upward of six or seven generations. As long as people continue to breed Golden Retrievers to Poodles or Pugs to Beagles, these designer dogs will remain mixed-breed dogs.

The University of California at Berkley, the University of Oregon, and the Fred Hutchinson Cancer Research Center in Seattle, Washington, studied the inheritance of approximately 31 canine traits or characteristics by crossing a female Newfoundland with a male Border Collie, two breeds that exhibit entirely different behaviors. The first litter of seven puppies, known as the F1 generation, all grew up to look similar to one another—smaller than their mother but bigger than their father and mostly black like their mother. All of the puppies showed the characteristic Border Collie "eye" and crouching behavior of their father and were water loving like their mother. Those puppies were then bred, producing an F2 generation, which was more diverse, with offspring being bigger or smaller and with more white markings than their F1 parents. There were unique combinations of behaviors, too. One F2 dog showed eye, loved people, and was indifferent to water. A second F2 dog carried his tail like a Border Collie, did not show eye, loved people, but did not swim.

By understanding the characteristics that distinguish one breed from another and individual characteristics within a breed, you will be better equipped to identify predictable breed-specific behaviors and also deal with any of your dog's quirks and idiosyncrasies.

3

The Human / Canine Relationship

When it comes to living with dogs, nothing is more important than a strong human–canine relationship. For the most part, we all make adjustments and adaptations so that we can live harmoniously with our dogs, and sometimes that includes giving up things—things like our time and energy and precious sleep and money and any notion of owning dark-colored clothes not littered with dog hair. What we should never give up is the love and respect our dogs deserve in order for the dog–owner relationship to prosper.

ogs love us unconditionally. Dogs don't question our decision to take a nap in the middle of the afternoon—in fact, they are happy to accommodate us. Dogs don't growl at our political preferences. Dogs don't care if we eat ice cream for breakfast, if our hair is a fright, our clothes are out of style, or we've gained a little extra weight. And unlike friends and in-laws, dogs don't rearrange our furniture or chatter incessantly. (Okay, a few bark incessantly, but at least they can be trained to be quiet.)

While dogs ask for little and are willing to give us everything in return, if you read the fine print, the owner–dog relationship does come with a few conditions attached.

First and foremost, a healthy human–canine relationship means that you must be a good leader to your dog. Otherwise, your life is doomed to be filled with turmoil and chaos. But setting the foundation for a good human–canine bond isn't about throwing your weight around, dominating your dog, or creating a fearful dog. It's about establishing a clear-cut communication system, laying down the rules, and maintaining them on a daily basis in a fun, positive, and humane manner.

We owe it to our dogs—especially high-drive, high-energy dogs—to invest time and energy in providing them with a relationship that is nothing short of fair, honest, and humane, which includes setting clearly defined rules and boundaries. Human

Agility handlers know that forming a strong bond with their dog is important to succeed in the sport.

Rare Breed Turbo-Charged Dogs

Generally, when we think of high-drive, high-energy dogs, Labrador Retrievers, Border Collies, Australian Shepherds, and Dalmatians are a few who come to mind. A few whom you may or may not recognize include:

- **Plott:** A member of the American Kennel Club's (AKC) Hound Group, the Plott is one of the six types of Coonhounds. Of German heritage and named after Jonathan Plott, an émigré from Germany who settled in North Carolina, the Plott works as a single hunter or in packs for small and large game. These natural-born hunters are high-energy dogs who need to be kept in a securely fenced yard; otherwise, they have a tendency to run off and hunt.

- **Norwegian Buhund:** Used primarily as a herding dog, the Norwegian Buhund is intelligent, lively, and full of character, with plenty of energy and stamina. The breed requires plenty of daily exercise and consistent handling and training from puppyhood.

- **Pyrenean Sheepdog:** A superb athlete, the Pyrenean Sheepdog is a high-energy, intelligent herding dog, with a cunning, mischievous attitude. He is always on alert, suspicious, and ready for action.

relationships require constant attention and maintenance, and so too does the partnership you have with your dog.

How the Pros Do It

Dog fanciers who compete in the sport of dogs, such as agility, obedience, herding, and so forth, make training look easy, which could not be further from the truth. While it may look like the handler is doing nothing while the dog does all the work, good trainers know how much training and precise physical and verbal control goes into a flawless— or seemingly flawless—performance.

For the most part, you may not care too much about precision. Perfect *sits*, flawless *downs*, and high-speed *recalls* may not be a priority for you. Most owners are quite happy when their dog sits, downs, or comes when told to, even if he has to be told seven or eight times to do so. And there is nothing wrong with that, if that's what you want. Everyone decides for themselves which behaviors they will and will not accept from their dog.

Although you need not be interested in competitive dog sports to have a well-trained dog, there is a lot to learn from the training methods utilized by competitive dog handlers and show people. Their success starts with a strong human–canine relationship. Given the proper ingredients, a good human–canine relationship is well within the capabilities of most owners.

Timing Is Critical With Puppies

The methods and techniques for establishing a great human–canine relationship are pretty much the same, regardless of whether you have an adult dog or puppy. That said, time is of the essence when it comes to bonding with your puppy. Your job begins the day your puppy arrives at your home, so you need to maximize your time and use it wisely.

When it comes to puppies, you have a narrow window of opportunity to develop a strong bond.

Oftentimes an owner will acquire an eight- or ten-week-old puppy, and the first thing she'll do is go on vacation without the puppy. Yikes! That is one of the worst things to do, and here's why: Puppies must learn important socialization skills between 8 and 16 weeks of age. Once this small window of opportunity has passed, it can never be recaptured. Puppies mature faster than humans. On average, humans take about 18 years to reach maturity, while puppies take about 1 to 1.5 years, depending on the breed and individual dog. An eight-week-old puppy is eight weeks old for exactly seven days. The same goes for being 9, 10, 11, and 12 weeks old. Although one week may seem insignificant in the life span of a child, it represents a significant portion of puppyhood. Once those seven days have passed, they can never be recaptured. Failing to maximize your opportunities during this critical time means that your puppy will suffer in the long run. You run the risk of having him develop bad habits and associations that will be difficult, if not impossible, to correct later in life. Boarding him in a kennel or leaving him in the care of friends or relatives during this time puts him at a serious disadvantage later in life. You will have missed a prime opportunity to shape his future character, instilling all of the behaviors you want your puppy to possess as an adult dog.

Bonding With Your Dog

Have you ever noticed how some dogs seem to really love being with their owners, while other dogs are utterly oblivious? Some dogs interact with and respond to their owners, regardless of what else is going on around them. The juvenile delinquents, on the other hand, saunter around the park peeing on anything and everything in sight, ignoring their owners' frantic and pitiful pleas to come. What separates the well-behaved dogs from their unruly counterparts is a strong human–canine bond built on a foundation of mutual love and respect.

For a strong bond, your dog must see you as the dispenser of all things fun and exciting, be it playing, training, retrieving, running, tugging, eating, swimming, grooming, or riding in the car. You must truly love your dog, and he must love being with you. You must be the center of his universe—the most exciting person in his world. Although some behaviorists and trainers pooh-pooh this concept, if you think about it, it makes sense. It does not mean that your dog must focus on you 24 hours a day or that you must become the only thing he can enjoy. But let's face it: Some owners are, well, boring. It is difficult for them to be funny and silly and engaging, but you should try to be more exciting than a tree stump. If you act like a zombie, chances are high that your dog will run off and find someone or something more exciting to play with. Simply put, your dog should enjoy being with you and *want* to be with you. He should enjoy engaging with and interacting and playing with you. His eyes should light up when he sees you, and vice versa.

Accomplishing this requires you to spend a significant amount of time each day investing in quality one-on-one time with your dog. If possible, keep him with you as much as you can throughout the day. Handle him at every opportunity. Kiss him. Snuggle with him. Revel in his puppy breath. Take him for walks in the park and rides in the car. Train him. Brush him. Feed him. Love him. Talk to him. Tell him he's wonderful. Teach him that everything you do together will be fun and exciting. If he thinks that you are the most important person in his world, he will be less inclined to ignore you or wander off to be with other dogs or people who are (obviously!) more exciting.

This necessary task becomes more difficult if you work full time and have a spouse and a houseful of kids. You will need to manage your day efficiently so that you have time and energy to devote exclusively to your new puppy or adult dog. The process is time consuming, but the time invested today establishing a strong human–canine bond will reap enormous benefits down the road.

Bonding With Multiple Dogs Can Be Challenging

If you have multiple dogs, the process becomes doubly challenging because you must be certain that your puppy bonds with you and not your other dog(s). (This is a point that dog trainer Bobbie Anderson, author of *Building Blocks for Performance*, continually points out to her students.) Let's say that your puppy or new adult dog spends the majority of his day in the backyard playing with another dog. Or perhaps you purchased two puppies so that they could keep each other company eight or ten hours a day while you work. A puppy who spends the majority of his day unsupervised with another dog will bond with the other dog rather

Bonding is much harder when you have multiple dogs because there is a strong chance they will bond with each other before they bond with you.

than you. He will look to his canine sibling for all of his fun and excitement and bad habits. That is not to say that your puppy won't love you or look to you for food and snacks and kisses and snuggling on the couch, but it will be on his terms. The other dog—not you—will influence his behaviors. His allegiance will be to his canine buddy, and he will look to him for direction and leadership. Subsequently, establishing yourself as a leader, which is the foundation of all successful dog training, will become more difficult. A dog who does not respect his owner will have little or no desire to do as his owner asks, be it coming when called, sitting, or walking nicely on leash.

One-On-One Time

It's true that a lot of people work and can't spend 24 hours a day playing and training and bonding with their dog. If you work at home or taking your dog to work is an option, bonding should be a snap. Otherwise, you will need to find clever ways to spend time establishing a strong bond with your new dog. For the first several months, for example, after dinner (and after you have spent time playing and loving all of your dogs), you and your new puppy or adult dog could spend 30 minutes or so of quiet time snuggling and bonding while your other dog(s) chews on yummy Nylabones in his crate or in the yard. Also, take your new puppy or adult dog someplace new each day, such as for a walk in the park, hike in the woods, or swim in the lake. Take him anywhere and everywhere it is safe to do so. Do something special with only your new dog several times a day, such as fun training and play sessions. Of course, you'll need to rotate this alone time so that each dog gets individual attention.

Running, playing, and interacting with other dogs is okay under your watchful eye. However, you must teach him that you—not the other dogs—are the dispenser of all things fun in his life. When you choose to own a high-drive, high-energy dog, you must take responsibility for him, and that includes finding the time and energy to train and exercise him. Sure, most of us would rather flop on the couch after a hard day's work, but remember that the clock is ticking. Time invested building a strong and mutually respectful relationship today will reap benefits down the road, which is doubly important when you own a high-drive, high-energy dog.

It won't be long before your puppy will be able to run and play unsupervised with your other dogs, but until he is thoroughly bonded with you, it is highly recommended that you do not allow him free and unsupervised access to other dogs.

How Long Until We Bond?

The great thing about dogs is that they have a strong desire for companionship, be it with humans or other animals. No doubt you've heard stories of dogs forming strong bonds with a cat or a horse or even a goat. But dogs are individuals, too, which is why it is impossible to put a time limit on the bonding process. One cannot, for example, set a time limit of, say, three days or three weeks for a dog to form a lasting attachment to you. Much depends on the dog's breed and temperament. And of course, much will depend on your commitment—how much time and energy you are willing to invest forming a strong bond.

Generally speaking, herding, working, and sporting dogs, who were originally bred to work closely with their owners, tend to bond quite quickly. Hounds and terriers were originally bred to work independently of their owners and are therefore not always willing to happily respond to their commands. Establishing a mutually respectful attachment usually takes time, energy, and an unwavering commitment.

That said, dogs, be they young or old, who have been rescued from shelters or abusive situations, have been known to

Dogs have a strong desire for companionship.

bond almost instantaneously with a stranger. Even if he is set in his ways, an older dog can become your best friend in a matter of days—or minutes. Dogs who were never—or not properly—socialized as puppies can form a strong bond with some individuals, even though they may remain uncomfortable around strangers.

The time invested today establishing a strong human–canine bond will reap giant benefits down the road when your high-octane dog hits his peak energy years, which for the most part include anything between two and six years of age. (Unless, of course, you own a Border Collie, who normally peaks at seven or eight years old—if you think he is going to calm down when he's seven, think again.)

Leadership—It's all About Respect

Here is where dog training gets a bit confusing but nonetheless fascinating. Remember those early European ethologists and American comparative psychologists mentioned in Chapter 2? Well, those learning theories forged by early pioneers still govern the scientific practices of learning, with each having its use in a trainer's program. However, dog trainers (those people who have hands-on experience training dogs) and behaviorists (those who typically study animals and apply scientific theory to training) still disagree at varying lengths on a number of topics, including the social and/or hierarchal system of dogs and how it pertains to canine behaviors and human leadership.

Some of the most recent and intriguing information is detailed in Temple Grandin's book, *Animals Make Us Human*. She explains that dogs are "genetic wolves," and all of our images and preconceived ideas about how wolves live in packs with an alpha male are completely wrong. She goes on to raise the questions: "If dogs are wolves and wolves don't have pack leaders, why do dogs need a pack leader? Dogs evolved to live with humans, but what does that mean? Did dogs evolve to live with humans in *families?* And if they did, does that mean dogs living with human families need a mom and a dad, not an alpha? Or are dogs living with human families more like a forced wolf pack than a family, in which case somebody has to be the alpha?"

Respect is a key component in establishing yourself as a leader.

More than a few dog trainers will have a good laugh at the thought of dogs living without an alpha, top dog, or leader. Chaos and turmoil are sure to prevail—just as chaos and turmoil are guaranteed to triumph when children have no guidance or designated leader. Granted, 100 years ago most dogs lived a fence-free life, wandering ranches and farms and the streets of most towns and following kids to school. Dogs were allowed to be dogs, much more than they are today. It's possible that family dogs (as opposed to working dogs) required less guidance or direction at that time. After all, many dogs were ranch or farm dogs, living outdoors and sleeping in barns or under porches. However, today's dogs live different lives. They are expected to live in closer quarters (sometimes with other dogs), and their territory is sometimes no bigger than a fenced yard or an apartment balcony.

You must give your high-energy dog direction, guidance, and leadership.

Don't Get Caught Up in Terminology

Here's the bottom line: The terminology you choose, be it *parent*, *guardian*, *top dog*, *pack leader*, or *alpha*, probably isn't that important, as long as you are giving your dog direction, guidance, and leadership. How you go about instilling and enforcing your leadership is what makes a dog's life pleasant or unpleasant. Just as good parents are good leaders—setting limits for their children and teaching them to behave nicely—good dog owners must teach their dogs good manners. A dog needs to learn that he can't run amok, pee from one end of the house to the other, or fight with other dogs. He can't swipe food off the counter, bolt out doors, or bark incessantly. He can't harass livestock, ransack trashcans, or destroy your personal belongings. Without boundaries and a firm leader, dogs run amok and do whatever is in their best interest (including all of the behaviors just mentioned). It doesn't make them bad dogs—it simply makes them dogs without good leaders.

Respect is a key component in establishing yourself as your dog's leader. Think how much more pleasant and easier life is when your children (or spouse or boss or friends) respect you. When children understand the concept that Mom and Dad make the rules, they are more willing to do what is asked of them. The same concept applies to dogs. A dog who respects his owner—who views his owner as the leader—is more willing to do what is asked of him.

Establishing Yourself as a Leader

Establishing yourself as a leader is a critical ingredient in a successful human–canine relationship and one of the most important things you can do for your dog and your family. A dog who views and respects his owner as a leader is easier to train because he will be more willing to obey commands. As a well-behaved dog, he is more likely to be considered a valuable family member, thereby included in family outings and activities.

Problems arise when owners fail to establish right away—and maintain—their position as a leader. A dog who sees no clearly defined leader has no problem sliding into the driver's seat. He will take over and do as he pleases when he pleases, with utter disregard for your expectations or concerns. Trying to train a dog who thinks that he is in charge—a dog who believes that he is allowed to make decisions—is nearly impossible. A dog who never learns to respect his owner will not obey commands or do anything he does not want to do. That same dog may behave aggressively—snarling, growling, or snapping—to get his point across. This is a disastrous situation for any dog, let alone a highly intelligent, highly complex, high-drive, high-energy dog.

The Clock Is Ticking: Be a Leader Starting Today

Some dogs—especially high-drive, pushy, bossy, dominant-type ones—are highly skilled at getting exactly what they want. They can quickly and easily take over a household whose members are not experienced in the art of handling these types of personalities. Therefore, in a fun and humane manner, you must begin establishing yourself as a leader

Some bossy, high-drive dogs become highly skilled at getting what they want.

right away. Ideally, you should start the day your new puppy arrives in your home.

It's worth reiterating that pushy or dominant dogs are not bad dogs. Like people, some dogs know exactly what they want and how to go about getting it. Perhaps you know a few relatives or friends with this trait!

What Is Dominance?

The word *dominant* is often a catch-all phrase for anything and everything that goes wrong in the human–canine relationship. Owners often say "He's too dominant to walk on leash" or "He pees in the house because he's so dominant." In the simplest of terms, dominance is defined as exercising the most influence or control. For example, when two dogs want the same thing, say, a bone or toy, the dominant dog is usually the one who gets it. In the human–canine relationship, the human and the dog may want the same—or different—things. For example, an

Training helps establish a bond with your dog and reinforce your position as a good leader.

owner may want her shoe back but the dog is not willing to give it up. Maybe the owner wants to sit in her favorite chair but the dog thinks otherwise. Or perhaps the owner wants the dog to come but he'd rather play with his canine buddies. Is this dominance or lack of training? It's hard to say because a lot depends on the dog, his temperament, personality, and how much training the owner has done. Perhaps it's a bit of both. It can be a fine line between a lack of training, lack of respect, owner ignorance, and dominance-related issues. That's why it's unfair and even a bit hazardous to lump or generalize specific labels onto dogs without understanding the dog as an individual.

That said, generally speaking, if you acquire a puppy at eight or ten weeks of age and have laid the proper groundwork and instilled the behaviors that build a solid and mutually respectful human–canine relationship, by the time he is three and a half or four months old, he will have developed a foundation of respect for you. He will have assessed all of the family members and decided where he fits in the hierarchy. If your puppy learns to respect you at an early age, he will respect you throughout his life, provided, of course, you continue to reinforce your position as a leader. This is important because the hierarchy in a dog is not fixed. When circumstances change, the position of top dog is likely to change, too. In your household, you must reinforce your top dog position daily in a fun and humane manner. Otherwise, a dog who thinks that he should

What's Your Dog's Temperament

All high-drive puppies and adult dogs are different. They are individuals, and they must be treated as such. Some dogs are dominant, pushy, and bossy and will exploit every opportunity to take over and control the household. Other dogs are more submissive and generally content being subordinates. Less willing to exploit their pack position, they can be given a bit more leeway and allowed to get away with much more, and they will not take advantage of the situation. By understanding and continually assessing your dog's personality and temperament, you can decide how much leeway he gets.

be the leader will exploit every opportunity to stick his paw in the proverbial door.

How Long Until He Accepts Me as Leader?

Again, timetables in dog training are counterproductive because dogs are individuals and must be treated as such. Some puppies, depending on their breed, temperament, and the owners' commitment to the process, may take longer to understand their position in the household. An adult dog coming into a new home may arrive with unexpected baggage, quirks, and leadership issues. Therefore, establishing the foundation of respect may be more challenging and take longer. Perseverance and consistency in a firm but fun and humane manner are key.

What Makes a Good Leader?

Living harmoniously with a high-drive, high-energy dog (or any dog who tends to have a strong or independent personality) requires a strong leader. This does not imply the use of force or intimidation. Owners must never be mean or cruel or bully or berate their dog. Those are crimes in progress, not training techniques. Understanding your dog—his temperament, personality, and why he does what he does—is key. No doubt he is cute and irresistible, but he is still a dog, not a furry little person with four legs.

A good pack leader is benevolent. Confident. Tolerant. Loving. A firm disciplinarian—tough and uncompromising when need be but always fair and consistent. Gray areas have no place in dog training. You cannot be wishy-washy. You cannot be a leader today but not tomorrow or be top dog only on Tuesdays and Thursdays. Your dog must see you as the leader at all times. Just as you set ground rules for toddlers and teenagers, you must set ground rules for your dog and reinforce them throughout his life. Your dog must understand that you love him, you will protect him, and you will be his best friend, but you call the shots and you will tolerate no nonsense. You will not negotiate or compromise your position. This is so important to the overall scheme of dog training that it bears repeating. Your dog needs to think that it is impossible for him to be top dog.

In the simplest of terms, as a leader, your dog is looking to you for guidance and direction. Therefore, you must teach him that being sassy, cheeky, pushy, bossy, or obnoxious will not be tolerated. He must learn to play nicely, act like a gentleman, and not run wild. He must follow the rules of the household that you set.

Of course, you will need to teach him all of these things without stifling his zany personality. After all, he should be respectful but not fearful. He should be confident, fun, and lively, not dull or robotic.

How to Be a Good Leader: Controlling the Resources

Dogs have different priorities than humans. They don't worry about carpools or soccer practice. They don't fret about traffic jams, business meetings, or their carbon footprint. Dogs establish or maintain their superiority by fighting over stuff that is important to them. Their lives revolve around things that are seemingly unimportant or insignificant to humans. After all, they sniff other dogs' bums, lick unmentionable body parts, and will gleefully eat another dog's poop, if you let them. To be a strong leader, you must be in charge of all aspects of life that a dog considers important.

Attention-Seeking Behaviors

In a household situation, pushy, bossy, or dominant-type dogs will often demand attention from their owner by pawing or using their nose to nudge or flip their owner's hand. Some dogs will stare or bark or growl at their owner in an effort to demand attention. The dog is saying "Hey, you! Pay attention to me!" By acknowledging him in any way, you are reinforcing his demands for attention and thereby reinforcing his position of control.

It is worth noting that there is a difference between demanding attention, such as "Pet me right now!" and trying to get your attention because your dog needs to go outdoors to potty. You must read your dog's body language and recognize when he needs your help or when he's trying to control the situation by demanding attention.

Try to initiate most of the interactions between you and your dog, and ignore his demands for attention, especially when you are doing something else, such as working at the computer, paying bills, cooking dinner, watching television, sewing, reading, and so forth. During these situations, if your dog demands attention, try to ignore him. Do not give him eye contact, pet his head, or give him a kiss before telling him to lie

Identify Your Criterion and Stick to It

Identify the behavior that you want to teach, such as walking nicely on leash or sitting politely at the door, as opposed to bolting out it. Some trainers call this *establishing your criterion.* Simply put, have a clear picture in your mind of the behavior you want to teach, and try not to deviate from that behavior as you set about making it happen. For instance, if your goal is for your dog to wait at the door and not rush out while you open it, what if he whines and yips and yaps? Technically, he is waiting, but he's very vocal about waiting. Is that acceptable? If so, that's great. If not, then whining and barking at the door should never be acceptable. Owners often get in a hurry and allow a behavior, such as bolting out the door or whining and barking, because they are late for work or they want to get to the post office before it closes. They think "I'll fix that next time." It is much easier to take the time to reinforce the desired behavior—or criterion—than it is to go back and retrain it once it becomes ingrained.

down and be a good boy. Do not yell or holler or reprimand him either. By ignoring his demands, he will quickly learn that pestering or demanding attending will not buy him anything. When he gives up and lies down, calmly tell him "Good boy. That's what I wanted."

Comings and Goings

Dogs are territorial. They like marking and guarding their territory, be it a fenced yard or the inside of the house or car. Dogs also seem to get territorial about doorways and gateways, and some experts suggest that doorways may separate territory boundaries—a demarcation line, so to speak, from one territory to another. Dogs also like barging in and out of those doors and gateways and charging past you as you go upstairs. These behaviors are not only disrespectful, they are potentially hazardous. Dogs who charge through doorways or bolt out car doors run the risk of darting into traffic and being seriously injured by a car. A dog underfoot while going up or down stairs is an accident waiting to happen. For these reasons, your dog should learn early on that when you come to a doorway together, he must wait for you to go through first. Then he can follow. The same concept applies to stairs—he should learn to walk behind you when ascending or descending stairways.

You can do this by teaching your dog the *wait* command. (See Chapter 10.) Eventually, when reinforced consistently, your dog will learn to wait for you to pass through a doorway or walk behind you going up stairs. By doing so, not only is he learning good manners, but he is accepting you as his leader. However, some dogs will test their owners on a daily basis, checking to see if the household rules really do apply. If your high-drive dog sits and waits today, it may not carry over to the next day—you may have to go through the routine each and every day. A pain in the rear? Absolutely! But don't give in. Reinforce the household rules daily, and your dog will soon be a model citizen and a joy to live with.

Food

A lot of trainers and behaviorists disagree on the topic of feeding dogs, or more specifically, the order of feeding dogs. Some subscribe to the theory that in a pack situation, dominant animals eat first and the subordinate dogs get what is left, and they believe that's the way your household should be run. Not surprisingly, others disagree with this concept. Perhaps what is most important is that at the very least, you should control what and when your dog is eating. When he turns those pathetic doggy eyes on you during mealtimes it may be difficult to resist him, but you must do so. Sharing people food with your dog is not good for his waistline, encourages begging (a difficult and annoying habit to break once it becomes ingrained). Also, your dog—depending on his personality—may consider you to be a weaker animal because you have just given up some of your food. Again, much will depend on his individual temperament.

If you can't resist sharing your food, put it in the refrigerator and share it later as a treat for doing something productive, such as a fun trick, a *sit*, or a *down*.

Power Games

There are plenty of differing opinions on canine posturing—it's another area where dog training can get a bit confusing for new or first-time owners (and even some experienced owners, too!). Basically, posturing is a way dogs try to establish or exert superiority. Examples of posturing include mounting another dog or placing the head or forepaws on the shoulder of another dog and trying to maintain that position.

When playing tug-of-war, a bigger dog will often allow a smaller dog to win to prolong the game.

Play Versus Posturing

Social play is different from posturing. Dogs frequently

roughhouse and win and lose play fights. A bigger or more dominant dog will occasionally roll over on his back and lose on purpose, or when playing tug-of-war, a larger dog will let the smaller dog win to keep the game going. Most of the time it is great fun for the dogs provided both are enjoying the game. Understanding canine body language and knowing when your dog is playing nicely or when the play has crossed over into a pack status-type brawl will go a long way in helping you raise a puppy who grows into a well-behaved adult dog. (See Chapters 4 and 8 for more on the intricacies of play and body language.)

When in doubt—and depending on your dog and his personality—you should discourage posturing behaviors from other dogs toward your dog and from your dog toward other animals. By discouraging these behaviors from day one, you are setting boundaries and teaching him good manners. As your dog's leader, you are also his guardian. Your job is to keep him safe and prevent him from becoming fearful by being bullied by stronger, more willful dogs. He should also not be put in a position where he is allowed to develop bad habits, such as intimidating other dogs.

Posturing With Humans and Other Dogs

Your dog may have tried some posturing maneuvers on you, and you may not even be aware of them. Similar to dog-to-dog posturing, dogs will try to place their paws on your shoulders or put their paws on your lap and stare down at you. Many dog trainers will tell you that very dominant dogs need to be kept down low because height advantage is important to them. For example, a dog may show little or no interest in you, but if you lie down on the floor where he can tower over you, his entire demeanor will change. That is why dogs often try these types of maneuvers while a person is sitting or lying down on a couch or bed. Again, depending on your dog's temperament and personality, you may want to discourage this behavior from the beginning.

Posturing frequently occurs in multiple-dog households. Say, for example, a puppy is chewing on a bone. When another dog walks by, the puppy looks up, glares, or curls his lip ever so slightly as if to say "This is my bone, don't even think about it!" Some owners think that this behavior is cute or funny. "He's got such a deep growl for such a little puppy!" Or "Isn't he funny when he curls his lip?" Others, including a number of trainers and behaviorists, think that this is simply a matter of dogs establishing the rules of the house, establishing their pecking order within the dog pack. Their thinking is that as long as one of the dogs is not launching a full-blown attack, the growling is fine, and if things escalate, then it will be time to call in a professional. This is a recipe for disaster.

Prevent Problems Before They Start

The goal is to prevent problems *before* they escalate. Aggression problems take a nanosecond to get out of control—it is a very short leap from a curled lip to a full-blown attack. Once hostilities commence, owners often quickly become overwhelmed and discouraged, and the dog ends up on the fast track to the humane society. Furthermore, you should not let another dog in your household put a puppy in his place—it gives the older dog way too much power, and if you have a pushy dog, it makes him even more controlling. Remember, *you* set the rules, *you* are the leader, and *you* control all of the toys. Some might argue that aggressive behavior is normal canine behavior in wild animals, but in a domesticated environment where dogs are living in social contact with humans, aggression is unacceptable.

To be a good leader, you must pay attention to these minute details. Growling at another dog (provided it is not play growling) is not funny or cute. It is a sign of things to come. The dog is testing the fence to see if there are any weak spots. He is setting the ground rules and establishing himself as the CEO of the household. Unless immediately nipped in the bud, the puppy will grow into an adult dog who thinks that he rules the roost. Your puppy must understand that growling is unacceptable and it will get him nothing. If handled properly, he will quickly learn that you are the pack leader, not him. You control all the bones and toys, not him.

Some owners can have multiple dogs chewing bones or playing with toys without a shred of trouble. Others cannot. If you have leadership problems in your household, it is best to keep all bones and toys picked up until you resolve the problem.

Sleeping Places

Not surprisingly, another area that has sparked spirited debates among trainers is where dogs should sleep. Some of the top trainers in the country allow their dogs to sleep on the bed or furniture and would never dream of altering that arrangement. Other experts will tell you to avoid this practice, and here is why: They believe that some dogs—especially those strong-willed, highly driven dogs who like to try to control or manipulate situations to their advantage—will take advantage of your generosity. By allowing a dog to sleep on your bed, it theoretically reinforces his position of superiority. Feeling superior, he may not give up his newfound power easily or willingly. He may think that he

It's up to you to decide whether or not to allow your dog on your bed.

Sleeping Arrangements

As a puppy, your dog should be crated at night to facilitate housetraining and prevent any accidents. If keeping your adult dog off the bed is an ongoing problem, consider crating him at night with a Nylabone to chew on.

can ignore your commands. Worst-case scenario, he may resort to growling, snarling, or biting. It's his way of saying "No way! I'm not sleeping on the floor and you can't make me."

At the end of the day, where you allow your dog to sleep is your call, and your decision should be based on your own preferences, as well as your dog's personality and temperament. Some dogs, as we have learned, are opportunists and will maximize every situation to their advantage. However, some dogs do not view sleeping on the bed as an opportunity to take control. This is why it's critical to know and read your dog's personality and temperament.

What's important is that you are making the decision, not your dog. You control the resources—he does not. If you want him sleeping on the bed, that's okay, but it is you who should make that call. If you don't want him on the bed, that's okay, too, but it's your decision—not your dog's.

Be Consistent

If your decision is to designate your bed, as well as all of the furniture in the house, a dog-free zone, then set a clear pattern of behavior by not allowing him on the furniture from day one. Avoid confusing your dog by allowing him on the bed on Tuesdays but not Thursdays or allowing him on the bed tonight but not tomorrow because you just changed the sheets. It is equally unfair to allow your adorable puppy on the furniture today but scold him for the same behavior six months down the road when he is 60 pounds (27 kg) with four dirty feet. If you do not want your dog on the bed, you should discourage the behavior when he is a young, impressionable puppy. Always insist quietly, calmly, and consistently that he stays on the floor, and praise him for doing so: "That's my good boy!" If you want to snuggle, get on the floor with him. By insisting from day one that your dog not get on the furniture, he will develop the habit of staying on the floor, even when you are not home.

Toys and Games

Puppies play fight with their littermates as they grow up. Observing a litter of puppies, you can see how they chase, nip, body slam, yip, yap, and prepare for mock battle. These "play" sessions help teach each puppy about his strengths and weaknesses relative to other members in the litter. It is evident, even at this young age, that some puppies are more dominant and will try to control or dominate the more submissive puppies. These puppies play to win. When a strong-willed puppy goes to his new home, he will try to take control, pushing the same buttons with his human pack. Possessing all of the toys and winning all of the games reinforce his position as top dog.

This doesn't mean that you need put away the toys or stop playing—quite the opposite. Interactive play is a great way to establish yourself as a leader. Play also teaches your puppy or adult dog control. Learning to control him as a puppy helps ensure that you will be able to control him as an adult. Play is excellent for bonding and building a strong human–canine relationship by establishing early on who is boss in a positive and fun way. By understanding what to expect, you can take steps to establish and reinforce yourself as pack leader. A few key rules will help:

- You must always control the games.
- The games must be interactive.
- You must both win equally. You win. Your puppy wins. You both win.

To Tug or not to Tug?

Tugging is a favorite canine game but has fallen out of favor with a lot of trainers because it is a test of strength. The theory is that dogs who win strength games will assume that they are equal to their owners, or worse yet, stronger than their owners, both physically and mentally. Being stronger, the dogs will naturally assume that they are more suited to be pack leader, with some dogs willing to exploit this opportunity to take over as top dog.

As long as your dog doesn't get out of control, tugging can be a fun and interactive game.

Not all trainers and behaviorists agree with this theory. Interestingly, in her book *Animals in Translation*, Temple Grandin cites a British study of 14 Golden Retrievers that proved the "tugging leads to dominance" idea as not true. (At least not true in the 14 Golden Retrievers cited in the study.) Winners and losers were more obedient after playing tug-of-war games, and none of the dogs suddenly became more dominant. Of course, one study does not settle this debate conclusively. In addition, Golden Retrievers differ from Border Collies, Australian Cattle Dogs, Miniature Schnauzers, German Shorthaired Pointers, and any number of high-prey-drive dogs.

Whether the dominance theory holds true or not, what tugging can do is stimulate or create arousal in some dogs, especially high-octane dogs. When a puppy or adult dog gets too wound up, owners usually lose control of the game, thereby losing control of their dog. At this point, the dog is beyond his threshold and outside the area of any possibility of learning.

Nonetheless, tugging can be a fun and interactive game that helps release stress and boredom. Chances are your dog will enjoy it, too, and it might just be good for him. The key to success is to understand and correctly read your dog's personality, temperament, and body language. You must control all of the games, and you must win equally. It does not take a genius to figure out that when a dog never wins, he will lose interest in playing, which proves that even dogs don't like losing all the time.

Pick Up Your Toys

To establish and maintain your position as leader, you must control all of the toys with which you and your dog play. Do not leave them lying around so that he can play with them whenever he wants. Remember, you want to establish yourself as the dispenser of all things fun in his life. If all of his toys are available anytime he wants, he will not need you. Give your dog one or two toys that he can play with by himself, such as a tennis ball or chew toy. Keep the "special" toys that are reserved for interactive play put away until you play together.

Pulling It Together

Separately these canine priorities for certain resources may hold little importance or significance to you. Collectively, however, these positions, which are very important to dogs, help you establish and maintain control, which reinforces your position as the dispenser and re-enforcer of all the rules.

Dogs—especially high-drive or high-energy dogs—need guidance and boundaries. Dogs who have boundaries seldom grow into obnoxious,

Life Is a Reinforcement

Living harmoniously with a high-drive dog is more than a ten-minute-a-day training session. It must be a 24-hour-a-day relationship because for your dog, everything in his life is a reinforcement. Every second spent with him is a training session in which you are either adding or subtracting from the human–canine bond. No experience is neutral. Your dog depends on you entirely for all of his needs. When he wants to eat, you feed him. When he wants outside, you open the door. When he wants to play, you interact in a game of tug or fetch. Kisses, hugs, tummy rubs, walks, games, sweet nothings in his ear—these all represent opportunities to bond and instill specific behaviors.

Use your time wisely—when your dog wants to eat, teach him to sit before you put down the bowl. Or teach him to run to his crate to get his food. Teach him to sit nicely while you open the door. Let him know that jumping or rebounding off your body parts is not permitted.

By utilizing these countless day-to-day opportunities to set the ground rules, training will become a snap because you have built a bond of mutual respect in your daily activities.

annoying hooligans, which makes them a joy to live with. However, by giving up ground in one or two or three areas—for instance, allowing a high-drive or high-energy dog to sleep on the bed or allowing him to bolt through gates and doorways—you unwittingly allow your dog to get his foot in the door. Once that happens, it will not take long for him to take total control of the household. He will do as he pleases, when he pleases, and for however long he pleases, with little concern for your expectations. Someone once said that Border Collies were so smart that they could pick your pockets clean and leave you smiling about it. That philosophy could easily apply to most high-drive, high-energy dogs. No doubt we all know one or two friends or relatives who have a dog who runs the household. By the time the owner realized that she had been hoodwinked, the dog was already sitting at the supper table and making his own list of rules. Reestablishing yourself as top dog can be a long and time-consuming task. Remember, it is always easier to instill desired behaviors than to go back and correct unwanted behaviors.

You should never feel guilty about setting ground rules and asking your dog to do as he's told, provided the command is reasonable. You love him, feed him, kiss him, pay his vet bills, groom him, train him, buy him chew toys and tennis balls, and take him on vacation. It is not too much to ask him to respect your leadership position, obey the ground rules, and not run amok.

4

Dog Talk: Speaking Your Dog's Lingo

How many times have you said—or heard someone say—"If only my dog could talk, he could tell me what he's thinking"? Dogs can't talk to us with words, but they can give us a pretty good idea of what they are thinking and feeling by communicating with us through body language, which is a dog's specialized communication system.

Absent mental telepathy or a scientific breakthrough, the truth of the matter is that what dogs are really saying when they bark or growl or what they are thinking when they cock their head at a piece of lint will always remain a bit speculative. We can't get into a dog's head, therefore we can never know for certain what they are thinking. However, by studying a lot of dogs in different situations, experts have built a mosaic of knowledge—and a pretty detailed picture—of their body language, expressions, and actions that help us deduce what our dogs are most likely thinking or feeling.

Decoding your dog's body language takes a bit of practice and can be tricky. However, it's easier than you think, and it's well within the capabilities of most owners. After all, reading body language is something humans do every day, and most do it exceptionally well. For example, you know from everyday life with your family, friends, and coworkers that information about how they feel is often given nonverbally. By reading subtle and not-so-subtle signals, such as posture, gesture, breathing, and energy, you know when they are happy, sad, or irritated, even though they say nothing. You know from their body language when you can push your luck a little more or when you should drop the subject, immediately.

Communicating With High-Drive Dogs

High-drive dogs are smart and inquisitive, and owners need to stay two steps ahead of them at all times. Otherwise, these dogs are likely to get themselves into trouble, which makes communication doubly important. These dogs are like sponges—they love to learn and interact with their owners, and they relish a challenge. Mental stimulation is as important to them as physical activity. They love to be included in daily activities, whether walking, swimming, mowing the lawn, or running errands.

High-drive and high-energy dogs can also become bored and nervous quite quickly, and owners can run into all kinds of trouble if they think that they can sit back and let their dog do his own thing. Quite the opposite is true when you own a turbo-charged dog. You must become proficient at tuning into your dog and reading his body language and knowing what he's going to do *before* he does it. Otherwise, you will likely lose control quickly. Your verbal or physical cues must be clear and consistent, too, or you will likely send confusing signals.

Reading your high-drive dog's body language will help you prevent or manage many problem

But I Said "Sit"!

Australian Shepherds are sight sensitive, which makes them keenly aware of your body language. They can pick up on the slightest change in your deportment. So while your verbal command said *sit*, your body language may have said *down*.

behaviors before they become major issues that put you and your dog on the fast track to a broken human–canine relationship.

Communication Is Everything

Reading a dog's body language is an essential and key ingredient to building a strong human–canine bond. If you've ever tuned in to a self-help show on television, you know that relationships are built on communication. A mutual communication system connects us to others, be it to other people or animals, and feeling connected is an integral part of any good relationship.

Problems arise because many owners expect dogs to understand their ever-changing rules and endless verbal commands, but they fail to take into account that dogs don't speak human. As a result, dogs are often getting blamed for something they didn't do or weren't thinking because owners misread their body language and actions. Because the smartest dog in the world will never master human language, the responsibility of becoming bilingual rests squarely upon your shoulders. In order for the human–canine relationship to flourish, you need to learn to speak dog…so to speak.

Learning to read your dog's body language will make you a better and more effective owner because you will have a communication system that both you and your dog understand. Think how much easier your life (and your dog's life) will be when you understand when he is asking for help (*I'm nervous. I'm anxious. I'm scared. I'm confused. I'm sick.*) as opposed to making a choice to disobey (*I heard you call me. I'll be there as soon as I finish playing with my canine buddies.*).

When you have a common communication system, your dog will be more willing to trust and work with you to learn new behaviors, be they obedience commands or fun tricks and games. Integrating dog training into your daily routine will also become much easier. Owners are happy. Dogs are happy. Everyone wins because a well-trained dog is more likely to be included in your day-to-day activities, and that means that the human–canine possibilities are endless.

Can You Hear Me?

Dogs are pack animals, so cooperating and coexisting are essential to them. Although canine communication is primarily accomplished through body language,

Reading Your High-Drive Dog

Successfully living with a high-drive, high-energy dog (or any dog) requires owners to communicate in the clearest, most effective way. One key component in doing so is the ability to read or interpret accurately what a dog is saying with his behavior and the context in which the behavior is displayed.

verbalization, such as howling and growling, is also part of a dog's repertoire. Yet it appears to be a smaller part, with some breeds (such as Alaskan Malamutes, Siberian Huskies, and Beagles) being more vocal than others. That said, verbalization is pretty standard, regardless of whether it's done by a Beagle or a Border Collie. Here are a few examples of common canine verbalizations.

Barking

Barking conveys different meanings. A dog protecting your car, for example, will usually display deep explosive barks that are frequently accompanied with a frantic charge toward the door or window. Dogs, especially small ones who are doted on by their owners, bark to get attention. Dogs who like to be the center of attention will bark incessantly until their owner responds. Dogs also bark when they are bored, frustrated, excited, and to release excess energy.

Growling

Growling, especially a menacing growl, tells another dog—or heaven forbid, a human—"This is mine. I'm not giving it up without a fight." Growling can also warn intruders that coming any closer may be a hazard to their health.

Dogs often prevent altercations through body language: (1) A terrier and Golden Retriever approach each other and their body language conveys confidence and curiosity. (2) They sniff each other. (3) A Nova Scotia Duck Tolling Retriever approaches cautiously. (4) They go their own way without incident.

So That's What My Dog Is Thinking!

Dogs do not think like humans. They think like dogs because they *are* dogs. The smartest dog in the world will always think like a dog. While it's always fun to guess what your dog might be thinking, avoid anthropomorphizing—attributing human characteristics to animals. It goes without saying that your dog is charming and delightful and no doubt the smartest and cutest dog in the world, and no one is saying not to love him or talk to him or call him by funny, rhyming names. That's what dog lovers do. But he's still a dog—not a little person in a fur coat. Try thinking like a dog rather than trying to get your dog to think like a human. Learn to view the world through his eyes and see what he is really seeing and thinking— not what you want to think that he is seeing and thinking.

Howling

Howling is frequently used to communicate with others who are far away—a doggie GPS system, so to speak. If separated from the pack, howling and waiting for other dogs to respond helps the lost one know in which direction to travel.

Decoding Canine Body Language

Canine body language is a fascinating yet complex topic. Entire books have been written offering in-depth information on the intricacies of a dog's native language. This section is intended to introduce you to the basics of canine communication. By familiarizing yourself with the fundamentals of canine body posture and facial expressions, you can develop a better relationship and understanding of your dog, as well as other dogs.

The positioning of a dog's ears, eyes, lips, nose, tail, head, and legs tell you a lot about what he is thinking or feeling. In a relaxed state, dogs have an overall calm, easygoing appearance. Their body lacks tension. Their lips, eyes, and ears are relaxed and comfortable (as opposed to being forced or held into a specific position). Their eyes are blinking, which is good because blinking indicates friendliness or a nonthreatening intention. Their ears fall naturally and may be at half-mast. The head is lowered and the mouth may be slightly open. A relaxed tail carriage is displayed. Everything about their body conveys a relaxed, stress-free neutral state.

Notice how the body language signals of a relaxed dog contrast with the descriptions that follow, which are a few of the more common canine behaviors. Note also that many of the body language signals can cross over, with the same signal applying to multiple

This rescue Nova Scotia Duck Tolling Retriever's body language and facial expression convey an overall calm appearance. His ears, eyes, mouth (1) and body (2) are relaxed and lack tension.

behaviors. Signals can also have multiple intents depending on the dog's overall body posture, position, and the context of the situation—all of which must be considered when reading a dog. Depending on the individual dog and the situation in which the behavior occurs, the signals may be subtle, not grandiose or obvious. Signals indicating that trouble is brewing generally start out subtle but are overlooked by owners until they increase in intensity. For instance, it's easy to interpret your dog's behavior when he jerks the leash out of your hand, charges and scares another dog, or worse yet, bites and causes serious physical injury. Chances are the warning signals started as a curled lip, a low growl, or an intense stare, yet these signals usually go unnoticed by an owner until the dog explodes. By then the damage is done.

Dogs may exhibit all or only a few of the cues, with some signals happening in the blink of an eye. This is why it is important to pay close attention to and understand your dog's mannerisms in all situations.

Aggression

Aggression is a tricky topic because many types of aggression exist, with entire books written on this one topic. Fear aggression, for example, is a defensive type of aggression. Dominance-related aggression, which is often (albeit incorrectly) categorized as an emotion, is a reaction to a social situation. There's also possession-related aggression or what's often called territorial aggression, or guarding or resource guarding aggression. There's also protective-type aggression, pain-related aggression, predatory aggression, and redirected aggression, to name a few.

Further complicating the topic is the not-so-simple act of categorizing aggression. While people tend to lump dogs into a specific category, dogs aren't machines, so it's not quite as simple as labeling a behavior as a particular type of aggression. For example, a dog may be fearful and angry at the same time and may thereby send conflicting signals. A dog's temperament and upbringing influence how he reacts in a particular situation, too.

That said, aggression does have a few common denominators. Attack-mode aggression, for instance, is pretty easy to identify. Few people mistake the significance of a lunging, snarling, teeth-baring, snapping, salivating dog. Like humans, dogs have different triggers that trigger an aggressive state. Some dogs are mellow and nonconfrontational. Others short-circuit with little provocation (or little provocation in the minds of humans). Intact male dogs frequently posture and challenge each other for the right to mate with a female. If neither male is prepared to back down, fighting that results in serious injury is highly likely.

What Are You Grinning At?

Some breeds, such as Australian Shepherds, have a characteristic grin that exposes their teeth. This friendly behavior is frequently, albeit incorrectly, mistaken for aggression.

On the other hand, some dogs who have been trained on electronic collars will expose their teeth in a grin-like gesture while occasionally snapping at the air as a means of displacing the stress and anxiety caused by these types of collars.

These two similar-looking behaviors communicate different messages.

Cues

Aggression is a serious problem and can escalate from a lip curl to a full-blown attack in the blink of an eye. By learning to recognize the subtle warning signs of impending danger, you can prevent problems by intervening before your dog unloads on another animal or person. You can also prevent him from being on the receiving end of an attack. Aggression signals can include but are not limited to several or all of these cues:

- tense body language, generally oriented in a forward motion and fully adrenalized
- ears drawn back
- eyes strong, staring, and making direct contact with the other animal or person in case further aggressive action is needed
- lips drawn back to expose the teeth
- tail raised, usually held over the dog's back
- explosive barking or growling, which is intended to make the aggressor move away so that a fight does not ensue

Do not wait for signs of aggression to escalate before you call a professional for help.

It is important to note that aggression typically does not happen overnight. Granted, some dogs are born with sour temperaments or a skewed view of the world. Generally speaking, however, dogs are permitted by their owners to develop improper behaviors and subsequently follow a designated path to aggression. A dog's brain is not hardwired to wake up one morning and think *I plan to bite my owner today.* Or *I think I'll rip my canine sibling's ear off after lunch.*

Some aggression signals can be less subtle but equally important to recognize. Look for these cues that indicate that your dog may be headed down a wayward path:

- object guarding, be it food, toys, or furniture. Signals include a puppy or adult dog who snarls, growls, snaps, or displays other guarding behaviors toward objects when people or other animals approach. Don't ignore the first signs, which can be as subtle as a dog lowering his head or crouching over an object, flicking his eyes, glaring, or turning his head in the direction of another animal
- growling at or biting you or other animals
- pushy, bossy behaviors, such as pawing, nudging, whining, and demanding attention
- ignoring learned obedience commands

Breeds and Aggression

Dogs were originally bred for a specific purpose, be it hunting, herding, guarding, fighting, retrieving, and so forth. Although aggression can be seen in any breed of dog, some breeds have been selectively bred for or against aggressive tendencies. For example, many scenthounds are housed and worked in large packs and therefore tend to be peaceful, rarely getting into altercations even with unfamiliar dogs. Their lack of agonistic behavior makes managing large groups of hounds easier. Can you imagine a pack of 30 English Foxhounds on a foxhunt scraping, quarreling, and outright fighting with each other? Mayhem would be inevitable.

Some hounds have long, pendulous lips that help with scenting but tend to inhibit fighting because an opponent could easily grab them. Similarly, retrievers are selectively bred for a "soft mouth," which prevents birds from being mangled when carried back to the hunter. Pointers, which are not allowed to attack birds, are taught to stand still.

That's not to say that hounds and retrievers never fight. Aggression is possible in any breed and any dog. However, many of these selected traits, such as pendulous lips and a soft mouth, tend to reduce contentious or argumentative-type behavior.

On the other hand, terriers have been selectively bred for courage and tenacity, to attack prey and keep on attacking regardless of any injury suffered. Herding dogs have been selectively bred to "bite" livestock to move a particularly stubborn bull or cantankerous ewe. They need to be tough enough to chase down a running bull and make him turn the other way yet controlled enough so as not to attack and kill the livestock.

Some herding breeds guard livestock against predators as opposed to moving it. Their ancestors tended to be larger and more aggressive, not unlike their guard-dog counterparts that were used to protect houses and families. Guard dogs, such as Rottweilers and Doberman Pinschers, bred for their ferocity and size, were also bred to show less fear than other breeds, which can make it harder for owners to tell what they are thinking.

Although dogs display similar patterns of aggression, because of their ancestry and the original purpose for which they were bred, some breeds are more easily stimulated than others toward aggression. Understanding your dog's origin, purpose for which he was bred, and temperament will help you better read his body language.

Ignoring obedience commands or pestering you for affection doesn't mean that you have the makings of Satan's cousin on your hands. However, obeying obedience commands means that your dog accepts you as a leader and is less likely to challenge your authority.

The earlier you recognize these signs, the sooner you can put a stop to them, thereby making your life and your dog's life safer and more enjoyable.

Aggression-type behaviors are a serious problem. Most dog owners—even experienced ones—are not adequately skilled or qualified to handle aggression-based behaviors. Therefore, if you suspect that your dog has aggressive tendencies, it is highly advisable that you seek professional advice from a trainer or behaviorist who is specifically trained in dealing with canine aggression. Do it at the first sign of trouble—do not wait until it has escalated into a bigger problem. Also, choose a trainer who is knowledgeable about your breed and its characteristics.

Anxiety, Fear, and/or Stress

Dogs become anxious, fearful, or stressed for a variety of reasons, including lack of socialization, unfamiliar surroundings, isolation, crowds, strange or loud noises, other dogs and animals, unfamiliar people, and rambunctious toddlers running about. If a human or another animal crosses the fearful dog's perceived safety zone, he may show defensive or aggressive behaviors, such as barking, growling, lunging, biting, or air snapping, which is biting at a threatening object, be it a person or another animal,

(1) This Australian Shepherd's ear position and facial tension indicate that he is not comfortable with the Border Collie's close proximity. (2) Once the Border Collie looks away, the Aussie relaxes slightly.

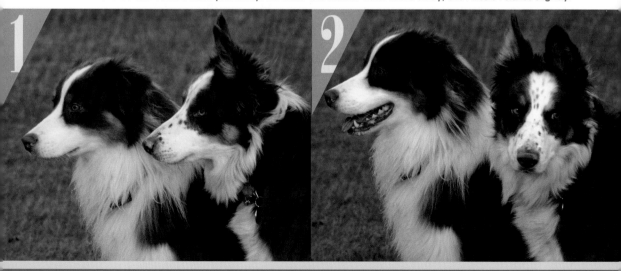

without making contact. Air snaps are a warning signal; they are an inhibited bite, meaning that the dog is restraining himself, but he could easily make contact with his teeth if he wanted to.

Learning a new task or making a mistake while training can cause some dogs stress. Something as simple as a person or another dog passing by too closely can trigger fear or stress in some dogs. *Down* is a vulnerable position because it is more difficult for dogs to run away. Therefore, dogs who are asked to lie down during stressful situations can become even more stressed and worried. Injured dogs frequently become fearful and highly stressed.

Cues

When you know what cues to look for, you can take steps to diffuse the situation. Typical signals that indicate a dog is stressed or fearful can include:
- panting, drooling, and/or yawning
- ears tense, flattened back, and out of the way should the dog be attacked
- eyes open wide, with a lot of the white part showing, dilated pupils; the dog's eyes may be fixed on whatever is scaring him
- in stressful situations, the dog may be looking away to avoid eye contact, which usually means "I'm minding my own business. I'm not approachable. I don't want any trouble"
- tail down and generally tucked between his legs
- sweaty paw prints on floor
- rounded topline (a hunched-over look)

In addition, dogs who are anxious or stressed may sniff the ground, scratch or dig at themselves, and may have dandruff or loss of hair. Also, like some people, some dogs mask their fear by attempting a display of confidence and bravado, but underneath that facade they are worried. Some dogs, depending on their temperament, will display an array of signals, which to some owners can be confusing to decipher. Understanding your dog's temperament and personality, how he reacts to specific situations, the positioning of his tail and ears, and his overall body language will help you unravel what might be going on in his head.

Curiosity

Dogs are curious about all kinds of things, such as strange smells, birds chirping, horses whinnying, sticks, bugs, rocks, puddles, grass, clouds rolling by, and so forth.

Cues

Typical body language cues for curiosity can include:
- ears are alert and erect but not tense, and they may be floppy or asymmetrical
- eyes are inquisitive (not wide open in fear but not squinting); eyes are blinking and/or pointing in the direction of interest

Calm Down!

Dogs use body language to calm another dog or person or to postpone, pacify, or break off conflict with another dog. Experts classify these signals differently. Nikolaas Tinbergen, a noted ethologist, described them as "cutoff signals." Turid Rugaas, a Norwegian dog trainer, refers to them as "calming signals." Dogs engage many common signals to calm another dog or person and can include:

- averting their eyes or head or their entire body away from the other dog or aggressor
- licking the lips of another dog
- sniffing the grass or something on the floor as a threatening dog or person approaches
- flicking their tongue, which is difficult to see in real time but frequently shows up in photographs, as some dogs find posing for photographs stressful
- walking away from the aggressor or troublesome situation very slowly
- yawning

- mouth may be slightly open
- head tilted or cocked to the side (a head tilt can also indicate an attempt to hear a specific sound, or a predatory cue if body posture is tense and directed at another animal or person)
- body position may be directed forward as if ready to pounce or give chase

Excitement

Different things excite and please different dogs. Herding dogs, for example, are easily stimulated by anything that moves, be it a vacuum, livestock, or a fleeing child. The scurrying movement of a rodent can cause terriers to become manic. Most retrievers get wound up at the sight of water or a training dummy, which can only mean one thing—retrieving! Some dogs get excited when they hear the jingle of car keys, when they see their canine buddies, or when their owners arrive home.

Cues

Typical body language cues that indicate excitement include:
- eyes bright and alert
- ears up or forced out to the side—often referred to as airplane or helicopter ears; may be forced backward if locking on a scent or object

- lips loose and relaxed, may appear to be smiling
- tail held over body with a buoyant or self-confident air
- head tilted or cocked to the side
- body radiates playfulness and/or curiosity, may be relaxed or intense, depending on the dog and situation; can turn to predatory behavior, which presents more serious and intense body cues

Predation

Dogs are pack animals. As carnivores, long before they were domesticated, much of their time was spent hunting and scavenging for food, which required strong predatory instincts. Despite thousands of years of domestication, most dogs, be they purebred or mixed breed, still retain many of the predatory instincts of their ancestors, including:

- scenting
- stalking
- chasing
- biting
- killing
- shredding or dissecting

This Shetland Sheepdog's herding instinct means that he loves playing the "catch me if you can" game.

Investigative, agonistic, and ingestive behaviors are all closely associated with predation or predatory-type behaviors. Most often associated with hunting, they can also be seen in play and work behaviors, such as herding and retrieving.

Typical Behaviors

Watch closely and you might see your dog engaging in some of these common predatory-type behaviors:

- tug-of-war between another dog and an object, such as a toy, sock, shoe, etc.
- resource guarding (e.g., food bowl, bone, toy, bed, favorite chair)
- grab bites to the neck, holding bites to the jugular area, bites to the rear leg while playing with another dog
- shaking and "killing" a stuffed toy, ball, tug toy, etc. (very characteristic of terriers)
- rolling in stinky stuff (e.g., rotting carcass of another animal, deer droppings, etc.)
- circling, gathering, and driving behaviors (herding traits)
- chasing games, including chasing a ball, fleeing kids, or another animal running
- retrieving
- carrying objects, such as a toy, slipper, shoe, etc.

Depending on your dog's temperament and personality, some of these traits may or may not escalate into a problem. Terriers, for instance, were originally bred to catch and kill small animals, such as rats and other vermin. If you own a terrier, you know that the scurrying movement of small animals can drive him crazy. Their predatory instinct is strong, so they enjoy playing with squeaky toys that simulate captured prey. In the presence of inexperienced owners, shake and kill games may escalate into aggressive behaviors. Therefore, knowing your dog's temperament and personality allows you to intercede if necessary long before trouble starts brewing.

Rather than correct or punish your dog for doing what comes naturally, try channeling his predatory energy and instincts into fun chase recall or retrieve games that burn excess energy and stimulate his mind. For example, use his natural retrieve instinct

Understanding your dog's instincts will make living with him much easier.

Dogs greet each other by sniffing each other's bum and groin areas.

to fetch your slippers or the newspaper or pick up his bowl after eating. Use his chase instinct to chase you, thereby teaching him a reliable *come* command. Use his tugging instinct to instill a strong desire to play.

Peculiar? Only to Humans

Dogs have what humans perceive as peculiar or offensive behaviors. In reality, they are normal communication signs for dogs. Remember, you must think like a dog. Here are a few of the more common canine behaviors and what they mean.

Bum Sniff

Dogs greet and introduce themselves by sniffing each other's bums. They spend a lot of time doing it, which may make you think that they learn a lot more about each other from sniffing bums than sniffing faces. Someone once referred to bum sniffing, a sign of confidence and courage, as the equivalent of a human handshake. (Surely you'll never shake another hand again without thinking of your dog or cringing.) Some dogs are quite bold and assertive with their sniffing, often advancing to a mounting behavior. Some dogs take offense to being sniffed and will tuck their tail and hindquarters and

This Border Collie is displaying a prey bow. He's looking at sheep and anxiously waiting for a command from his owner.

round their back as if to say "Back off!" If a dog is reactive, he may turn and snap at the sniffing dog.

Groin Sniff

Dogs also engage in groin sniffing as a way of greeting and checking out another dog. Between males, this seems to be a particularly important behavior that induces a type of social inhibition, causing the dog being sniffed to stand still throughout the greeting.

Play Bow

When dogs play bow—elbows touch (or are close to) the ground with their hind end sticking up in the air—they are initiating play. The dog is saying "I am friendly. Let's play!" The dog's tail is down, ears are alert, and eyes and nose are pointed in the direction of the dog with whom he is communicating. A play bow appears to be an innate universal signal, with dogs everywhere seeming to recognize it as an invitation to play.

Prey Bow

A prey bow, which looks slightly different from a play bow, signals that a predatory behavior, such as hunting or attacking, is about to commence. Dogs often use a prey bow when playing, but they also send other signals to their canine buddies that they are not really prey and they are playing, not intending to kill them.

Rolling in Stinky Stuff

Some dogs love rolling in stinky stuff, and it seems the more disgusting the pile of stink, the better. And if they've just had a bath, that is even better yet! (Better for the dogs, that is.) Rolling is a nonthreatening behavior, and it usually means that there are interesting scents lurking about. Dogs roll because it feels good to scratch their bodies, and they also roll to release anxiety. Some dogs, especially those who are easily overstimulated, exhibit strong predatory behaviors and can become overexcited when watching another dog roll. When rolling, a dog is in the *down* position, which is a submissive position and may be misinterpreted by some dogs as an invitation to attack.

Yum! Stinky Stuff

Stool eating (yes, some dogs do this!) isn't a communication skill, per se. However, it is a behavior that's worth mentioning because it can tell you something about your dog. Known as coprophagy, stool eating is incomprehensible to most owners. Theories abound, but many experts believe that dogs develop the distasteful behavior as puppies. A good mother dog naturally consumes all of her puppies' waste material. As puppies grow, they become inquisitive, sniffing, touching, and even eating their own stool. It can also be indicative of two common assumptions:

- a dietary deficiency
- boredom, which high-drive, high-energy dogs—as well as most dogs—are highly susceptible to. If a puppy or adult dog is kenneled in an area that is not cleaned regularly, he may develop the habit of entertaining himself by eating his—or his canine buddies'—stools. Some experts note that stools can become even more fascinating to dogs in cold weather, when they are frozen

Feeding a high-quality, palatable, and nutritious food may help eliminate the problem. Plenty of exercise will ward off boredom, and being conscientious about picking up after your dog will keep eliminate the temptation.

Sniffing Stinky Stuff

Dogs have superior olfactory skills, which is why they are frequently employed to sniff out explosives, drugs, and cadavers. Dogs, such as scenthounds like Bloodhounds, still scent game to hunt. They also sniff as a calming signal, especially if an owner is yelling loudly or a threatening dog is approaching. Dogs sniff as a negotiation and/or greeting signal (the bum and groin stiff) and to identify canine buddies and canine intruders. They also sniff another dog's excrement and urine, especially on fire hydrants, lampposts, and mailbox posts (dubbed as "pee-mail") to find out what's happening in the canine neighborhood. Think of it as 24-hour cable news for canines.

Know Your Dog

Knowing your dog's temperament and personality, his threshold, and what triggers his manic behavior, anxiety, fear, stress, aggression and so forth will go a long way in helping you become a more knowledgeable owner. It also will improve the human–canine relationship by fostering a better understanding between you and your dog. Is he pushy, bossy, cheeky, nervous, dominant, or aggressive? Does he have ants in his pants? If you come on too strong with a timid dog, you will frighten him, thereby creating more stress and anxiety. If you are sweet and overtolerant with a pushy, bossy dog, he will take advantage of you.

Yawning can be a stress signal.

Don't Misjudge His Behavior

Misjudging your dog's personality interferes with the communication/ learning process, which reduces your chances of getting the desired result from your training. For example, high-drive or high-energy dogs are not all brutes. Some are sensitive and quite submissive— sometimes to the point of submissively urinating, which is a reflexive sign that a dog accepts his owner's authority. Most common in young puppies, junior dogs, and shy dogs, a dog will excitedly greet his owner or a visitor by running up to them and urinating on the floor. A submissive dog may also greet a more dominant dog by piddling on the floor as he excitedly licks the dominant dog's muzzle. Owners often read this as a behavioral disorder, a housetraining problem, or a willful act of disobedience. They mistakenly believe that the dog can control himself and he is simply urinating on purpose. Owners immediately go into freak-out mode and scold the dog, telling him that he is a naughty boy, which only exacerbates the problem by causing the dog to become even more submissive. In the dog's mind, he has acknowledged the owner's authority by submissively urinating. When scolded for doing so, he becomes even more submissive in an effort to appease his owner.

Understanding his personality and temperament, plus his quirks and idiosyncrasies, will allow you to intercede quickly and eliminate things your dog perceives as a threat or problem. By doing so, you will protect your dog from potential harm and he will feel less threatened and better able to cope.

Now that you have a basic understanding of canine body language, build your own mosaic of knowledge by watching and observing lots and lots of dogs. Watch dogs on television, at the park, or in your neighbor's yard. Look at them in books and magazines. Look beyond their obvious cuteness to their body posture, head, and ear and tail position. See you if you can pick out any of the characteristics and behaviors noted earlier.

What's His Body Saying?

A dog's body parts tell you a lot about what he is thinking or feeling. The positioning of his ears, eyes, mouth, head, and tail tell you what's going on in his brain. While this list is in no way complete, it will help get you thinking about what your dog is thinking. Watch him when he's playing, eating, sleeping, interacting with other dogs, and so forth, and see if you can pick up on any of these cues:

Ears

- Ears hanging relaxed, coupled with a relaxed tail, indicate a neutral or comfortable state.

- Ears forward (perked-up ears) without excess tension and the head tilted to one side usually indicate curiosity, excitement, playfulness, confidence, and/or interest.

- Ears tensely drawn forward, coupled with a lowered head, can indicate confidence and/or guarding. Can also indicate a predatory/stalking position in which a chase is about to begin.

- Ears pulled back close to the head indicate tension or fear. Can also indicate an attempt to calm or turn off any interaction with another dog, depending on the remaining body posture.

Eyes

- Direct eye contact (often showing the white of the eyes), coupled with staring, usually indicates alertness and/or dominance. Can also indicate a predatory position.

- Wide-open, sparkling, mischievous eyes, coupled with no body tension, usually indicate a dog who is ready for fun—perhaps a game of fetch or a wrestling match with his canine buddies.

- Narrowed eyes, coupled with ears drawn back, generally indicate fear, anxiety, or submissiveness.

- Squinty eyes, coupled with drawn-back ears, relaxed jaw, and tail at half-mast, usually indicate a nonconfrontational greeting.

Head

- Head tilts generally indicate curiosity. Dogs often tilt or cock their head when trying to hear a specific sound better.

- A head tilt, coupled with stiff body posture and teeth showing, may indicate that an attack is forthcoming—especially if this behavior is directed at another dog or person.

Mouth

- Open, relaxed mouth, coupled with a wagging tail at half-mast and lack of body tension, indicates joy and acceptance.

- A closed mouth may indicate stress and/or concentration, depending on the dog's body positioning.

- Lips drawn back can indicate stress and/or appeasement, depending on the overall body position and context of the situation.

- Lip licking (a dog licking another dog's lips) can be a sign of submission and/or acceptance. It's also an expression of bonding.

- Yawning can indicate stress or uneasiness about a situation.

Tail

- Tail raised means that he is confident.

- Tail wagging indicates that he is excited.

- Tail lowered or tucked between his legs means that he is frightened or submissive.

2

Part II

Training Your
High-Energy Dog

5

A
Multitude
of
Methods

Dogs learn through repetition and consistency, and of course, from their successes and failures. That almost sounds simplistic, doesn't it? Yet with dog training, there are countless ways to get from point A to point D, all of which can cause owners—and dogs—an inordinate amount of frustration. After all, there is positive and purely positive motivation, negative motivation, food training, play training, toy training, and clicker training.

The terminology alone—shaping, marking, luring, bribing, reinforcing, and upping the ante—is enough to make your head spin. Throw in the endless paraphernalia employed, from electronic gizmos to metallic gadgetry, and the entire training process can seem more complicated than computer science. However, with a bit of canine behavior and training info—what works, what doesn't, and why—being a savvy trainer is well within the capabilities of most owners.

This chapter is not intended to present you with one absolute method of training, as many wonderful training methods exist. And not one single training technique works for every dog because dogs are individuals with different personalities, temperaments, quirks, and idiosyncrasies. Rather, this chapter is intended to point out some general principles that are the cornerstone of all good training. The starting point for all good owners and trainers is to understand that no two dogs are alike. Terriers do not work like German Shepherd Dogs, Nova Scotia Duck Tolling Retrievers do not behave like Border Collies, and on and on through the breeds. What works for an Australian Shepherd may not work for a Belgian Tervuren, even though both are herding breeds. What works for your current dog may not work for your next dog. What works for your neighbor's dog may not work for your dog.

Serious problems can arise when owners limit themselves to one trainer or one type of training. That is why it is important to take every opportunity to learn about different training techniques and canine behavior.

Classical Conditioning

Think of a lemon. Does it make your mouth tingle? What about chocolate? Does it make you drool? What about the sound of a dentist's drill or finger nails scraping a chalkboard? Does it make your cringe? Grit your teeth? Maybe you contracted food poisoning from eating spoiled shrimp, and the sight of shrimp now makes you nauseous. These are examples of classical conditioning, or establishing a conditioned reflex. The behaviors involve the learning of involuntary responses—responses that you have no control over. You are responding reflexively or automatically.

Russian scientist Ivan Pavlov, best known for his drooling dogs, first described the most notable example of classical conditioning in the early 1900s, when he discovered that a dog salivates at the anticipation of food. In his well-known experiment, Pavlov rang a bell immediately before feeding a dog and found that in time—after about 30 repetitions—the dog would salivate at the sound of the bell alone. The dog had no control over this reflex. Salivating at the sound of the bell became a conditioned reflex.

In retrospect, Pavlov's thesis seems so simple. What he did was take something that had absolutely no meaning to the dog (the bell ringing) and paired it with something really good (the food) over and over and over again until the dog began to equate the meaningless thing (the bell) to the really good thing (the food).

Bribe:
A misuse of a reward or reinforcement. You are bribing when you show a trained dog what you are offering to get him to do what you want. For example, let's say your dog understands the come command. You call him, but he chooses to ignore you because he is busy sniffing the grass. If you whip out a tasty chunk of food or his favorite toy and show him what you have, you are bribing him to come to you.

Correction:
To take a behavior that is wrong or incorrect and make it right. A correction should never mean that a dog is "bad"—only that he did something wrong. You correct the wrong choice and make the right choice happen.

Latent Learning:
When a dog learns something but the knowledge is not immediately expressed until one or two days or even a week later—as if the dog learns a behavior after the fact.

Lure:
Enticing a dog with a reward. Luring is frequently used to show an untrained dog what you want—for example, using a tidbit of food to lure a puppy into a sit or down. Once the puppy understands the behavior, the lure quickly becomes a reward.

Marking:
A signal (usually your voice or a sound) that tells the dog that's the behavior you want. When using a clicker, the click sound "marks" correct behavior. It's an exceptionally efficient way of telling the dog "That's right! That's exactly what I want!"

Reinforcement:
A stimulus—clicker, treat, toy, praise—that alters the probability that a behavior will be repeated. The terms reinforcement and reward are frequently used interchangeably. However, some trainers prefer one term or the other.

Reward:
A piece of food, a toy, physical or verbal praise, or play that is given after the dog performs a desired behavior, such as coming when called.

Shaping:
The process by which dogs (or any animals) are taught behaviors in order to receive a reward. Luring (see above) uses food. Pure shaping—or free shaping—does not involve luring, compelling, or prompting the action but rather rewarding each small increment of a behavior that will eventually add up to the complete behavior.

Verbal Marker:
A word, such as "yes!" or "yea!" that marks the exact second your dog does the correct behavior. A verbal marker is generally used in place of a clicker or to fade out the use of a clicker.

It's Happening all the Time

You might be surprised at how easy it is to teach your dog through classical conditioning. Think of all the things he might already have unwittingly or inadvertently learned. For instance, does he go berserk at the sound of your car keys? If so, he's no doubt associated the jingling with a fun ride in the car. Does he pace and whine and pester you the closer it gets to his dinnertime? Perhaps contrary to academic pessimists, he can tell time! If he's like most dogs, he probably associates the sound of the doorbell with someone arriving because it rings before they enter the house, not afterward.

Classical conditioning is not always associated with something positive. A dog who is petrified of riding in the car may run and hide at the sound of keys jingling. The sound of thunder may paralyze a dog with fear or send him into a frenzy of barking, cowering, pacing, or destructive behavior. A noise-phobic dog may start to shake long before he hears the thunder. A trip to the veterinarian may be enough to cause a dog to shake or whine uncontrollably.

Does your dog know when it's dinnertime? He may have been conditioned by the sounds of his meal being prepared to associate them with food.

In these instances, a dog's conditioned fear response prevents him from thinking or performing a previously learned behavior, such as *sit* or *down* or *come*. Think of something that terrifies you. Maybe it is snakes or spiders or frogs. The presence of a snake, for example, may be so terrifying that you are paralyzed by fear, unable to think or remember something as simple as your telephone number or street address. Your fear overrides your ability to think. The same concept applies to dogs; a dog who is fearful is not in a state to learn anything or even remember previously learned behaviors. It is important to recognize that these dogs are not dumb, willfully disobedient, or stubborn. Their fear overrides their ability to think. Regardless of how much you sweet-talk him or how yummy your treats are, the conditioned fear response will override any previously learned behavior.

Turning Negative Into Positive

That said, classical conditioning is a wonderful and frequently utilized method to teach dogs to overcome emotional issues that interfere with learning. It changes how a dog physiologically responds to something by changing a negative reaction into something positive. For example, if you take your new puppy or adult dog someplace new where he is nervous or worried, such as an obedience class, a park, or a veterinarian's office, his fight or flight hormones will kick in and he will be beyond terrified. There will literally be no reasoning with him because in a terrified state, he will not be capable of thinking, let alone responding to your pleas to behave. However, if you immediately feed him some incredibly tasty tidbits of food each time he walks in the door of a new place—even if he is acting crazy and out of control—and you do that hundreds, maybe even thousands, of times, eventually he will relax and be able to think and respond to training. On the other hand, if you get upset or correct or scold him for being terrified, your counterproductive behaviors will only create a more terrified, insecure dog.

Operant Conditioning

In contrast to classical conditioning, operant conditioning presents a consequence for a dog's actions, teaching him to think about his choices and choose the one that pays a reward (e.g., treats). In the simplest of terms, the essence of operant conditioning is that a dog (or any animal) is required to perform a behavior to receive a reward. Think of it as a cause-and-effect relationship where the dog causes a behavior, such as walking backward, and is rewarded with a positive reinforcement, usually a tasty tidbit. The dog quickly learns that his own behavior causes a reward to happen.

Pioneers of Operant Conditioning

Operant conditioning has been around for more than 150 years. Around 1855, long before the term was coined, Herbert Spencer described an animal learning a response through operant conditioning. However, B.F. Skinner, a noted American psychologist who developed his infamous "Skinner Box" to study operant conditioning in the laboratory, and American scientist Edward Thorndike, who developed the *Law of Effect*, a cornerstone of operant conditioning, are most closely associated with this theory of learning. Thorndike's basic notion was that behavior is driven by consequences. When a behavior has favorable consequences, the probability that the act will be repeated is increased, and a behavior that results in an unpleasant outcome will be avoided by the animal in the future.

Basic Principles

In the simplest of terms, the basic principles of operant conditioning are:
- A behavior that is rewarded will repeat itself.
- A behavior that is ignored will go away.

- The behavior you reward is the behavior you get, which is not necessarily the behavior you want.

Operant conditioning is most closely associated with clicker training, a training method we'll discuss later in this chapter. The idea is to have a dog connect a clicking noise (the conditioned reinforcer) with a yummy tidbit of food. Once the dog understands that the click equals a reward, you can then employ operant conditioning to teach him everything from fun tricks to basic obedience commands. You do this by reinforcing any desired response that the dog offers.

The big advantage to this type of training is that the dog gets rewarded incrementally for figuring out what you want. Most dogs quickly become obsessed with trying to figure out what behavior will produce the "click" and subsequently the tidbit of food. Eventually, the dog fires off a bunch of behaviors, and you mark (click) and reinforce (reward) the behaviors you want. Operant conditioning requires spot-on timing because the behavior you click is the behavior you teach, which requires you to pay close attention to the behaviors your dog is offering. If your timing is off, you are likely to click and inadvertently reward undesired behaviors.

One of the basic principles of operant conditioning is that a behavior that is rewarded will repeat itself.

In almost every situation, classical conditioning will override operant conditioning. When a dog is stressed, be it from fear or excitement, classical conditioning will have a more powerful influence over his behavior than anything he learned through operant conditioning. If a dog is truly terrified, you can dangle sautéed liver in front of his nose and it won't make one iota of difference. The conditioned fear response will overpower any previously learned operant conditioning.

Free Shaping

Operant conditioning is about shaping and marking behaviors by rewarding small increments of a behavior that put the dog on the path to the desired behavior, without luring. True operant trainers never lure, feeling any manipulation of the dog is a corruption of the learning process and doesn't produce a dog who is predisposed to work for you. The key to operant conditioning is that the dog must think that performing a behavior is his idea—not yours—because the behavior must be spontaneously expressed and not elicited by a stimulus, as in classical conditioning. Experts note that this creates a thinking dog: "What do I have to do to get her to click and give me a yummy reward?"

Free shaping can be lengthy and sometimes frustrating for some dogs because it requires a certain mental makeup and a willingness to think independently. Detailed in *Genetics and the Social Behavior of the Dog*, John Paul Scott and John L. Fuller attempted to measure, among other things, the relative intelligence of various breeds of dogs. A complicated maze/obstacle course was set up and food was placed at the end. The four hunting breeds, which generally work independently of their owners, did great. By contrast, the Shelties "…whose ancestors have been selected for their ability to perform complex tasks under close direction from their human masters, performed rather badly."

That's not to say that hunting dogs are smarter than herding dogs, or vice versa. Some dogs, for whatever reason, prefer to be shown what to do. They can find free shaping a chore, and on occasion, a stressful chore, to boot. In these instances, many trainers still free shape quite a bit but also use more luring and showing the dog what is expected of him. After that, the dog catches on right away.

Training Methods

Learning theory is learning theory. Once you understand how each method works, be it classical conditioning or operant conditioning, you can utilize different training methods to accomplish the end result. While many wonderful methods are available for training puppies and adult dogs, the hardest part is deciphering among the enormous variety of methods and trainers. What works, what doesn't? Who is right, who is wrong?

In today's canine-friendly environment, it seems as many trainers and training methods exist as breeds of dogs.

Years ago, the accepted methodology of dog training was that a puppy had to be at least six months old before you began teaching him obedience skills. That concept has since been debunked, and modern-day trainers now recognize the important benefits of early training, as early as eight weeks of age. Additionally, past trainers usually employed the standard pop-and-jerk-type training that involved a choke chain, force, and a total domination of the dog—what is known as training through corrections. If, for example, you wanted to teach a dog to walk on leash, you would put a choke chain and leash on him and start walking, and when he got in front of you, you would jerk him back beside you. The theory was that if you jerked the dog by his neck enough times, he would eventually figure out that staying beside you (i.e., *heel* position) was what you wanted. Although that method usually produced desired results, it often came at a hefty price that included stifling a dog's personality, as well as his willingness and desire to please.

Trainers still exist who adhere to the ideology of force and domination as a means of training, but most trainers today employ gentler training methods that include positive motivation and positive reinforcement. Good trainers allow dogs and owners to be themselves, rather than imposing the same training method, regardless of temperament.

Clicker Training

As we discussed earlier, clicker training, which is based on the laws of learning and operant conditioning, is a great way to train your dog using positive motivation. And it's fun, too. You can train almost any behavior, from basic obedience commands to retrieving to fun and entertaining tricks. A clicker, which is nothing more than an inexpensive plastic device that makes a clicking noise, is a training tool that rewards or marks a behavior—a snapshot, so to speak, of a specific behavior you want to capture. The click tells the dog exactly which behavior you liked. It also tells a dog that a reward is on the way, be it a treat or a toy.

Clicker training starts by pairing classical conditioning with the sound of a clicker. This means that you want to create a positive association from the sound of the clicker for your dog. Trainers do this by clicking, then delivering a tasty tidbit to the dog, then repeating the process again and again—perhaps 25 or 30 times in rapid succession. You are classically conditioning the dog to respond to the sound of the clicker, just as Pavlov conditioned his dogs to respond to the bell. In a relatively short time, the dog will make the positive association between the sound of the clicking noise and a yummy treat. In training terminology, this process is known as *priming the pump, loading the clicker*, or *powering up the clicker*.

Theoretically, you don't even need to use a clicker. A verbal cue or marker word, such as a crisp "yes!" or any perfectly timed one-syllable word like "yea!" works, too. The clicker's slight advantage is that it marks the behavior in an unemotional manner.

The key is that you need something—a clicker or a verbal word—that marks the behavior and tells your dog that the behavior he performed is the behavior you wanted and the behavior you would like him to repeat. Without a marker (a click or verbal cue) that distinguishes a small piece of behavior, it will be more difficult to train the behavior.

Timing is just as important because the theory of operant conditioning is that reinforced (rewarded) behaviors are more likely to be repeated behaviors. Your timing must be spot on, or you are likely to mark behaviors you do not necessarily want repeated. For instance, if you are teaching your dog to sit and you click at the exact moment he paws your leg, you just told him that pawing your leg is the behavior you want. You can't then go back and scold him for pawing your leg. That's not fair. Or if you click at the exact moment he stands up, you are telling him that standing up is the behavior you wanted. If you click at the exact moment he barks, you are teaching him to bark. Do you see the pattern?

A number of good books are available that

Instead of a clicker, you can say the word "yes" to mark your dog's correct behavior.

delve into the intricacies of clicker training. Sometimes, however, books are not enough, and you may need a trainer who can set you on the path to proper clicker training.

Positive Training and Reinforcement

Ideally, all dog training, be it basic obedience commands or fun games and tricks, should be taught to dogs positively. But the concept of positive training can be a bit confusing for some owners because they occasionally misinterpret positive to mean being permissive, thereby allowing their dog to run amok and do whatever he wants, whenever he wants. Just because you use positive rewards like yummy treats and fun toys and interactive play doesn't give your dog permission to be out of control.

The concept behind positive motivation and reinforcement is that when a behavior has favorable consequences, the probability that the behavior will be repeated is increased. For example, if every single time your puppy comes to you he receives a ton of positive reinforcement in terms of verbal praise and a tasty tidbit or interactive play, he will learn to repeat the behavior because in his mind, coming when called is always fun, positive, and rewarding. The dog learned a behavior through positive motivation and reinforcement.

It's worth clarifying that in dog training, *positive* simply means adding something, such as cheery praise, a favorite toy, or a tidbit of food, that will make a behavior, such as a *sit* or *down*, more likely to occur in the future. *If you sit, Mummy will reward you with a cookie.* Positive does not necessarily mean being nice. Think about the owner who smiles while she's jerking her dog into a *sit* with a choke chain and then rewards with a yummy tidbit. Is that positive training? Any owner or trainer can be upbeat and sweet, but that doesn't mean that they are positive trainers. This is a point worth remembering when you are searching for an obedience trainer.

Without getting too bogged down in the complexities and terminologies of positive motivation/reinforcement, let's just say that the general concept of positive motivation and reinforcement is teaching dogs without corrections or harsh handling. It's about training dogs primarily or exclusively by positive motivation and reinforcement to reinforce the behaviors you want. The reward can be a combination of verbal or physical praise coupled with a tasty tidbit of food or his favorite toy.

At one time correction training (jerking a dog into the *heel* position) was standard operating procedure in many dog classes. Now, the dog is lured into the *heel* position with a tasty tidbit or favorite toy, and through positive reinforcement and a lot of patience, repetition, and consistency, the dog learns that walking beside you is where you want him to be. Positive motivation teaches dogs how to choose the correct behavior, as opposed to avoiding the wrong behavior because of correction training.

Treats are one of the most popular motivators used in dog training.

Purely Positive Training

The essence behind purely positive training is that everything is positive and a dog is never, ever corrected regardless of the circumstances. That sounds wonderful, right? After all, no one wants to scold or correct a dog. We all want our puppies to grow into adult dogs who never misbehave or get into trouble or embarrass us in public. That's paradise, and unfortunately it rarely exists in the world of raising and training dogs (or teenagers!), and therein lies the problem.

Purely positive has been compared to raising kids without ever telling them no or setting any boundaries. While this might look good on paper, when you send it down the runway, it does not always fly and here is why: Dogs need boundaries. They understand boundaries. They are happy when they have rules and boundaries. Rules give a dog freedom. Dogs without boundaries grow into unruly hooligans.

Granted, all training should be positive. And purely positive training is great for dogs who have been trained harshly in the past because it provides a safe way to let them know that the rules have changed and that training is fun, and more importantly, safe. However, it's highly probable that your hound will find chasing a deer or a paper bag blowing in the wind more fun than any cookie you could ever offer. Or your terrier will find chasing a rabbit or unearthing a rodent more exciting than a piece of steak. Or your herding breed will finding chasing anything that runs fun because it is more entertaining than the tidbit of cheese you are attempting to dangle in front of his nose.

As a result, purely positive training may not serve you well in all instances. That's not to imply that you should train through force, corrections, or intimidation. That's old-style training and counterproductive to a happy, harmonious, and mutually respectful human–canine relationship.

Positive Motivation Versus Purely Positive

The key difference between positive motivation trainers and purely positive trainers are the corrections or lack of corrections. And this is where many trainers part company. Purely positive trainers never, ever correct a dog, regardless of the circumstances. If they ask a trained dog to come and he chooses to ignore the command, they wait until he does the command or any other command they can reward, or they distract him with another command. That said, a number of trainers advocate purely positive training and have had, in their opinions, great success.

On the other hand, the philosophy behind most positive motivation/reinforcement trainers is that when a trained dog thoroughly understands a command, such as *down*, yet he chooses to ignore the command, they feel that a correction is warranted. *Yes, you can run and play and swim and we will have a barrel of fun, but you cannot kill my chickens, bolt out doors, bark incessantly, or fight with other dogs. When I ask you to come, you must come. When I ask you to down, you must down.* Rules are black and white, and if a trained dog chooses to willfully ignore a command, there are consequences. The consequences for ignoring a command, depending on the dog's temperament and personality, can range from a mild *"Aahhhhhh"* to a stronger *"Knock it off"* command, or as some trainers advocate, a time-out, which is when the dog is taken

Understand Your Dog

No two dogs are alike. Even littermates can be as different as night and day. One may be dominant, the other submissive. One may have a high play drive, the other a high food drive. One may be gregarious, the other may be timid. Understanding your puppy's personality and temperament is key to developing a training program that works for you. For instance:

- Miniature Schnauzers are very athletic and can have tons of drive and attitude, but they are terriers. A lot of dog in a little package, you cannot force a Miniature Schnauzer—or any terrier—to do something he does not want to do. It is a battle you will not win. Schnauzers—along with most terriers—must think that everything is their idea.

- Australian Cattle Dogs are tough little dogs, which they need to be for their jobs. The puppies tend to look like grown-up dogs, so owners then treat them as if they were adults rather than the puppies they truly are. They can be argumentative, and they don't like to be forced into anything. They too must think that everything is their idea. You can't make them come into your space—you need to encourage them into it.

- Border Collies are born with an intense desire to work. They come with lots of problems, but work ethic is not one of them. You must stay two steps ahead of them at all times and give them the impression you are on top of every situation.

- Bull Terriers, while not the first breed that leaps to mind when talking about high-drive, high-energy dogs, are energetic, determined, and always on the go when it comes to something they want, which usually conflicts with what you want.

away from the work, game, or job that he loves. (For more information on corrections and discipline, see Chapter 6.)

Combining Your Options

The great thing about dog training is the options. You can use any combination of training that works for you and your dog, provided, of course, they are fun, fair, and humane. You can lure a dog into a *down* or strictly go the route of clicker training and operant conditioning. You can use food and toys and physical and verbal praise. You can try purely positive, too, if that better suits your dog and his temperament. The more you learn about canine behavior and training, the more you customize a training program that best suits your dog's personality and temperament.

You Need to Control the Reinforcements

Dogs are learning all the time, whether or not you are present. If, for example, you fail to restrict a dog's freedom, he is likely to learn bad habits, such as peeing on the carpet, eating the wall, or chewing the upholstered furniture.

Some behaviors are self-rewarding, which means that you—the trainer—may not be in control of all of the reinforcements your dog receives. For example, barking at the mail carrier is self-rewarding because when she leaves, the dog thinks *Look how clever I am. My barking made her leave!* Raiding the trashcan reaps mounds of yummy, spoiled garbage, which is self-rewarding. Fence fighting with the dog next door, swiping food off the counter, bolting out doors, and digging in the garden are also self-rewarding behaviors. Remember, any behavior that is rewarded will continue in frequency.

As a savvy dog trainer and owner, it is your job to be on the lookout for behaviors that are self-rewarding so that you can eliminate them by managing your dog's environment. Set your dog up to succeed so that you can reward him for positive and desired behaviors, thereby teaching him in a fun and humane manner which behaviors are acceptable and which should be dropped immediately.

You Are the Primary Motivator

Just like people, dogs need motivation to learn. After all, would you go to work every day if you didn't receive a paycheck? If you stopped getting paid at noon, would you go back to work after lunch? Ideally, a dog's primary motivator should be you—pleasing you and working for you for verbal and physical praise, for play, for fun, and for the love of working. Therefore, you must have a good relationship. He must enjoy being with you and vice versa. He must see you as his leader. He must respect you but not fear you. He must see you as someone who is important enough to issue commands.

When you are your dog's primary source of fun and motivation, you build a strong human–canine bond that helps carry you through the trouble spots. Dogs, especially puppies, are easily distracted by environmental stimuli, such as birds singing, car noises, kids playing, lawn mowers, other dogs, clouds rolling by, and so forth. Motivating your dog with your voice and/or body language allows you to get his attention when he is distracted, such as at the veterinarian's office or when walking in the park.

To remain your dog's primary source of motivation, you must motivate him throughout his life. Depending on your dog's breed and barring any unforeseen disasters, he will likely live somewhere between 10 and 15 years. That is a long time to be his primary motivator. However, dogs who do not continue to receive positive interaction and motivation from their owners shut down, tune them out, and frequently refuse to do the simplest of commands. This is especially true for high-drive, high-energy dogs, who tend to become bored quite quickly. Therefore, you must be funny, silly, animated, engaging, and two steps ahead of them at all times.

The goal is to keep your dog's attention on you, which means that you must be more exciting and stimulating than his surroundings—and there is a lot of competition out there. As he grows and matures, you can begin asking for longer periods of continuous attention.

Verbal Praise and Tone of Voice

Your tone of voice is the greatest motivator and training tool, more so than any treat or toy. What you say and how you say it can make the difference between a dog who is motivated to respond to your commands and one who wanders off to find something (or someone!) more exciting. You might not have a treat at the veterinarian's office or when walking your dog, but you always have your voice.

You should be the primary motivator for your dog—which means that you need to establish a mutually respectful relationship.

Some dogs become happy and wag their tails when their owner speaks to them in a normal tone of voice. Other dogs get excited or cock their head at the sound of a high-pitched voice. Others strut around bursting with pride when they are rewarded with a simple "Good boy!" Some dogs are more responsive to low, soothing tones—staring adoringly at you as they wait to see what you will do. Harsh voices make some dogs cower and run for cover. Others consider a harsh or angry voice as threatening and may bite. If your voice and mannerisms are too pushy, some dogs will take offense. In their mind, they are thinking *Look how hard I can push back!*

What constitutes praise for one dog is completely different for another. Therefore, pay attention to the sound of your voice and how your dog reacts. Is your voice happy? When your dog retrieves a ball, does your voice squeal with excitement? "Look at you! Aren't you clever!"

Motivation and Praise

Socially oriented dogs respond actively to praise and rewards—they make a dog want to keep trying and working for you. If a dog receives praise and a reward each and every time he comes to you, he will associate coming to you as something good and fun. If he comes to you but is scolded for peeing on the rug ten minutes ago, chances are high that he will not want to come the next time he is called.

At the veterinarian's office, is your voice calm and reassuring? When your dog comes tearing back to you, does your voice motivate and encourage him? Are his ears and tail up? Is he pleased with himself? Or is he frightened and cowering? Do you bludgeon him to death with your harsh, angry voice? Or bore him with a monotonous voice that drones on and on, regardless of his achievements?

Bored to Tears

When dogs hear a boring, repetitive tone of voice for every command—"Good boy," "Come," "Good dog," "Sit," "No," "Fido, don't do that," "Good dog," "Heel," "Stop that," "No, come here"—all the words run together, and the dog hears "Blah, blah, blah, Fido, blah, blah, blah, Fido." Besides being excruciatingly boring, which has zero motivational power, the dog is unable to decipher between obedience commands and praise. Therefore, he never gets a sense of what behaviors you really like.

High-drive, high-energy dogs are unique, and you must temper your voice and mannerisms to suit their individual temperaments and personalities. A high-pitched, animated voice may be perfect for motivating an English Cocker Spaniel, but some dogs, such as Border Collies, Australian Shepherds, and Labrador Retrievers, are frequently on the verge of being out of control. Therefore, calm praise works best because even the tiniest excitement in an owner's voice will excite the dogs even more, causing them to become too revved up to concentrate on the task at hand. Some high-drive dogs are very sensitive, and they need calm, soothing praise. All they want to know is that they are doing a good job.

Physical Praise

Physical praise is a great motivator, too, especially when combined with verbal praise. Tap your dog on the shoulder as you tell him he is wonderful. Kiss his nose, or get on the ground and hug him when he comes tearing over to you or brings his ball back. Some dogs dislike being tapped on the head, which is what owners naturally want to do. Instead, stroke his back or chest area lightly, or scratch under his chin as you tell him he is brilliant.

Physical praise is a personal thing with dogs. Some dogs love it; others dislike it. Some dogs like a little physical praise, but give them too much and they crumble. Depending on your dog's temperament and personality, physical praise may be too stimulating and exciting. For some dogs, especially young puppies, the anticipation alone of physical praise is enough to send them into uncontrollable wiggles, unable to concentrate on the task at hand. If this is the case, modify your physical praise so that it is calm and reassuring, or eliminate it temporarily until your dog has matured and can handle small doses without losing control of his body.

Do you bore your high-drive dog to tears? Don't be afraid to act silly and have fun with him.

Please Don't Touch

Some dogs—especially herding dogs—enjoy physical interaction if they have a toy but dislike being stroked, patted, petted, or otherwise touched when they are working. It annoys them. Generally speaking, herding dogs want to work. Most are not interested in physical praise—it distracts them from their job. All they want is an enthusiastic "Good boy!" and a chance to get their toy or get on with their work.

Finding what works best for your dog involves reading his body language, as well as a bit of trial and error (and error and error).

How he reacts is the best indicator. Does he lean into you—happy, relaxed, panting, eyes open? Or does he lean away, trying to avoid physical contact? Shelties, for instance, are notorious for disliking physical praise and will usually pin back their ears, lower their head, or avert their eyes. In these instances, verbal praise alone is your best bet. If you want to teach your dog to enjoy physical contact, teach it separately from obedience training and do it in a fun and humane manner. It's okay when dogs dislike physical praise—they shouldn't be forced to endure it, just because we enjoy it.

Toys, Games, and Food

Toys, games, and food are excellent motivators, too. Often referred to as secondary motivators, they help stimulate and excite puppies and adult dogs. As trainer and author Bobbie Anderson likes to say, they are extensions of yourself—that little extra perk that puts some oomph into your training. They can include any type of toy— tennis ball, soccer ball, ball on a rope, stuffed toy, tug toy, a piece of rubber garden hose, or even an empty plastic water bottle.

Food is probably the most popular motivator. Dogs tend to like smelly foods, so any tasty tidbit will work, such as boiled chicken or liver, cheese, hot dogs, leftover steak, tortellini, and so forth. Use something other than your dog's daily food or kibble. Think of training treats as $100 bills. If, for example, a friend offered you $1 to bathe her dog, would you do it? What if she offered you $100? That would up your motivation considerably, wouldn't it? Apply the same concept when training your dog. Use $100 bills (figuratively, not literally!) to motivate him.

Soft foods work better than hard, crunchy dog bones. You want your dog to chew and quickly swallow the tidbit in less than a second or two. You don't want him standing around for 20 seconds crunching a hard dog bone. Use tiny pieces of food about the size of a raisin or small pea. The goal is to motivate, engage, and reward your puppy, not fill him up with big treats. That said, be generous with your treats in the beginning so that your puppy understands that you "pay" well. Learn to spit or toss food with precision, too. Not only will this teach your puppy to catch (a fun trick) and to watch your face (no telling when you might spit something yummy), but it will help you quickly reward him when he is beyond your reach.

Consider keeping tasty treats or your dog's favorite toy in your pocket, or have containers of food or toys strategically

It's All About the Job

A lot of high-prey-drive dogs, such as Border Collies, Belgian Tervurens, Australian Shepherds, and Labrador Retrievers, are extremely driven. Many of these dogs don't care about food or toys, preferring instead to work for their owner or for the sheer joy of doing their job. That said, some dogs are born with a natural and strong desire to play, while with other dogs, that desire and enthusiasm must be nurtured and encouraged.

placed around the house or yard. This way you will always have a tidbit or toy handy when your puppy or adult dog does something clever. Surprise him by "finding" a tidbit or toy on a shelf or behind a planter box. Ask him "What's this?" Have him do a quick *sit* for a treat, or engage in a quick game of tug or retrieve.

It's Not About Bribes

It is worth mentioning that food has fallen out of favor with some trainers, but the food is not the problem. Where owners inadvertently run amok is by allowing the food (or toys) to become the primary motivator. Hopefully your dog comes when he is called because he thinks that being with you is more fun than anything else in his world—not because bribing or luring him with a chunk of food or a favorite toy works better. The problem with luring and bribing is that when the food or toy is not forthcoming, most dogs have little or no interest in coming when called, sitting, downing, walking nicely on leash, or doing anything whatsoever. That is why you must work hard to establish yourself as his primary motivator—to motivate him with your voice and mannerisms, to be the most exciting person in his world.

Find What Motivates Your Dog

Different things motivate different dogs. A ball on a rope may motivate one puppy, while his littermate brother may go wild at the sight of a flying disc or piece of rubber garden hose. Some dogs like funny noises. Others will do backflips for a tidbit of food. Some breeds care little about food in the presence of toys. Some dogs love food and toys equally and will work for either one. Others will work for toys as long as food is not visible. Once the food comes out, it is difficult to get them tuned in to a toy again.

Generally speaking, terriers tend to like "shake and kill" games, most sporting and working dogs like to tug, and herding dogs usually favor movement, such as chase and prey games.

Find out what motivates your puppy—discover what excites him and what is most rewarding to him, and use it to your advantage. If you have multiple dogs, you will need to find out what works best for each dog. Once you find that magic button, use it only when playing or training. For example, if his favorite toy is a piece of rubber garden hose, do not allow him free access to it. Save it for those times when you interact together, such as during play or training sessions. If he has access to it anytime he wants, he will lose interest in it.

It is perfectly acceptable to combine motivators, too. Keep your dog guessing by using a tasty tidbit of food for a *sit* and then whipping out his favorite toy when he comes tearing back to you on a *recall*. Or use different toys—a tug toy for a *down* and a favorite squeaky toy for a *sit*. Hide toys or treats around the house or yard, and when your dog does something exceptional, run and find a treat. Excitedly say "Look what I found!" or "What's this?"

The Art of Timing

Dog training is all about timing. Correct timing tells your dog exactly which behavior you are rewarding. Poor timing—praise that is given too soon or too late—confuses dogs. Good timing can be a bit tricky, but given a bit of practice, it is a skill anyone can learn. It also helps to look at it from your dog's perspective. What is he doing at the exact moment you are telling him he is a good boy? Is it a behavior you want to reinforce?

Find out what motivates your dog. For many high-drive breeds, toys will do the trick.

Remember, you get the behavior you reward, which may not necessarily be the behavior you want. If, for example, you verbally reward your dog with "Good boy!" as he charges out the door, he will think that charging out the door is what you like, and he'll keep doing it. If you give him a tasty tidbit each time he barks, he is pretty much guaranteed to bark when he sees you. If he jumps on you and you say "Off" yet praise him while he is still jumping on you, you are reinforcing the behavior of jumping on you—you are telling him that this behavior is what you like. You must be aware of what you are reinforcing when you train your dog.

On the other hand, if your puppy comes tearing over to you, his tail and ears up with an attitude that screams "Here I am!" and you lavish him with a potpourri of kisses and treats and plenty of praise—"What a good come!"—he will think that coming to you is fun, and that is definitely a behavior you want to reinforce.

Continuous Praise

Continuous praise is problematic because chances are high that you will praise at the wrong time, thereby reinforcing the wrong behavior. For instance, if your praise is: "Look at you! What a good boy. You are the best and cutest and smartest dog in the

Time your praise right so your dog understands what he's being rewarded for.

world! I love you so much, and you are doing such a good *sit*! What a perfect boy. Keep doing your *sit* and I'll give you a yummy treat!" Chances are your endless chatter will cause your dog to become excited and unable to concentrate on the task at hand, and chances are equally high that he will move. If he stands up or moves away while you are chatting, you will inadvertently be praising and rewarding the movement rather than the *sit*.

Nagging

Nagging is also problematic. For example, constantly saying your dog's name—"Fido, Fido, Fido"—without putting a command to it teaches him to become indifferent to your voice and ignore his name. Ideally, every time you use his name, put a command to it, such as "Fido, come!" or "Fido, sit" or "Fido, here!"

That said, if you say your dog's name—"Fido, come!"—and he ignores you, and you say it again, and he continues to sniff bugs and ignore you, and you say it again and still nothing happens, you are inadvertently teaching your dog that it is okay for him to ignore you and do as he pleases because nothing happens to him when he is inattentive.

Think of the kid who runs amok in the grocery store while the mother repeatedly yells his name. "Johnny!" "Johnny!" "Johnny!" Johnny ignores his mom, so her voice gets louder and more demanding. "Johnny, come here!" "Johnny! Come here right now!" "Johnny, you better come here right this minute or else…." Johnny continues to ignore his mom, so she gives up, ignores the situation, and continues shopping. What message is she sending? Johnny quickly learns that there are no consequences to his behavior.

Try to look at your actions and the timing of your praise from your dog's point of view. What message are you sending? What behaviors are you reinforcing?

Remember that every dog and owner is different. What works for you and your dog may not work for your friend and her dog. Therefore, find what works for you. It is okay to pick and choose from each of the methods. Experiment until you find a way to get your dog doing what you want, but use only humane methods. Using force or punishment is counterproductive, and you will only end up hurting your relationship with your dog.

Chapter 6

Doggy Discipline: Corrections and Your High-Energy Dog

The term *correction* means a lot of different things to a lot of different people in the world of dog training. In the simplest of terms, it means taking a behavior that is wrong and making it right. It should never mean that a dog is "bad" or you are punishing him—only that his choice was wrong and you're going to help him make the right choice.

Although this idea seems easy enough, the use of corrections is one of the more hotly debated topics in the dog-training world. Passionate owners and trainers argue endlessly about the pros and cons: corrections versus no corrections; corrections versus discipline; and correcting adults versus correcting puppies are just some of the enduring discussions. In spite of these differences, correcting a dog remains a touchy yet timely topic because it is you who will have to make the decision about corrections and your high-drive dog. Here's how to make sense of this complex topic.

Set Your Puppy Up to Succeed

Before you even decide how to deal with your dog when he's done something you don't want, figure out ways to get him to make the right choice from the beginning. In other words, set him up to succeed. Ideally, you should take every opportunity to manipulate his environment so that he develops the habits you want rather than put him in a position where he can get himself into trouble and develop the habits you don't. Set him up to succeed so that you can praise and reward the behaviors you want to instill rather than correct the undesirable behaviors.

Set your puppy up to succeed by preventing him from getting into trouble in the first place.

For example, giving a puppy free run of the house puts him in a position to develop bad habits, such as peeing from one end of the house to the other, ransacking trashcans, swiping food off the counter, and chewing furniture, shoes, electrical cords, walls and anything else he can sink his teeth into. Owners immediately scold or correct a puppy for being bad, which is unfair. After all, why is your puppy (or an untrained adult dog) the bad one when it was you who failed to manage his environment? He's a puppy. He doesn't know any better. Would you expect a six-month-old human baby to be toilet trained? I think not. So why would you expect a young puppy to act like a well-behaved adult dog? Instead, set him up to succeed by using baby gates or an exercise pen to corral his movement, thereby preventing him from chewing or pottying on your expensive Oriental rug.

Prevention Is Key

To foster good habits and minimize destruction, follow these simple guidelines, which are geared toward puppies but apply equally well to untrained adult dogs:

- Before bringing your new puppy home, plan ahead. Have an exercise or playpen and a crate ready. Do not wait until you think that you need them. If you have a puppy or adult dog—especially a high-drive or high-energy breed—you will need them.

- When you cannot keep a constant watch on your puppy, keep him confined in an exercise pen, playpen, crate, or puppy-proofed area with a yummy chew toy like a Nylabone. This includes when you need to run to the mailbox, while you make dinner, or when you need to dash outside for two minutes to move the sprinkler.

Keep your interactions with your puppy positive.

- Once your puppy arrives at your home, know where he is and what he is doing at all times. You would not dream of taking your eyes off a toddler, and you should never take your eyes off a puppy or an untrained adult dog when he is not safely confined.

- Puppy-proof your home before your puppy arrives. Puppies are ingenious when it comes to finding items to chew. Pick up anything and everything he is likely to put in his mouth, including shoes, purses, backpacks, jackets, candles, rugs, magazines, books, electrical cords, toys, medications, and so forth.

- A tired dog is a happy dog. Make sure that your puppy or adult dog receives plenty of physical exercise and mental stimulation each day. Lacking adequate and appropriate exercise, dogs release pent-up energy through chewing, digging, barking, or any number of destructive or annoying behaviors.

- Never allow him to run around unrestricted inside your house (with or without other dogs).

- Never put him in a position where he can ignore your commands.

Did you know that there are four reasons a trained dog does not respond correctly to a command? They are:
- The dog is confused.
- The dog is nervous or afraid.
- The dog is distracted.
- The dog feels that he has a choice.

Keep It Positive

Only on very rare occasions should you need to scold or correct a young puppy. Ideally, you should keep all negative interactions to a minimum. (If your puppy hears "NO!" enough times, he'll think that is his name.) The majority of your interactions should be fun and exciting as you foster his madcap personality, mold his future character, and lay the foundation for a strong human–canine bond.

Another reason to avoid corrections and keep interactions positive is the nature of your dog. High-drive, high-energy puppies and adult dogs are smart and quick to learn, but they are sensitive. As a result, many of them don't like to be wrong. Some of them end up worried and stressed if they are wrong or make a mistake, which can cause problems down the road. Rewarding the right behaviors allows you to reinforce the behaviors you want, and as a result, your dog isn't getting frustrated or worried from continually being wrong.

Are You the Problem?

Dogs are a product of what we put into them. If you are having problems with your dog, always look to yourself first for what is wrong. Did you provide adequate training? Does he understand your commands? Are the commands wishy-washy, too harsh, not demanding enough? Did you manage his environment sufficiently?

If you have done a good job establishing yourself as a leader and you have laid the foundation for a respectful and mutually trusting relationship with your puppy, there should be little need for corrections as he grows and matures. Remember, it is much, much easier and more effective to create and reward good habits than it is to try to fix unwanted behaviors once they become ingrained.

When Is Discipline Warranted?

Two instances come to mind for which discipline might be warranted. First, serious infractions such as biting someone or biting another animal should be stopped immediately. Otherwise a puppy will grow into an adult dog who thinks that biting is acceptable, which is a disastrous situation for any dog. Milder problems, such as chewing, digging, or barking—behaviors that are natural for dogs but viewed as problematic by owners—should be prevented by manipulating and managing a puppy's or adult dog's environment so that he cannot develop or continue these bad habits. (See Chapter 11 for more information on problem behaviors.)

Secondly, there comes a time in nearly every dog's life, especially during adolescence, when he deliberately chooses to ignore his owner because he has his own agenda and would rather do something else. He is testing the rules to see if they still apply. For example, you have diligently taught your young dog to come, and after 900 or 1000 repetitions (when he is about five or six months old), he understands that the word *come* means "Stop what you are doing and run as fast as you can to me, right now." One day you call him and he decides to ignore your command and sniff the grass, pee on a bush, or run off and play with his canine buddies. Immediate correction will teach him that he must respond to you when you give him important commands.

However, before you decide that a correction is warranted, there are two things you must be absolutely, positively certain of: your dog understands the command and you didn't inadvertently ask for the wrong thing.

Does He Understand the Command?

The golden rule of dog training is that you never, ever correct a puppy (or adult dog) for something he does not know or understand or if he is confused or frightened. It does not matter if he is eight weeks, eight months, or eight years old. If you have not thoroughly taught a command, it is unfair to correct him for failing to comply. Puppies do not come preprogrammed. They do not magically understand "Come" or "Sit," or "Down," or

Dogs aren't born knowing the *come* command—they must be taught to obey it.

"Get off the couch!" Nor do they understand "Oh honey, Mommy loves you but please don't piddle in the middle of the carpet" or "Don't run out in the street, honey, you'll get hit by a car."

Equally unfair is correcting a puppy for your temporary lapse of good judgment. If, for example, you leave your puppy unattended while you shower or run to the post office, you should not be surprised when you return to find epic amounts of destruction. To correct a puppy or adult dog in these situations is unfair. After all, it was you who left him unattended. He was simply doing what comes naturally to dogs—chewing, digging, exploring, and pottying.

A good rule of thumb is to encourage and help a puppy (or an untrained adult dog) who is learning a new task or is confused or worried. Honest errors, which are almost always a result of confusion, should not be corrected. Instead, they should come with information, such as "I'm sorry sweetheart, that isn't right. Let's try it again." When you correct a dog who does not understand a command or who is confused or afraid, you run the risk of losing that dog's trust. The dog, depending on his temperament, may become afraid to be wrong and may stop trying for fear of making a mistake.

When a dog has thoroughly mastered a task, be it *sit*, *down*, *stay*, or *come*, yet he chooses not to comply, then and only then is it fair to correct him. Again, you must first be absolutely sure that your dog heard and understands the command.

You should never correct a dog if you've given him the wrong message.

Did You Send the Wrong Message?

You must also be careful not to correct a dog who is doing what he thinks you want because you gave him the wrong message. There are a number of reasons a dog may not respond to a command. He may not have heard you, or he might be confused or too fearful to respond. Perhaps your voice said "Sit" but your body language said "Down." This is particularly applicable to many high-drive dogs—especially herding breeds—who are sight sensitive. They are acutely aware of movement, and many of them will zero in on the slightest shift in your body language rather than your

Many high-drive dogs are sensitive and will shut down from harsh corrections.

voice command. A Border Collie can see sheep on the horizon at 400 yards (366 m)—do you think that he can't see your arm twitch from 10 feet (3 m) away?

You also must be certain that what you thought you taught is what the dog learned. For example, when teaching the *down* command, if you unconsciously turn your head every time you say "Down," your dog is likely to assume that when you turn your head, he is supposed to down. All of these situations must be taken into account before you jump to a correction.

What Type of Correction Is Right?

Ask a dozen trainers how to correct a puppy or adult dog and you are guaranteed a dozen different answers. No two trainers will agree on the sort and dose required. Further complicating the matter, some trainers subscribe to the purely positive viewpoint of training where a dog is never, ever corrected—verbally or physically—regardless of the situation. Some trainers adhere to the philosophy of training only through corrections (definitely not recommended). Others use verbal corrections but no physical corrections. Still others are middle-of-the-road trainers and correct in a manner similar to how a mom would correct a cheeky or misbehaving pup.

Eye Contact

Staring directly at a dog can be challenging and threatening, especially when it comes to terriers! Therefore, you should seek every opportunity to foster nonthreatening eye contact with your dog. They say that the eyes are the windows to the soul, and puppies tend to instinctively focus on the faces of those who greet them, which makes establishing eye contact relatively easy. If you have ever gazed into the eyes of a loving canine companion, you understand the emotions and value associated with this type of eye contact. This nonassertive eye contact helps lay a solid foundation and foster a strong human–canine bond. Competition dog trainers use nonassertive eye contact to direct a dog over the correct jump or to show a dog exactly where to down or even to maintain a *stay* when told to do so. As your puppy grows and matures, he should look to you for direction, and if he is in the habit of doing so, your eye contact, coupled with a verbal correction, may be enough to veto any undesired behavior.

Some owners are heavy-handed and quick to correct, which is not fair or productive. Others are reluctant to provide any discipline or structure, instead choosing to make excuse after excuse for their dog, who eventually grows into an out-of-control adult.

Like everything else pertaining to dogs, the type of correction will depend on the dog's temperament. What's too harsh for one dog may not be objectionable to another, and what discourages a behavior in one dog may actually encourage it in another dog. For example, Shelties, as a general rule, resent corrections and have been known to hold a grudge for months. (Okay, maybe a day or two, but it seems like months when you own a Sheltie.) Some dogs, such as American Pit Bull Terriers, Border Collies, Australian Shepherds, German Shepherd Dogs, and Labrador Retrievers, are physically tough but mentally sensitive and can be crushed with a firm verbal scolding.

Verbal Versus Physical

If you have done a good job establishing yourself as leader and you have done a good job reinforcing all of the behaviors you want to instill, a verbal correction, such as "Aaahhh" or "Ecckkkkk!" or "No!" should be sufficient.

Physical corrections are not recommended for several reasons. People who don't train dogs for a living rarely get the timing right to make a physical correction effective. And there's risk involved—too much of a correction may scare, or worse yet, injure a puppy or adult dog, which will damage the bond you've been trying to establish with your dog. Plus, what may discourage a behavior in one dog may actually encourage that same behavior in another dog. Therefore, it is best to leave physical corrections to the experts.

Try Scolding the Object

An alternative to verbally correcting your dog is to scold the offending object (as Sylvia Bishop, England's top obedience trainer, dog expert, and author, advocates). For example, say that your dog decides to swipe some tasty leftovers off the kitchen counter. Rather than scold him, scold the counter. Bang on the counter and give it a good telling off. "What in the world do you think you are doing! Bad, bad counter! Don't you ever do that again. Shame on you." Or if your dog gets on the sofa—a behavior you want to discourage—go after the sofa, not the dog. Bang your hand on the cushions and give them a good verbal lashing. Seriously, if done correctly, this works. Your dog will be so stunned and surprised that he will be afraid to go near the counter or couch again. It's true that your friends will think you are certifiable, but if it works and you do not need to physically correct your dog, quite frankly, who cares if you look like a nut?

Use your imagination to come up with self-corrections—corrections where the dog thinks that the unwanted behavior itself is causing the correction.

Longtime obedience trainer and competitor Patty Russo used to say that it is a shame that our dogs get all of our attention when they are doing something wrong, but we tend to forget about them when they are behaving well. Shouldn't it be the other way around? Ideally, you should spend the majority of your time instilling, encouraging, and rewarding the behaviors you want to foster in your dog. And by manipulating his environment, you can set him up to succeed. This way you will have little need for corrections as he grows into an adult dog.

Pay attention to your dog when he's behaving well, not just when he's doing something wrong.

7

Socialization:

An Investment

in Your

Puppy's Future

Did you know that how well your dog gets along with other dogs and people has a lot to do with how he is socialized as a puppy? Granted, much will depend on his breeding. Generally speaking, however, a combination of good genetics and good canine parents, proper socialization, and a happy, safe environment usually produces a puppy who grows into a well-adjusted adult dog who is friendly toward strangers and other animals.

Important Developmental Times

Certain periods in a puppy's life are critical in his social development. What happens within these individual stages has an enormous and significant impact on his future behavior as an adult dog. Research has shown that puppies are capable of learning at an early age, and they form lasting impressions during these critical periods. These impressions are remembered throughout a dog's life, be they good or bad.

A puppy who is exposed to positive experiences during the socialization period, such as positive handling, grooming, and different sights and sounds, stands a better chance of developing the socialization skills and coping mechanisms necessary to grow into a mentally sound and confident adult dog. Older puppies who have not been adequately or properly socialized during these periods tend to be more cautious. They generally grow up shy, fearful, and frequently nervous. As adult dogs, they find it difficult to cope with new experiences. They rarely, if ever, reach their full potential or live their lives to the fullest—a disastrous situation for any dog, let alone a high-drive or high-energy dog.

Socialization is the single most important process in a puppy's life. You owe it to your puppy to take advantage of these critical periods to maximize his future, foster his zany personality, and instill desired behaviors. How much time and energy you invest during this critical period directly impacts the future character of your puppy.

Your job of socializing your puppy begins the day you bring him home.

How your puppy is handled early on has a tremendous impact on him as an adult.

Foundation Fundamentals

By the time your puppy is ready to begin his new life at your home, usually between seven and eight weeks of age, the process of socialization will have already begun. The breeder will have seen your puppy through the neonatal (approximately 0 to 13 days old) and transitional (approximately 13 to 20 days old) periods and halfway through the critical socialization period (approximately 3 to 12 weeks, although some experts consider it up to 16 weeks). During this time, responsible and knowledgeable breeders will ensure that their litters are handled daily to accustom them to human contact and imprint trust, which is essential when it comes to raising a sound dog. They may have a radio or television playing to accustom them to different voices and sounds. They make sure that the puppies receive individual attention and are exposed to a variety of sights and smells in a safe and stress-free environment. Many breeders will have accustomed their young puppies to crates, thereby facilitating the crate-training process. For this reason, you must make careful choices about where you acquire your high-drive or high-energy puppy. How your puppy is managed during the neonatal, transitional, and socialization periods has a tremendous impact on how he reacts and interacts to various situations and people as an adult dog.

Socialize your puppy to everything he is likely to encounter as an adult dog, including wheelchairs.

Your Role

Your job begins the day your puppy arrives at your home. There is much to accomplish and a very small window of opportunity, so it is important to use your time wisely. Your puppy must learn important socialization skills between 8 and 16 weeks of age. Once this small window of opportunity has passed, it can never be recaptured. Squandering your opportunities during this critical time means that your puppy will suffer in the long run. You run the risk of having your puppy develop bad habits and associations that are difficult, if not impossible, to correct later in life.

As the owner of a new puppy, you are assuming the role of parent and leader. You are assuming an enormous responsibility that includes protecting him from bad or traumatic experiences while simultaneously instilling desired behaviors, fostering his madcap personality, and providing him with every opportunity to grow into a well-adjusted, mentally confident adult dog.

How to Socialize Your Puppy

Before taking your puppy outdoors and around other animals, consult your veterinarian about any necessary puppy vaccinations to ensure that he is protected from disease. Then, in a fun, safe, and stress-free environment, begin exposing your puppy to a wide variety of people, including toddlers, teenagers, women in floppy hats, and men in uniforms. Expose him to other animals in the household, such as cats, birds, horses, goats, chickens, and so forth. Expose him to the clapping of hands, the jingling of keys, and the clatter of dog bowls. Let him explore a variety of surfaces, including grass, cement, gravel, tile, carpet, linoleum, sand, and dirt. Many dogs, especially herding dogs, are attracted to moving objects, which incite their chase instinct. Therefore, your puppy should be exposed to these objects, including strollers, wheelchairs, shopping carts, vacuums, bicycles, and kids on roller skates and skateboards. A puppy who is not exposed to moving objects may be fearful of them and try to attack them as he gets older.

He should also be exposed to stairways, elevators, paper bags blowing in the wind, honking horns, garden hoses, sprinklers, wind chimes, and everything else he might come in contact with as an adult dog. Let your puppy play in and around empty boxes, tunnels, or buckets. Allow him to investigate trees, rocks, bushes, branches, leaves, and fallen fruit. He should explore bugs, animal odors, pastures, wooded areas, city sidewalks, and sandy beaches.

Enlarge your puppy's world and challenge his curiosity by taking him for rides in the car and walks in the park. Take him to the bank, post office, flower shop, veterinarian's office, and an outdoor cafe for a cookie and a kiss. Take him anywhere and everywhere that is safe, dog accessible, and dog friendly. Enroll him in a puppy kindergarten or puppy socialization class so that he is exposed to other puppies in a safe and supervised environment.

Special Concerns for High-Drive Puppies

High-drive puppies and adult dogs are smart and inquisitive, and most are acutely aware of their surroundings. Some of them even develop obsessive-compulsive behaviors. Therefore, during the socialization process—and throughout the dog's life—it is best to prevent these behaviors from developing, or at the very least, from continuing. For instance, never allow your dog to fixate on cats or other animals, chase his tail, chase shadows, or run fence lines. High-drive breeds prone to noisiness should be discouraged from incessant barking before it becomes a problem. If your dog tends to be aloof, like some working breeds can be, you'll probably need to socialize him to a wider variety of people so that he does not develop fearful reactions. Some herding breeds are sight sensitive, meaning that they are acutely aware of movement. These dogs must be socialized to all types of movement, such as vacuums, strollers, wheelchairs, and so forth so that they don't become fearful or obsessive.

Balancing Act

As your puppy's guardian of safety and well-being, you will want to protect him from potentially harmful or fearful situations but not coddle or reward fearful behavior. (The handling games discussed in Chapter 8 will help socialize and accustom him to being handled.) Ideally, you want to find a balance between the right amount of exposure and stimulation while still providing a safe, stress-free environment. It's important that your puppy not be exposed to a barrage of constant

Introducing strange dogs in a safe, controlled environment is key.

noise and stimulation every waking moment. Puppies have short attention spans, and they need plenty of downtime to sleep and recover from their busy day of being a puppy. When they're awake, however, they need enough physical and mental stimulation and socialization to grow into healthy, happy, sound adult dogs.

Finding that balance will depend on your dog. You will need to read his body language by observing his reactions to different situations. Watch his ears and tail and body posture. Is he fearful? Apprehensive? Courageous? Inquisitive? Submissive? By understanding and reading your dog's body language, you will be able to evaluate and adjust the situation accordingly. For instance, if your puppy or adult dog was raised in a childless environment, a room full of rambunctious children may be overwhelming or downright scary. By coddling or otherwise rewarding a puppy who shows fear, you reinforce that fear. For example, when a puppy is fearful and you attempt to comfort him by saying "It's okay, honey. Don't be afraid. Mommy won't let anything happen to you." In the dog's mind, he thinks that you are rewarding or encouraging his fearful actions, which compounds the problem by reinforcing his fear. It is also important never to scold or correct a puppy who shows fear or is apprehensive. Again, this only compounds the situation. Ideally, modify or restrict the exposure to one quiet, well-behaved child in the beginning until your puppy is confident enough to handle more. Manage his environment so that he is not put in overwhelming situations. Instead, set him up to succeed so that you can praise and reinforce him for being brave and inquisitive: "Good puppy!" or "Look at you. Aren't you clever!"

Social Traits of Different Breeds

Breed characteristics, genetics, whelping conditions, breeder diligence, and socialization all factor into a dog's overall temperament and sociability. Obviously, any breed can be born with a sour temperament and a skewed view of the world. Also, dogs of any breed can be born with temperaments ranging from aloof to independent to aggressive to highly sociable—and anything in between. That said, some breeds—because of their original purpose and function—tend to be more social than others. Other groups are more difficult to generalize because they encompass a diverse lot. Here is a look at a few of the more popular high-drive, high-energy breeds and their social traits.

- American Pit Bull Terriers are known for their intelligence, loyalty, and strong personalities. They can show aggressive responses to dogs, cats, rabbits, and other household pets. Because of the breed's characteristics and (often undeserved) bad-boy image, diligent socialization and obedience training from puppyhood are important.

- Australian Cattle Dogs are tough dogs in little packages. They were bred to be exceptional biters (for controlling and moving cattle), with stamina and resilience. They are bright, intelligent, and hardworking but rather aloof with strangers.

- Australian Shepherds are social, but a key characteristic of the breed is that they are reserved and watchful with strangers or in a new environment. However, they should not be timid or shy.

- German Shepherd Dogs, while seemingly outgoing and social, should display an aloofness and not out-and-out friendliness.

- German Wirehaired Pointers are gentle, affectionate, and even-tempered dogs. They love to be included in every activity, but because they still have some guarding instinct, they tend to be aloof with strangers.

- Labrador Retrievers, Golden Retrievers, and Nova Scotia Duck Tolling Retrievers are friendly, social, and outgoing.

- Pomeranians are extroverts with large personalities in tiny bodies.

- Salukis are one of the most aloof of the sighthound breeds. Although affectionate and loyal to their owners, they are not overly friendly to people in general.

It's worth repeating—understanding your dog's history, origin, and the purpose for which he was originally bred will go a long way in helping you not only socialize him but also understand why he might be behaving in a certain way.

Make It Positive

Most importantly, and this point cannot be stressed enough, the socialization process must be positive and productive. Taking your puppy to a state fair, city park, or outdoor market and allowing him to be bombarded by strange sights and weird sounds and hordes of screaming, rambunctious children grabbing at him or stepping on him is not a positive experience. These types of experiences can permanently traumatize him, and the only thing he will learn is to be afraid, deathly afraid of everything, especially people.

Sometimes with unsocialized dogs, triumph is measured in baby steps.

A Dog's Limitations

What if you are considering or have already adopted an older high-drive, high-energy breed that suffers from many of the behaviors associated with a not-so-great upbringing? Perhaps your precious Labrador Retriever was rescued from a puppy mill, where her entire life was spent pumping out puppies every six to nine months. Possibly your Australian Shepherd was relegated to a kennel for nine months, deprived of significant human interaction. Maybe your lovely Border Collie developed obsessive-compulsive behaviors and was surrendered to a shelter because his previous owner lacked the knowledge to deal with his abundant energy and drive. Perhaps you know nothing of your dog's past—only that his mannerisms tell stories of a really crummy upbringing.

Many dogs with nightmarish beginnings have become magnificent, loving companions cared for by equally loving owners. Some have flourished in one-dog homes, while others have become a guardian and best friend to a houseful of kids. Others have gone on to prove their mettle in canine competitions, including obedience, herding, and agility. However, some dogs—because of their compromised upbringing—lack the confidence and coping skills necessary to deal with the stress and pressure associated with different situations.

That's why it is important to see your dog for who he is and assess his individual victories accordingly. Oftentimes your greatest success will be measured not in blue ribbons but in helping your dog learn to trust another human being, to relish in the comfort and pleasure of being petted, or to sit comfortably at your feet or nap in your lap. Perhaps a great accomplishment will be teaching him to enjoy riding in the car or to tolerate being left alone for short periods without destroying your household. Triumph is often measured in baby steps and knowing that you have given your heart and love to a dog who had never before known the joy of human companionship.

Desensitization

Socializing an adult dog with phobias or behavioral issues follows the general format of socializing a puppy. However, the process differs somewhat because rather than prevent a puppy from developing hard-to-manage fears through socialization, you are now dealing with an adult dog who is already fearful. Common sense must prevail, and you must continually modify or restrict the dog's exposure so that he is working within his threshold. Behaviorists call this *desensitization*, which is exactly what it sounds like. You expose the dog to tiny doses of his fear, such as children, men in hats, garbage cans, other animals, etc., building up gradually to larger and larger doses but always working within the dog's threshold or limitations.

First, however, you must identify the dog's specific fear, which may not be as easy as it sounds. Is he fearful of all people or one person in particular? Does he love women but show fear around men, or vice versa? Is he fearful of people in black hats? Not all hats—just black hats? Is he terrified of flies or hot air balloons? What about loud noises? Is his fear genetically inherited or a result of lack of socialization? Once you identify the fear, you can manage your dog's environment so that he is not put in a position where he becomes reactive and more fearful. Instead, set him up to succeed so that you can praise and reinforce him for being brave—"Good boy!" or "Look at you. Aren't you brave!"

There are plenty of good books that offer in-depth information on this topic. However, depending on how ingrained your dog's fears are, books may not be enough. If you are hesitant about going it alone, don't hesitate to call in an expert. You and your dog will be much happier in the long run.

Managing Obsessions and Manic Behavior

High-drive or high-energy dogs can easily become overstimulated at the mere anticipation or sight of something they love to do—or even the sight of other dogs doing something they love to do, such as herding,

Border Collies have been known to become obsessive-compulsive.

swimming, retrieving, or agility. You see this frequently in Border Collies, and to some extent, in Australian Shepherds and Belgian Tervurens who train and compete in agility. Herding breeds are easily overstimulated by movement, be it livestock or a dog and handler in a competitive environment. Attending obedience or agility classes with some high-drive dogs is enough to send them into uncontrollable hysterics. Terriers are not exempt from this behavior and often become overstimulated with scurrying-type movements, such as those made by rodents. They also can become manic around other dogs who are running or playing or who are in a competitive environment. You may have seen this behavior in your dog—or other dogs—when you're walking around the neighborhood. Perhaps your dog goes nuts as you approach the dog park—he is anticipating swimming in the pool, running free, or playing with his canine buddies.

Dogs in this state of mind are often referred to as being "over the top," and they are not in any frame of mind to learn. Preventing these behaviors from developing while your dog is a puppy is key. Early socialization and obedience training will help, as will paying keen attention to his body language and understanding what activities are likely to set him off. However, if your dog already has problems controlling himself in certain environments, try these tips to help regain control.

- Have a clear picture in your mind of the behaviors you will or will not accept, and try not to deviate from that picture.
- Always work within your dog's physical and mental threshold, which differs from dog to dog.
- Work on the fringe of his comfort zone—that area where he can control himself without going ballistic. For instance, if he gets hysterical when he sees other dogs at the park, stay at a distance where you are able to maintain control. If he knows the *sit* command, have him sit. Otherwise, have him stand nicely without lunging, yipping, yapping, or screaming. If your dog becomes overstimulated, you know that you are too close to the stimulus. Increase the distance between your dog and whatever is causing him to become hysterical, be it other people, dogs, sprinklers, etc.

- When your dog is capable of maintaining control while on the fringe of his comfort zone, which can take anywhere from a few hours to a few weeks, gradually move him closer to the stimulus. If he gets out of control, you may need to lower your expectations. For example, if he goes crazy at obedience or agility class, perhaps your goal needs to be as simple as sitting quietly or walking him around the class, gradually moving closer to the equipment as other puppies or adult dogs have fun. Reinforce him for good behaviors, such as when he's not screaming, lunging, clawing, and acting like a lunatic.
- Always offer a high rate of reinforcement for the appropriate behavior, which in this case is calm, quiet control. Simply put, reward him with lots of tasty treats and *calm* verbal praise to reinforce the behavior you want. If your praise is exciting, it's likely to excite him, too, which is not your goal in these instances.
- Some dogs who are highly overstimulated have zero interest in food—even the stinkiest, yummiest piece of liver won't help. In these instances, reinforce with calm verbal praise while trying to keep your dog's focus on you.
- A high rate of treat reinforcement will help reinforce in your dog's mind the behaviors you want and will prevent him from becoming frustrated by continually being wrong.
- Rejoice in small steps of progress. With highly reactive and overstimulated dogs, progress is generally measured in baby steps.

Beware of Flooding

The opposite of desensitization is what some trainers call *flooding*, which is the concept of throwing a dog in headfirst and letting him flail about until he's dealt with the problem. Rather than gradually exposing a dog to specific situations, flooding exposes a dog in large doses to the object that causes him fear. The technique is highly controversial, but sadly, is still employed by some trainers. Flooding has different effects depending on the dog's temperament. A sensitive or fearful dog can become even more sensitive and fearful and subsequently unmanageable, and he may never be okay with whatever object or situation originally made him fearful.

If you do nothing else for your puppy, you owe it to him to make the time to properly and adequately socialize him during this critical life stage. Time consuming? Absolutely. Energy expending? You bet! However, it is a necessary and obligatory investment when you choose to own a high-drive or high-energy dog, or any dog for that matter. His future well-being depends on how much you do—or fail to do—during this critical period.

Chapter 8

Playing Your Part: Why Play Is Important With High-Energy Dogs

High-drive, high-energy puppies are such fun to watch because they are like miniature versions of who they will be as adults. They imitate their wild ancestors—running, crouching, stalking, freezing, and suddenly tearing off in an opposite direction. They twist, turn, pounce, and run in an all-out sprint as they body slam, yip, yap, and playfully nip as they wrestle each other to the ground and then collapse in a heap of sleep.

Watch closely and you will probably be able to spot the high-drive retriever puppies, be they Golden Retrievers, Labrador Retrievers, or even Chesapeake Bay Retrievers, who display stronger retrieving instincts than their littermates. They are the puppies who want to pick up and carry everything and anything. Herding dogs, such as Border Collies, Australian Shepherds, and Australian Cattle Dog puppies, often show their herding instincts early, too. Look closely and you'll probably be able to spot right away those puppies who possess high-drive or high-energy behaviors.

In the beginning, the play is fun and good-hearted. However, watch closely and you'll see that the ground rules quickly change as the puppies grow and mature, establish their own superiority, and hone their natural prey instincts, including retrieving, herding, and hunting. As a savvy owner, you can capitalize on these natural instincts to instill the behaviors you want while discouraging unwanted behaviors. Watching dogs play is more than just good fun. It's tremendously beneficial and informative once you know what to look for. Most dogs love to play, but play is much more than just a way to have fun. How dogs play, and more importantly, how you play with your puppy or adult dog—especially those breeds that tend toward high-drive, high-energy personalities—is more important than you might think.

This adult Australian Shepherd and 11-week-old American Pit Bull Terrier are having a friendly game of tug, which helps them form positive associations with other dogs and keeps them fit.

Why Play Is so Important

Play is essential for the physical, mental, and social development of healthy puppies. From an early age, your puppy should experience positive, playful interactions with a wide variety of people, as well as other puppies and dogs. This will help him develop into a well-behaved, happy adult dog and a treasured family member, welcome wherever he goes. Important for improving your dog's overall physical and mental health, exercise and play burn calories, stimulate circulation, build strong bones and muscles, and maintain flexible joints, keeping a dog fit and trim. Exercise strengthens a dog's respiratory system, aids in digestion, and helps get oxygen to tissues. It nourishes and energizes a dog's mind, keeping it active, healthy, and alert. Plenty of exercise and appropriate games between dog and owner can help eliminate loneliness, stress, and boredom, which are primary causes of unwanted behaviors, such as barking, digging, chewing, and ransacking trashcans.

Throwing a ball with this retriever and herding dogs will burn off their excess energy, but they also need other interactive games to challenge them mentally.

Building a Bond

Play also establishes and builds a strong bond and a mutually trusting relationship between dog and owner. The more you play with your dog, the more appealing, interesting, and fun you will become to him. You will become the center of his universe; the most interesting thing in his world. As a result, he will see you as his primary source of fun and entertainment, and he will want to be with you rather than wander off to play his own games, chase other dogs, or get into mischief. If he is excited about playing with the toy you have, he will be less inclined to run off to chase and bark at other dogs or kids on bicycles. If you are his primary source of fun, he will want to stay close to you in anticipation that you might throw his favorite toy or play a fun game with him.

Kids and Play

Do you know why dogs love to play with kids? Because kids run and scream and wave their arms, and these behaviors activate a dog's chase instinct. Dogs, especially herding breeds, enjoy chasing anything that moves. They love to bark, chase, and grab and tear the shirtsleeves of fleeing kids. Obviously, this isn't the type of play you want to encourage, but it explains why most dogs love chasing, playing, and roughhousing with kids.

Play is a wonderful releaser of excess energy for both dogs and kids, but kids must also learn what games are acceptable when playing with dogs. To prevent the situation from getting out of control, parents should always monitor and control the play between dogs and kids. Play should also be appropriate to the size and age of the dog as well as the child. Think active rather than rough, avoiding games that encourage or allow a dog to use his teeth, such as attack or wrestling games, where a dog can become overly excited and inadvertently learn to use his teeth. Under no circumstances should children be permitted to hit, kick, punch, pinch, bite, or harass a dog in the name of play or at any time.

The more fun your dog has with you, the more he will want to be with you. The more he wants to be with you, the easier it will become to control him. The more control you have, the easier it will become to train him. The easier it is to train him, the more obedience commands you can teach him. The more obedience commands you teach him, the better behaved he will be at home and in public, thereby growing into an adult dog you—and other people—enjoy having around.

Burn Energy Reserves

Most high-drive, high-energy dogs belong to the herding, sporting, and terrier groups. Most of these breeds remain physically and mentally active and retain their natural instincts to herd, hunt, chase, or retrieve. Exercise, games, and interactive play help burn abundant reserves of energy that these breeds would otherwise utilize doing the job for which they were originally bred. Remember, relocating a working dog to the city or suburbs does not squelch his desire to work or eliminate his need for physical and mental stimulation. In the absence of adequate physical and mental exercise, turbo-charged dogs quickly become bored and destructive. Then it is only a matter of time before they get into trouble, which can be very distressing to owners, especially if the dog decides to dig up the underground sprinkler system, relocate the patio furniture, or eat the wiring for the central air-conditioning unit.

Toys, Games, and Interactive Play

Your puppy's first playmate was most likely his mother, who used play to teach him important canine social skills and puppy etiquette. She showered him with affection, nudged him, pinned him, and if the occasion was warranted, she nipped or growled. By doing so, she taught him which behaviors were acceptable and which ones were in his best interest to drop immediately.

By utilizing interactive play—just like a puppy's canine mother—owners can continue to instill desired behaviors while discouraging unwanted behaviors. The same concept applies to adult dogs. Interactive play is the key. Throwing a ball and having your dog retrieve it is exercise; this is great for tiring out a dog, especially high-drive, high-energy dogs, but the dog is doing all of the work. Interactive play, on the other hand, is the two of you playing together, such as a game of tug, find me, chase recalls, fun obedience games, and so forth.

Keep Games Fun

First and foremost, games between you and your dog must be fun. But play should emphasize what is fun for your dog—not necessarily what is fun for you. Shoving a toy in a dog's face and expecting him to play is annoying. Dogs don't like that. After all, how would you react if someone shoved something in your face? Standing in one spot and expecting a dog to do all of the work is no fun either.

High-drive, high-energy dogs often have short attention spans and can quickly become bored. Therefore, owners must be entertaining, stimulating, silly, and uninhibited. They must be willing to jump up and down, spin in circles, clap their hands, hop on one leg, make funny noises, run away so that their dog chases them, roll around on the ground, tap the floor—whatever it takes to get their dog tuned in to them.

Movement excites dogs, so make the play/games interesting by keeping the toy moving— drag, wiggle, or roll it on the

Keep the games between you and your dog fun.

ground. Gently kick it or throw it a few feet (m) in front of you and race your puppy to it. Let your puppy get it. Clap your hands and tell him that he is clever: "You got it! You're too fast for me!" For very young or small puppies, sit or lie on the ground and play. This will keep you at eye level, which is less intimidating to them.

Active Versus Rough

Games should be active rather than rough, which is especially important for strong, dominant, high-octane puppies and adult dogs. If you roughhouse, wrestle, and play aggressive games with a puppy, and if you allow him to jump on you, get too excited and out of control, bite at your arms, legs, or clothing, he will play the same way as an adult dog. These behaviors might be cute and funny when he is a 10-pound (4.5-kg) puppy but not so charming when he is 70 pounds (31.5 kg), pushy, bossy, and snatching toys from your hand.

Don't Ask for Perfection

As your puppy matures, begin challenging him by adding more complex behaviors into the games. However, in the beginning, when your puppy or adult dog is first learning, the goal is to instill fun and enthusiasm for playing. Try not to add too many rules or ask for perfection from your puppy. For instance, do not insist that he do a *sit-stay* before chasing after a toy. Most puppies are not emotionally mature enough to handle a *sit-stay* until they are six or eight months of age. Foster the fun first. As he matures, begin asking for more and more control.

Stay Positive

Do not take your bad day out on your puppy or adult dog. If you do not feel like playing, wait until you are in a better frame of mind. If you become frustrated or upset while playing, which can sometimes happen if things are not going the way you intended, your dog will sense that you are upset with him, and he will not be as eager to play next time.

Young puppies, as well as some high-drive adult dogs, have short attention spans. Keep

Just Say No to Laser Light Pointers

Some dog owners use a laser pointer and have their dog chase the light. But laser pointers are a nightmare for many high-drive, high-energy breeds—especially Border Collies, who are prone to developing obsessive behaviors. Although it may look like a great "game" to play with your dog, high-drive, high-energy dogs can easily become overstimulated by the laser light. This game can actually lead to obsessive-type behaviors of chasing shadows and light reflections on the ground. Be smart—leave the laser light pointer games for the cats.

puppy play sessions short—three to ten minutes, depending on the dog. Adult dogs can usually play longer. Always finish a game/play session on a positive note, and always quit while your dog is still enthusiastic about playing and the game is still fun. This ensures that he will be excited about playing the next time the toys appear.

What's Your Game?

Some dogs, depending on their breed and personality, prefer different games and toys. Most retrievers, for obvious reasons, excel at retrieving. Yet more than a few terriers love to retrieve a ball or flying disc, too. Some dogs are more outgoing and eager to play than their low-prey-drive counterparts. If you're stumped for games, try a few of these suggestions, which might help you to come up with your own fun and creative games to play with your puppy or adult dog.

- **Herding Breeds:** Herding dogs were bred to control the movement of other animals, primarily sheep and cattle. Most herding dogs—like Border Collies, Australian Shepherds, and Belgian Tervurens, to name a few—are high drive and high energy, which means that most of them are ready for any activity at the drop of a hat. The sight of a tug toy or ball can send them over the top with excitement. Many of the breeds are highly sight sensitive, meaning that they are acutely aware of movement. As a result, they like games that involve movement, such as chase recalls and retrieving. They can go nuts when a toy is dragged or wiggled on the ground. They are smart, too, so they like thinking games, such as the "Find It!" or "Find Me!" games mentioned in Chapter 9.

Herding breeds, like these Australian Stumpy Tail Cattle Dogs, tend to love chase games.

- **Terriers:** Terriers are feisty, energetic dogs, and most of them possess a strong desire to play. Their ancestors were bred to hunt and kill vermin, with some terriers using their strong neck muscles to quickly shake and kill their prey. As a result, most terriers like shake and kill-type games, as well as decapitating or toy shredding-type games. Any type of scurrying movement, like that of a rodent or a toy being dragged on the floor, can make them manic. Most like ratting games where they are allowed to hunt and find a toy, such as a furry mouse or rat. Teach your terrier puppy to dig in a sandbox or mound of dirt to "find the mousey." Hide treats or toys around the house and teach him to use his excellent hearing, eyesight, and natural ratting instincts to find them. Generally speaking, terriers may have little tolerance for other animals, including other dogs. Therefore, caution, as well as keen observation, is highly recommended when terriers play with other dogs and children.

- **Sporting Dogs:** Pointers, retrievers, setters, and spaniels are in this group. Pointers find and silently point game. Setters find, point, and may flush game. Spaniels find and flush game. And as previously mentioned, retrievers retrieve downed game from land or water, which means that they love retrieving games. For the most part, sporting dogs love to retrieve, and the sight of a bumper (a training toy), tug toy, or flying disc can whip them into a frenzy. Pointers "scent" game birds, so try some fun scenting and/or tracking, "find it" or "hide-and-seek"-type games. Use a bird-scented cloth to encourage his enthusiasm for the "game." Play games that encourage holding, like holding and carrying his favorite stuffed toy. A sporting dog's training is built on prey drive, so encourage games that instill or increase a strong prey drive, such as retrieving and chase recalls.

- **Working Dogs:** Working dogs, for the most part, were bred to perform jobs such as guarding property, pulling sleds, and performing water rescues. The group encompasses a diverse and wide range of dogs, including some pretty high-drive, high-energy breeds, such as the Boxer, Doberman Pinscher, Portuguese Water Dog, and the Rottweiler, to name a few. As with the other groups, encourage games that utilize their natural instincts. For

Most terriers, like this Airedale Terrier, love to dig.

Most retrievers, like this Labrador Retriever, take to retrieving naturally.

Some working dogs, like this Portuguese Water Dog, love all types of water games.

instance, the Portuguese Water Dog was used to drive fish into nets, retrieve lost tackle and broken nets, and act as a courier from ship to ship and ship to shore. His innate retrieving skills make him a natural for exciting and stimulating retrieve games, as well as "find it" and "hide-and-seek" games. Try fun jumping games with these athletic and agile adult dogs. The Rottweilers' ancestors were used to move herds of animals by day and guard supplies by night. Movement-type games, such as chase recalls and dragging or wiggling a toy on the ground, are likely to incite this breed's prey drive.

Interactive play and fun games are not just about having fun. They should stimulate your dog's mind, instill specific behaviors such as *come*, *down*, and *sit*, discourage unwanted behaviors, establish control, and build a strong human–canine relationship.

Quit While You're Ahead

Always quit playing while your puppy is still interested in the game. This will ensure that your dog wants to play the next time the toys come out. You want your dog to think *Oh, no, don't stop playing now. I'm having so much fun!* rather than *I'm so tired. Please don't make me chase that ball one more time.*

Chapter 9

A Team of Two:
Fun Games to Teach
and Play With
Your Dog

Playing with your dogs seems so simple, doesn't it? Throw a ball and let him chase it, right? What you may not have realized is that play is the greatest training tool in your toolbox. Yet the benefits of play are often underutilized because owners fail to maximize the benefits of interactive play—*interactive* being the key word.

Play is more than throwing a ball and wearing out your dog; it is the perfect way to instill in a fun and exciting manner new behaviors and basic obedience commands, which are the foundation of a well-behaved dog. High-drive, high-energy dogs who are taught in a fun and stress-free environment are more receptive to learning. The more a dog learns, the more obedient he becomes, and an obedient, well-mannered dog is more likely to be included in family situations, such as walks in the park, rides in the cars, and vacations.

Formal Isn't Always Best

Training need not always be formal—and it most definitely should never be boring, especially when you own a high-drive or high-energy dog. Watch dogs playing together. They romp and body slam and play catch-me-if-you-can and hide-and-seek games. They don't put on a leash and do patterned behaviors like *sit*, *down*, and *come*. They don't run out in the backyard and start doing obedience commands by themselves. No demarcation line should exist between playing and training. Your puppy should never think *Playing is fun, but training is boring*. Or, *I'm done training, now I get to play*. Training and playing should be intertwined. If your training (or playing) is too rigid, the fun is lost. Your dog should never know the difference between the two. Make playing and training fun and exciting.

Although we will touch on more formal commands in Chapter 10, this chapter is meant to get you started training your dog without the pressure of performing a perfect

Training doesn't need to be formal—or boring.

What's That in Your Mouth?

When training your puppy or adult dog, giving him the treat from your hands works great in many instances. However, another great option (one used by a lot of competition trainers) is to stash a few training tidbits in your mouth. Yes, in your mouth! Cheese, hot dogs, turkey, leftover steak, and boiled liver (if you can stomach it) are a few of the great treats that can be cut into tiny bits and easily tucked into your cheek. The advantages are:

- A few tasty tidbits in your mouth leave your hands free for holding a leash, clicker, toy, your dog, and so forth.
- Treats stored in your mouth are easily accessible. Timing is essential in training, and you won't be fumbling around in your pockets after your dog has done something brilliant trying to give him the reward.
- Spitting treats at your dog (a tricky but easily learned talent with a bit of practice) is a great way to dispense them—again, no fumbling around in your pockets or treat bag.
- If spitting isn't your forte, take the food from your mouth, simultaneously feeding from both hands (another Sylvia Bishop trick). This teaches the dog that food comes from both hands and prevents him from learning the behavior of continually sniffing one hand or the other in anticipation of food.
- Showing your dog that the treats are in your mouth (such as during the "What's This?" game) will encourage him to look at your face, which gets him to pay attention to you.
- Your mouth is a great place for storing food when your clothes don't have pockets.

sit or a long *stay*. In fact, your puppy or adult dog doesn't need to know any command words to get started playing these games. They are fun and mentally stimulating and will lay the groundwork for more formal lessons in the future.

How Long?

When you use play to instill basic obedience commands, it won't take too long for your dog to learn. Five minutes here and there and you will be surprised how much your puppy (or adult dog) can absorb and learn in a short period. One trainer calls it the "string cheese" training technique. Each day, or multiple times throughout the day if possible, take one stick of string cheese and cut it into a lot of small pieces. Then, do as many *sits* or *downs* or chase recalls or fun retrieves as possible using that one stick of cheese. Ideally, one stick of cheese should break into at least 20 tiny pieces. That means that you can do five or six *recalls*, three or four *sits*, four or five *downs*, and maybe a few find me or find it games, all with one stick of cheese. (To teach *sit* and *down*, see Chapter 10.) When that stick is gone, you are done training for that session. Do this three or four times a day, and it won't be long until your dog will be able to do all kinds of commands and fun tricks.

Maximize your time. While watching television, do a few *recalls* or fun retrieves during a commercial. Or while making dinner, have your puppy do a twist or spin and reward him with a tasty tidbit of carrot or potato. "What a good *sit*!" or "What a good spin!" Again, five minutes here and there and you will be surprised how fast your dog learns.

Get Your Game On

High-drive, high-energy dogs love to learn and play challenging tricks and games that keep them mentally stimulated. Teach your puppy or adult dog to chase you, find you, or find a toy. Give him a job or some chores to do, such as carrying the mail from the mailbox, picking up his dog bowl when he is done eating, retrieving your slippers, and so forth. Become a fun detective! Find out what games your puppy or adult dog loves, and use them to train new behaviors. Be creative. Design your own games. When you incorporate interactive play, there is no end to the games you can play and the behaviors you can instill, which set the foundation for basic obedience commands.

High-Drive dogs love to learn challenging tricks.

A few fun games are listed in this section. However, by using your imagination, you can tweak or modify them or invent your own. Although these games are geared toward puppies, they work well and are equally fun for adult dogs, too.

Attention Games

The first trick in training a high-drive dog is to get his attention—after all, you can't teach any dog whose brain is focused on anything and everything but you. These fun attention games teach a dog to want to pay attention to you, and they reinforce the concept that for him to get what he wants (i.e., a cookie), he must first do something you want (i.e., look at you).

These games instill the behavior of paying attention to you in a fun and humane manner. When played consistently, it won't take long for your puppy or adult dog to realize that looking at you is not only fun but also a highly rewarding game. These games can be played anywhere—living room, kitchen, bedroom, hallway, bathroom, front yard, backyard, etc.—and they take less than five minutes, but your puppy or adult dog will quickly learn that paying attention to you pays yummy, high-quality dividends.

Remember, puppies and adult dogs are individuals, and they learn at different rates. Most puppies have short attention spans and may become bored after a few repetitions. Some puppies may get frustrated because they are too young mentally to play some of these games. If that's the case, play the ones he can play and wait until he matures mentally before playing the others. Most importantly, always play within your puppy or adult dog's mental and physical capabilities. Pushing your high-drive dog beyond his threshold may cause him to become stressed and frustrated, which is what you want to avoid.

Game #1: "Look at Me"

- Start with your puppy on leash. (Use a buckle collar, never a pinch or choke chain.)
- For a small or very young puppy, kneel on the ground so that you are at eye level, which is less intimidating to a puppy.
- Stand or kneel on the leash so that your dog cannot wander away.
- Have four or five tasty tidbits in each hand and in your mouth.
- Make sure that you have plenty of treats handy. (You don't want to be digging through your pockets searching for rewards while your precious pooch is paying attention to you.)
- When you are ready to play, say nothing. Simply wait for your puppy to look at you.
- When he looks at you, praise with "yes!" and reward with a tidbit from either hand or your mouth. (If you are clicker training, click the second he looks at you, which marks the behavior, and then reward with a treat.)
- If your puppy looks away, say nothing.
- Wait for him to look back at you then praise with "yes!" (or click) and reward from the opposite hand or your mouth. (For example, if you just fed from your left hand, next time feed from

When your puppy looks at you, reward with a treat.

Control Your Environment

When playing and training your puppy or adult dog, you will find that controlling your environment makes it easier to train him. These pointers can help you and your dog succeed:

- In the early stages, train in a distraction-free environment (or as distraction free as possible), such as a room with doors that can be closed or a small enclosed yard or patio.
- Keep your puppy or adult dog on leash. This controls his environment by preventing him from running off or doing his own thing.
- Try to avoid training where other dogs are playing and running willy-nilly. If your dog is distracted, it will be more difficult to get his attention, which you need to train him.

your right hand. Then the next time, feed with a treat from your mouth.)

Your puppy will quickly learn that looking at you (something you want) gets him a tasty reward (something he wants). Dispensing treats alternately between your left and right hand and your mouth keeps him guessing. If your puppy nudges or sniffs your hand, simply wait him out. When he looks at you, say "yes!" (or click) and then feed from the hand he was not sniffing. Never feed from the hand he was sniffing or nudging, as this encourages him to continue doing so. When all of the treats are gone, the game is over.

Game #2: "Look at Me, With Treat on the Ground"

This game is more advanced than Game #1. It may be too much for very young or emotionally immature puppies, so wait until your dog is ready to handle it.

- Start with a handful of tasty tidbits and your puppy on a short but loose leash. (The leash should be short enough that he cannot snatch a treat off the ground but loose enough that you aren't holding his head in place.)
- Again, if you have a very young or small puppy, kneel on the ground so that you are at his level.
- Feed him two or three treats in a row, then drop one on the floor. Treat. Treat. Treat. Ooops! Dropped one.
- Most puppies will dive for the ground trying to snatch up the treat, but because your leash is short, he won't be able to reach it.
- He'll probably spend a few seconds or so staring at the cookie; wait him out.
- When he looks back at you, praise with "Yes!" (or click) and reward with a tidbit from your hand.

Repeat this game several times until the treats are gone. Do not let your puppy pick up the treat off the ground, as this defeats the point of the entire exercise. When the game is over, pick up the treats from the ground and feed them to him.

Game #3: "What's This?"

- Have a yummy tidbit of food in your mouth.
- Put your index finger to your lips and ask your puppy "What's this?"
- When he looks at you, praise with "Yes!" (or click) and reward with the yummy treat.

This game was developed by trainer Sylvia Bishop. Eventually, as your puppy learns that "What's this?" means look at my face, you can begin incorporating it into your *come* command by saying "What's this?" and pointing to your mouth as your puppy is running toward you. Make the command exciting and your puppy will want to run to you to get his treat.

Game #4: "Go Back, Then Run"

A lot of energetic dogs like when you are physical with them—gently pushing, pulling, or playfully touching them to rev them up. To get your dog's attention on you, try gently pushing him backward or away from you and then running away from him. In most instances this behavior will excite, stimulate, and encourage him to chase you.

There are two important notes of caution with this game. First, dogs who are easily aroused may find this too exciting and may jump or nip at your body parts. If this is the case, you will need to temper the play so that he does not get too wound up, making learning impossible.

Always temper your play to your dog's physical and mental capabilities.

Second, many dogs dislike being grabbed. Gently play touching is okay. Harshly grabbing or pinching any dog is not only wrong, it's counterproductive, as it's likely to result in the dog avoiding you and your hands. Always temper the play so that you are playing within your dog's physical and mental capabilities. Pushing or shoving any dog too hard can injure him physically and deflate his self-confidence.

Handling Games

Most reputable breeders accustom their puppies to being picked up, held, touched, and examined as part of the socialization stage. Depending on where and from whom you acquired your puppy, this may or may not be the case. Handling games help a puppy learn in a fun, positive, and humane manner to be handled without a lot of squabbling or backchatting. You will find this especially helpful when your dog must be groomed, checked for stickers and burrs, vaccinated, loved, cuddled, or examined by a veterinarian. These games, unless otherwise noted, are just as fun to teach to older puppies or untrained adult dogs.

Game #1: "Kiss Your Puppy"

- Kiss your puppy all over his face and body, and encourage him to kiss you back.
- Put a command to the behavior, such as "Kiss!"
- It won't be long before your dog is performing the behavior on command.

You can teach your puppy to kiss you by rewarding him whenever he licks your face.

You can kiss him, but never blow in his face, which will either excite or annoy a puppy, causing him to bark, lunge, and nip at your face—a behavior you do not want to encourage. Also, some older puppies or adult dogs may be wary of your face being too close to theirs. Perhaps they've had a bad experience or are simply unfamiliar or uncomfortable with the behavior. Some inexperienced or untrained dogs may try to nip your face rather than kiss. Remember to assess your dog's limitations, and always play within his capabilities, gradually increasing his abilities as his comfort level dictates. (For overexuberant, rambunctious puppies or adult dogs who like to jump, you might need a crash helmet to teach this exercise!)

Game #2: "No Wiggling"

The goal is for your puppy or adult dog to sit or stand quietly—without struggling—while you pet him and inspect his feet, teeth, ears, tail, and so forth. Every puppy should learn this exercise—especially high-drive, high-energy, or overactive dogs who are always raring to go and often have trouble sitting or standing still. It makes life so much easier as your puppy grows into an adult dog.

- Start with your puppy on leash. (Use only a buckle collar and leash, never a choke or pinch collar.)
- Kneel on the ground with the leash tucked loosely under your knee to prevent your puppy from running off.
- Have a handful of treats handy. They should be out of his reach but easily accessible for you, such as off to your side (the opposite side your puppy is on) or on a nearby table or counter; food in your hand or mouth is too distracting for most puppies who are just learning this exercise.
- With your puppy sitting on your left side, use your right hand to lightly hold his collar while you use your left hand to gently pet him on his back for three or four seconds.
- Praise with a calm "Yes" or "Good boy" (or click) the instant he stops wiggling. The praise (or click) marks and reinforces the behavior you want, which is not wiggling.
- Timing and tone of voice are important. If you praise or click while he is wiggling, you are reinforcing the wiggling, which is the behavior you don't want. If your praise is too wild and exciting or high pitched, it will cause your puppy to become excited—causing him to wiggle—thereby defeating the purpose of the exercise.
- Immediately after praising him, change hands—use your left hand to secure his collar and your right hand to reach for a tasty tidbit and feed him.
- Switch hands again—holding his collar with your right hand and petting him with your left hand—and repeat multiple times. (If your cookies are on your right side, reaching across your body with your left hand for the treats is cumbersome and distracting to the puppy.)
- Progress to checking his ears and verbally praising his calm behavior with a "Yes" or "Good boy" (or clicking).
- Change hands, reward with a treat, and change hands again, and repeat.
- Progress to checking his feet, inspecting his toes, counting his teeth, touching his tail, rubbing

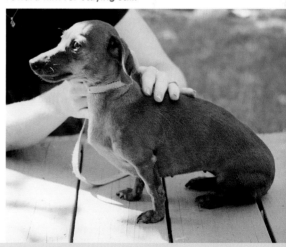

When teaching your dog not to wiggle, gently pet him for a few seconds, then reward him for staying still.

his legs from top to bottom, and so forth—each time praise the behavior of not wiggling with a "Yes" or "Good boy" (or clicking), changing hands, rewarding with a treat, and switching hands again.

- When he can sit calmly and accept physical praise and touching, progress to having him stand at your side, and repeat the previous exercises—pet him all over, check his ears, teeth, feet, and so forth while he is standing.
- Remember to praise (or click) and reward the behavior of not wiggling.
- Teach your puppy to accept being petted and touched while standing and lying down, too. This is especially helpful if he must lie down at the vet's office to be examined or if he must stand still to wipe his muddy feet before coming indoors or getting in the car.
- Practice these exercises on both your left and right side.

Some puppies are real wiggle bums and find it nearly impossible to sit or stand still for more than a nanosecond. The anticipation of physical or verbal praise is enough to send them into uncontrollable wiggles. Others dogs are much calmer. Either way, always progress at a speed that suits your puppy's temperament and personality.

For the serious wigglers, set a goal of simply sitting or standing next to you without wiggling, being sure to calmly praise and reward the calm behavior. Next time, progress to having him sit or stand calmly while you pet his back, calmly praising and rewarding as you go. Each time, progress a bit further, but always work within your puppy's capabilities.

Always do this exercise after your puppy has been for a walk or out to play. Never try this when he is revved up and wants to wiggle.

Game #3: "Pick Me Up"

Puppies need to learn to be picked up as part of their daily handling. You can play this game with smaller or lightweight adult dogs, too. To teach your puppy to enjoy this process:

- Pick up your puppy.
- Praise him for being brave: "Aren't you clever!"
- Set him down before he starts to object.
- Toss him a toy or treat as a reward.

You can combine this exercise with the "Kiss Your Puppy" game:

- Pick up your puppy.
- Kiss his nose.
- Praise him for being brave: "Good boy!"
- Set him down.
- Toss him a treat or toy.

You can also combine it with the "What's This?" game:

- Pick up your puppy.
- Kiss his nose.
- Praise him for being brave: "Aren't you smart!"
- Set him down.
- Toss a treat 5 or 6 feet (1.5 or 1.8 m) across the room or yard and let him run after it.
- As he's running for his treat, quickly put another treat in your mouth. Then, once he's retrieved the tossed treat ask him "What's this?" as you point to your mouth.
- When he runs back to you, praise him: "Good come!"
- Feed him the tasty tidbit from your mouth.

Some dogs, such as Shelties, dislike being picked up, which makes this exercise doubly important. If your puppy objects to being handled or picked up, begin slowly. Pretend to lift him up by putting your hands under his belly, say "Yes!" or "Good boy!" or "Look at you! Aren't you clever!" and then feed or play. Progress to the point where you can lift him a few inches (cm) off the ground, continuing to praise and reward with tidbits or a toy.

Similarly, picking up a puppy and putting him on different surfaces, such as a grooming table, examination table, countertop, and so forth conditions him to accept this behavior when he is older.

Game #4: "Hand in the Collar"

Early on, your puppy should be conditioned to wearing a leather or nylon buckle collar, and he should learn to accept your hand in his collar. He should associate a hand in his collar with fun games and treats. It should never mean that he is bad or in trouble. Ideally, you should start when he is a baby, but if you have an adult dog who dislikes your hand in his collar, it's never too late to begin. At every opportunity, nonchalantly slip your hand in his collar, praise, reward with a tidbit, and release. It's that simple. Do this when you are brushing, feeding, talking to him, and so forth. Do this several times in a row, multiple times throughout the day. When done correctly, your dog will become oblivious to your hand in his collar. Eventually, as you slip your hand in his collar, begin putting a command to it: "Give me your collar!"

An owner often goes wrong by grabbing for her puppy, which causes him to run off or stay just out

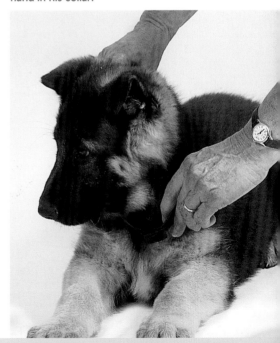

Teach your puppy to accept your hand in his collar.

of her reach. If this is the case, you need to condition your dog that coming close to you is safe and fun.

- Start by sitting on the floor with a tasty tidbit, and encourage him to come to you by showing him the treat.
- Hold the treat relatively close to your body so that he must come all the way to you if he wants the treat.
- Avoid stretching your arm out to feed him or coaxing him, such as "Come on, you can do it." Instead, let him figure it out on his own.
- When he comes to you, praise calmly and reward with the tidbit.
- If possible, encourage him to stay close to you by using your voice and saying something silly, such as "Look at you!" or "Aren't you brilliant!" Do *not* grab for him or touch him at this point.
- Repeat this exercise multiple times until he is comfortable coming to you.
- Progress to feeding him with one hand while you calmly touch his collar with the other hand—remember, do not grab his collar or try to restrain him.
- Touch the collar, then praise: "What a clever boy!"
- Repeat several times, progressing until your puppy accepts his collar being touched.
- Progress to the point where your puppy accepts—and enjoys—your hand in his collar.

You can make putting on your puppy's leash a fun game.

The *Come* Command Must Always Be Positive

The games mentioned in the "Come" section will help you begin instilling a fun and reliable *recall* or *come* command and will increase the probability that your dog will come to you each and every time he is called. A key component is that *come*—or whatever word you choose to mean "come to me," be it *come, here,* or *with me*—must always, always, always be positive. There is no wiggle room on this one. If you want your puppy to grow into an adult dog who reliably comes when he is called, the *come* command must always be positive. You cannot call him to you and correct him for peeing on the rug two hours ago. Or call him to you and then scold him for chewing your shoe, ransacking the trash, or any other heinous crime. You cannot call him to you and stick him in the bathtub if he hates a bath or call him to you and give him medications that he hates. If you call your dog to you and he comes, you must always praise and reward him. If you want to bathe him or give him medications or anything else he might find offensive, go and get him—do not call him to you.

Game# 5: "Leash On/Leash Off"
Teach your puppy or adult dog that putting on and taking off his leash is a fun game.
· With your hand in his collar, attach his leash with the command "Leash on" or any command you choose (or click), and reward with a yummy treat.
· Then take the leash off, using the command "Leash off," praise (or click), and reward.
   Increase your dog's vocabulary by doing this every time you put on or take off his leash, and it will quickly become a fun game. Gone will be the days of having your dog deliriously tear around the house when the leash comes out.

Games for Instilling the *Come* Command
Interactive play is one of the best ways to introduce the basic obedience command coming when called.

Come
Come is one of the most important commands you can teach your puppy (or adult dog). The goal is to have him grow into an adult dog who comes to you reliably, willingly, and immediately upon hearing the command while in a wide range of situations, such as at the park, at a friend's house, in an emergency, anytime he gets loose, and even when he is playing with his canine buddies. In your dog's mind, the word *come* should never mean

When Not to Use Come

Never use the *come* command for anything your dog might dislike or to end playtime. When you call your puppy, do something silly with him when he gets to you, such as a quick game of tug or a fun trick, or reward him with a tasty tidbit and then let him run off and play again. Owners often make the mistake of calling their puppy only when it is time to go in his kennel or to put his leash on and go home. In these situations, your puppy will quickly learn that the *come* means the end of his freedom, and he will likely avoid you the next time he is called.

"Okay, I hear you. I'll be there as soon as I finish playing with my buddies or peeing on this bush." You want your dog to understand that when you say "Come," it means "Stop what you are doing and run back to me as fast as you can, right now."

Owners often wrongly assume that a puppy comes preprogrammed with a reliable *come* command. When he doesn't respond to the word, they get upset and correct or scold him, which makes *come* not a lot of fun for the dog.

If you want a reliable *come* command, you can begin teaching it with fun games and tasty rewards or toys. As your puppy grows into an adult dog, he will come because you have made it a fun game and he wants to be with you—not just because you have a cookie. The "Cookie Toss," "Find Me!", and "Chase Recall" games in this section will help you begin instilling a fun and fast *come* command.

Before you get started with these games, here are some basic rules about the *come* command:

- Your puppy must always chase you. Avoid making a game of you chasing your dog, and never allow kids to chase your dog. It inadvertently teaches him to run away from you, which creates many, many problems down the road.
- If your puppy comes to you, you must always, always, always praise him—even if moments before he chewed your shoes, urinated on the floor, or ransacked the trash. There are no exceptions to this rule.
- Never call "Come" and then correct him for something he did, such as chewing your shoe or urinating on the floor. Punishing him when he gets to you will only make it less likely that he will come back the next time. If you need to correct your dog, go and get him. Never call him to you.
- Do not call "Come" if you want to give him a bath, administer medications, or anything else he might find unpleasant. Instead, go and get your dog and then put him in the tub, trim his nails, administer medications, etc.
- Never allow your puppy to run off leash in an unfenced or unconfined area. Doing so puts him at risk and teaches him bad habits because he is too young to reliably respond to the *come* command. The same goes for untrained adult dogs. Do not put them in a position where they can practice unwanted behaviors, which is not coming when called.

Ideally, you should play these games several times a day. And by following through with daily reinforcement (e.g., a high-value reward each and every time your puppy or adult dog comes to you), it won't be long before he begins to understand that the *come* command means "Stop whatever you are doing and come to me as fast as you can."

Come Game #1: "Cookie Toss"

Most dogs, particularly herding and terriers breeds and some hound breeds that are stimulated by movement, have strong food and chase drives. This means that they love food and chasing anything that moves—which makes combining the two a fun and easy game for both puppies and adult dogs.

If your puppy tends to wander off, play in an enclosed area, such as your living room, hallway, a fenced tennis court, playground, or your driveway (if your yard is fenced). Playing on grass is not as productive because your puppy won't find the cookie as quickly, and the momentum of the game will be lost. If grass is your only option, use treats that are light in color and big enough so that your puppy or adult dog can easily find them, such as chunks of white cheese. Absent a fenced area, or if your puppy tends to run off, play the game with him on an extendable leash or long line.

One important rule about *come* games is to always let your dog chase you.

Start with a handful of tasty tidbits, such as leftover steak, chicken, cheese, or tortellini, with pieces big enough for your dog to see at a good distance— anything tasty and solid in composition so that it does not fall apart when it is thrown. Crunchy dog bones or kibble is less effective because it takes a dog five or ten seconds to chew it, which slows down the energy of the game. The goal is speed, fun, and enthusiasm.

- Stand in the middle of the playing area. (It might help to think of your position as being in the center of a clock.)
- Rev up your dog by showing him the tidbit of food, then toss the food across the floor—about 8 or 10 feet (2.4 or 3 m) in front of him (toward the 6 o'clock position).
- The goal is for your dog to tear across the room and snatch up the food, which is what most dogs will do.

Set Him Up to Succeed

When teaching the *come* command, call your puppy only when you are absolutely certain that he will respond. For example, if you call your puppy when he is excited about greeting another dog, when a family member has just come to visit, or when he is eating his dinner, he will be too excited and distracted to respond to your command, and you will inadvertently be teaching him to ignore you. In the early stages when your puppy is learning the *come* command, wait until the excitement has subsided and then call him to you. If you must have your puppy during these times, it is better to go get him rather than call him to you.

Take advantage of opportunities where you can set him up to succeed by calling him back to you when he would be coming to you anyway, such as when you have just arrived home and he is running toward you or when you have his dinner or a tasty tidbit. Let him know how clever he is when he gets to you: "What a good *come!*"

A puppy who views the *come* as a fun game is more likely to develop a reliable response to the command. If this behavior continues throughout his puppyhood and you remain excited and enthusiastic each and every time he comes to you, you will have a strong and positive response to the behavior as he grows and matures into an adult dog.

- As your dog grabs the food, say his name enthusiastically: "Fido!"
- When he looks at you, show him a second piece of food and say "Quick, quick, quick!"
- As he runs toward you, let him see you toss the piece of food 8 or 10 feet (2.4 or 3 m) toward the other side of the room (toward the 12 o'clock position). This will cause him to zoom past you as he charges for the second piece of food.
- When he picks up the second piece of food, repeat the process.
- Say his name, "Fido!", and when he looks, say "Quick, quick, quick!"
- Show him the food as he is charging toward you, then toss it 8 or 10 feet (2.4 or 3 m) back toward the 6 o'clock position.
- Keeping yourself in the middle of the action will help establish you as the center of the activity.
  Once your dog is enthusiastically charging back and forth across the room for tidbits of food, begin incorporating fun behaviors. For example:
- As he is charging back to you, toss a piece of food between your legs and tell him "Go through," encouraging him to run through your legs.
- When he picks up the food, take off running in the opposite direction, saying his name, "Fido! Fido! Fido!", and encouraging him to chase you.

- As he charges toward you, throw another tidbit of food between your legs. As he matures, begin challenging him by incorporating obedience behaviors (which you'll learn in Chapter 10) into the game. (If your dog does not know basic obedience commands yet, you can lure him into a *down* or *sit* with a cookie. Eventually, the cookie will become a reward rather than a lure.) For example:
- As he charges through your legs for the tidbit of food, spin around and ask him to down.
- Praise lavishly: "Good *down*!"
- Repeat the process several times.
- Then let him see you toss a tidbit of food 8 or 10 feet (2.4 or 3 m) across the room as you tell him "Get it."

    Use your imagination to come up with fun and creative games that can be incorporated into the cookie toss game.

Come Game #2: "Find Me!"

"Find Me!", which is a modified hide-and-seek game, is great for building and establishing a strong bond, conditioning a puppy or adult dog that you are his primary source of fun, and instilling the *come* command. By capitalizing on a dog's natural chase instinct, you can utilize fun and excitement to teach him to always find you when you say his name. You can play indoors or outdoors, but when playing outdoors, always play in an enclosed area so that your puppy cannot escape.

When you start playing hide-and-seek, make sure that your puppy can find you easily.

- Start with a handful of tasty tidbits of food.
- Show your dog the food, then toss a tidbit down the hall or across the room.
- As your puppy runs to get the food, run in the opposite direction—go from one room to another, or hide behind a chair or door.
- Call your puppy's name enthusiastically: "Fido! Fido! Fido!"
- When he finds you, shower him with praise—"Aren't you clever! You found me!"—and a potpourri of kisses, and reward with a tasty tidbit or a tug on his favorite toy.

    In the beginning, your hiding spot should be obvious, making it easy for your dog to succeed. As he becomes more enthusiastic and proficient, make your hiding spots more challenging.

    When playing outdoors, wait until your puppy is distracted—sniffing the grass, exploring a bug—and

When playing "Chase Recall," have a friend hold your puppy, then let him go after you take off running.

then take off running or duck behind a tree, rock, building, or whatever is convenient while saying your dog's name in a happy, enthusiastic tone of voice. When he finds you, shower him with plenty of praise and enthusiasm: "That's my good boy! What a good *come*!"

A variation is to have a friend, spouse, or child hold your puppy at one end of the house while you run to the other end saying his name enthusiastically: "Fido! Fido! Fido!" As you say his name, the person holding your dog should let him go with the command "Find him!" or "Find your mummy!" If your puppy is reluctant to run and find you, make your voice more inviting and enthusiastic, make it easier for him to find you by letting him see you, or have the person holding the puppy run to find you, too. Most puppies will chase anyone who runs away from them. Again, this game can be played outdoors, but be sure to play in an enclosed or fenced area so that your puppy cannot run off.

Playing this fun, interactive game builds enthusiasm, fosters your puppy's zany personality, and builds an intense eagerness and unwavering desire for him to be with you. It helps puppies grow into adult dogs who are willing to climb over, crawl over, or go through anything to be with their owner.

Come Game #3: "Chase Recall"

Chase recalls are similar to the "Cookie Toss" and "Find Me!" games. The goal is to have your puppy or adult dog chase you. With this game, you want your puppy to burst out of your helper's hands and run as fast as he can to you.

- For very young or small puppies, have your helper kneel down and hold your puppy around the chest; for bigger or older puppies (and adult dogs), have a friend or family member hold your puppy by his leash. (Your puppy should be wearing a buckle collar, never a choke chain or prong collar.)
- Rev him up by showing him a tasty tidbit or his favorite toy.
- Tap his chest and growl at him, "Rrrrrrrrrr," then ask him "Do you want to do a *come*?"
- Take off running, saying his name enthusiastically: "Fido! Fido! Fido!"
- Don't worry if your puppy yips and yaps and carries on—this will tell you that his natural chase instinct is being engaged.
- Don't run too far or too fast or your puppy may be reluctant to run after you.
- About 10 feet (3 m) or so from your puppy, turn and face him while continuing to encourage him with your voice.
- The person holding your puppy should let him go, and if all goes as planned, your puppy should chase you.
- When he gets to you, lavish him with praise and reward him with a tasty tidbit of food or his favorite toy.
- As your puppy matures, you can begin increasing the distance between you and the person holding the dog.

For a variation on this game:

- Do the previous steps, but when your puppy is halfway to you, turn your back on him and run another 8 or 10 feet (2.4 or 3 m) as you encourage him to catch you.

This West Highland White Terrier puppy finds retrieving games fun.

- Stop, bend over, peek though your legs, and let him run through them.

Use your imagination to come up with fun and exciting variations to the chase recall game. For example, race across the yard, stop, get on the ground, and let him run right into your lap. Or run across the yard, stop, get on the ground, and bang the ground with your hands or his toy. Tell him "Quick, Quick, Quick!" Or run, stop, turn toward him, and encourage him to run between your legs: "Yea! What a good boy!"

Adding Distractions

In the beginning, play come games in an environment with few or no distractions. As your puppy grows and matures and is reliably coming, begin adding distractions, such as a toy or two lying nearby, a family member walking by, and so forth.

Categorize the distractions by their degree of distraction, which can vary for different puppies depending on their temperament and personality. For example, a toy on the floor may be a minor distraction, say, a 2 on a scale of 1 to 10. A cat running by might be a major distraction—an 8 on a scale of 1 to 10—for a sight-sensitive Australian Shepherd. Water, such as a puddle or kiddie pool or even a sprinkler, might not be a distraction for, say, a Weimaraner, but it will likely be a major distraction for a water-loving retriever.

As your puppy begins coming reliably during fun recall games, begin increasing the distractions. However, never progress to more difficult distractions until your puppy is coming reliably with low-grade distractions. If your puppy is distracted and not chasing or playing with you, try playing in a less distractive environment, or stay closer to your dog when he is chasing you, or get more attractive rewards, such as tastier treats or a toy your puppy is crazy about. Manipulate your puppy's environment so that you set him up to succeed, thereby always rewarding him for doing the right thing.

If you have no one to hold your puppy, simply take off running down the hall or across the yard as you encourage your puppy to chase you. Praise and reward when he catches you: "What a good *come*!"

Chase recall games are great for building motivation and drive and instilling the *come* command. However, as your puppy grows and matures, be sure to practice other fun, stationary *recall* games to teach him to come to you while you are standing still. Otherwise, you might be forced to run away anytime you want your puppy to come to you.

Come Game #4: "Recall With a Friend"

Another fun game that begins instilling a fun and exciting *come* command, "Recall With a Friend" is great for incorporating children into the training game.

- Sit on the floor with a friend, spouse, or child.
- Sit facing each other, with your legs as wide apart as possible and the bottom of your shoes touching. This forms a makeshift chute to guide your puppy.
- One person should start the game by holding the puppy, while the second person should show the puppy a tidbit of food and enthusiastically call his name: "Fido! Fido! Fido!"

- The person holding the puppy should release him, and the puppy should run to the person saying his name.
- When he gets to the person saying his name, shower him with an abundance of praise—"What a good come!"—and a yummy tidbit of food.
- Build up his confidence by telling him he is brilliant and clever, kiss his nose, and let him crawl around in your lap.
- Then repeat the exercise three or four times in succession.
- As your puppy matures and progresses, gradually increase and continue increasing the distance between the two of you.

Your puppy should be wearing his collar and dragging his leash as he runs between the two people—just in case he decides to escape, you will be able to grab his leash. (Never grab your dog.) This is a great game for playing indoors or outdoors, but when outdoors, always play in an enclosed area.

More Fun and Useful Games

As you can see, play is a great way to teach just about anything, including fun, interactive tricks and commands that utilize a high-drive, high-energy dog's natural instincts. For instance, most herding breeds (e.g., Australian Shepherds, Border Collies, Bearded Collies) and sporting breeds (e.g., Golden Retrievers, Labrador Retrievers, Flat-Coated Retrievers) love to fetch. Almost all breeds love to tug. Most high-drive, high-energy dogs are extremely clever, so they thrive on thinking games like find it, twist, or spin. That said, don't limit yourself to your dog's natural instincts. With some determination, stick-to-it-ive-ness, and intestinal fortitude, you can teach even your terrier to retrieve or sighthound to spin and twist.

Start playing retrieving games with your puppy before he learns to avoid you once he has the toy in his mouth.

Retrieving

Most dogs—especially retrieving breeds—love to fetch, be it a stick, tug toy, ball, or flying disc. Retrieve games are an easy way to exercise your dog, and they are the foundation of many other games you can play with him. By capitalizing on your dog's natural instinct to retrieve, you can get toys back easily and stay in control of the games. No need to worry if your dog is not a "natural" retriever. Some dogs have naturally high

Food? Toys? Try Both!

Depending on the breed and your dog's individual temperament and personality, he may prefer toys more than food. My Australian Shepherds are a great example. Moses is manic about toys—he'd much rather have his toys than food. That said, if I train him with food, he's happy to train with food. If I'm training with food and then whip out his toy, he'll go crazy for his toy. But not all dogs make the switch so easily. I got Moses' littermate, Miles, when he was nine months old. He had never played as a puppy, so he didn't even know *how* to play. He didn't know how to tug or retrieve. It took a lot of time and energy to get him to play with toys. It would have been much easier (on me!) to just use food, but I wanted the option of both food and toys in my training toolbox, so I worked really hard at getting him to play. To this day he prefers food, but I can now use food and toys interchangeably. Another of my Aussies, Jiggs, is two and a half years old and is not nearly as intense as Miles and Moses. He didn't naturally tug or retrieve as a puppy, so I had to teach him to do both. He'll do both now because I ask him to tug or retrieve, but he'd much, much rather have food any day of the week!

prey drives, while others need a bit of encouragement to flourish. By following a few simple guidelines, most dogs will quickly become enthusiastic fetchers.

Like any other game, retrieving must be fun for your dog and interactive—meaning the two of you should be playing together.

- Begin with your puppy or adult dog on leash.
- Use a toy he loves, such as a tug toy, ball on a rope, flying disc, rubber bumper toy, section of rubber garden hose, or empty plastic water bottle.
- Dogs love movement, so drag or wiggle the toy on the floor, encouraging him to get it.
- Put a command to it, such as "Fetch" or "Get it," so that he begins to associate the command with running out to pick things up.
- When he picks up the toy, praise him: "Good boy!" or "Yea for you!" (If he is reluctant to pick it up, give the toy a tiny kick to generate some movement as you encourage him to get it.)
- Back up, clap your hands, and use your voice to encourage him to come back to you.
- If necessary, get on the floor and encourage him to bring it back, or gently use your leash to prevent him from running off.
- Rather than reaching for the toy right away, allow him to strut around for 10 or 15 seconds savoring his mammoth achievement.
- Pump up his ego by praising him lavishly: "Look at you! Aren't you clever!" or "What have you got?"

- Sit on the ground and let him crawl around in your lap with his "prize."
- Praise him as he does so, but keep your hands away from the toy. (If he thinks that you will take the toy away from him, he will try to avoid you by running off or lying down with the toy elsewhere. Most dogs learn to avoid their owner because the owner is too quick to grab the toy when the dog returns.)

   Ideally, in the beginning, when puppies are first learning, toss the toy 2 or 3 feet (.6 to .9 m) in front of you. If you throw it too far, he may run partway out only to find the task too overwhelming or daunting. As he builds confidence and reliability, you can begin throwing it farther and making the game more challenging by tossing the toy under a tree, bush, or patio table. Most dogs will chase anything that moves, so to generate speed and excitement:
- Throw the toy.
- When he gets it, turn and run in the opposite direction, but don't run too far or he may be reluctant to chase you.
- When he catches you, praise him lavishly. Remember to keep your hands still.
- Allow him to strut around with his toy for a minute or two before taking it from him.

If He's Reluctant to Fetch

Competition encourages most dogs to try harder. If your dog is reluctant to fetch the toy, help and encourage him by racing after the toy with him, snatching it away just before he gets it. Hold the toy over your head or high enough so that he cannot reach it. Tell him "Too slow! I got it." Race for it again, but let him get it this time. Praise enthusiastically: 'What a good boy!" If he drops the toy, encourage him to get it by kicking it a few feet (m) and then racing him to it.

For a greater challenge you can move the "Find It" game outdoors.

You can encourage retrieving in young puppies by praising and rewarding everything they pick up, be it a shoe, tin can, garden gnome, or sheep poop. Ask him "What did you find?" or "Look at you!" If you have multiple dogs, tell them to look, too: "Look what Fido has! Isn't he clever?" If the item is something you do not want to encourage him to pick up, let him strut around for a moment, pump up his ego by telling him he is brilliant, and

What's He Distracted By?

Puppies are easily distracted by everything in life. As they grow and mature and become more aware of their environment, they get distracted by what's going on around them. Some distractions, however, are more enticing than others and can depend on their breed and natural instinct. Some dogs, even well-trained ones, find it difficult to concentrate on the task at hand when working around a particularly enticing distraction. Distractions and how enticing they may be will depend on your dog, his breeding, temperament, and training. Here are a few distractions your dog might find too enticing to resist.

Breeds	Easily Distracted By
Australian Shepherds, Border Collies, Australian Cattle Dogs, Shetland Sheepdogs, Corgis, Bearded Collies, and most other herding breeds	movement of any kind, including children playing, other animals running, joggers, bikers, etc. livestock, including sheep, ducks, cattle
Golden Retrievers, Labrador Retrievers, Nova Scotia Duck Tolling Retrievers, Flat-Coated Retrievers, English Springer Spaniels, and most other sporting breeds	birds water of any kind, including ponds, lakes, and pools, other animals
Parson and Jack Russell Terriers, Norfolk Terriers, Norwich Terriers, Schnauzers, West Highland White Terriers, and most other terriers	scurrying-type movements, other animals, high squeaks or squealing noises
Greyhounds, Salukis, Whippets, and most other sighthounds	moving animals, moving objects

then tell him to give it up. Be sure to replace it with something he can have, such as his own toy.

If He Won't Give Up the Toy

Ideally, you should start playing this game before your dog learns to avoid people once he has a toy. If he plays the catch-me-if-you-can game, do not encourage him by chasing after him. Instead, run in the opposite direction, clapping your hands and saying his name enthusiastically. (Remember, most dogs will chase anyone or anything that runs, so use their natural instinct to your advantage.) When he gets to you, praise him lavishly: "What a good boy!"

An alternative method is to get on the ground and pretend to pick at the grass with great interest: "Ohhh….what is this?" Dogs are curious, and their curiosity usually gets the best of them. Most dogs will come over to investigate what you are so excited about.

If so, avoid grabbing or touching your dog. Calmly pick up his leash so that he can't run off, and talk to him: "There you are! You're my silly boy."

"Find It!"

"Find It!" is a fun game and a good way to teach puppies and adult dogs to use their nose, which is great for future tracking skills and a good way to use up mental energy. "Find It!" is a similar game to "Find Me!", but rather than teaching your puppy to find you, you teach him to find an object.

- Start by sitting or kneeling on the floor next to your puppy.
- Hide a tasty, smelly tidbit of food, such as boiled chicken or liver, under a bucket, box, or plastic bowl, and encourage your puppy to use his nose to find it.
- When he does so, lavish him with praise—tell him he is brilliant and clever.
- As he becomes more proficient and understands the command, gradually increase the complexity and difficulty of the game—but never make it so difficult that he becomes bored or frustrated. Always set your puppy up to succeed by working within his physical and mental capabilities.

For a variation on this game:

- Gently hold your puppy by the collar.
- Let him see you toss a tasty tidbit down the hall.
- Let go of his collar and encourage him to find it.
- In the beginning, you might need to run with him to encourage or help him, saying "Let's find it!" or "Where is it?" on the way.
- When he finds the treat, tell him he is brilliant: "There it is! You found it! Aren't you clever!"
- Pump up his ego by encouraging him to strut around, savoring his colossal achievement.

If your puppy loves toys more than food (and some high-drive puppies and adult dogs do), use his favorite toy, rather than food, to play this game. Either is acceptable. When he finds the toy, interact in a fun game of tug as you tell him he is smart and clever. Then gently snatch the toy away, hold his collar again, toss the toy down the hall, and run for it again. As his skills increase, make the game a bit more challenging by tossing the toy or food under a chair or table or behind a door.

Toy Motivation

If your puppy is not motivated by a toy, try putting a tasty hunk of food, such as boiled liver, a chunk of steak, or a whole hot dog, in a specially designed toy or an old sock, and encourage him to tug or retrieve the toy. Or try boiling the toy in some chicken or beef broth to make it more appealing. Play with this "special" toy only when you play together. Never leave the toy out where your puppy or adult dog can chew or swallow it. Doing so may result in a life-threatening situation that requires an expensive, not to mention painful, surgery.

For a more advanced trick, teach your dog how to put his toys away in a toy box.

"Toys in a Bucket"

Build on your puppy's retrieve and find it skills by teaching him to put away his toys by retrieving them individually and dropping them in a bucket or toy box.

The steps for teaching this are, well, backward, meaning you start from the finish point of the trick (the toy in the bucket) and build the sequence of the trick backward—a process known as back-chaining. You'll need a bucket or toy box that your dog is comfortable being around and one that isn't so high that he can't drop the toy in it.

- Start by kneeling on the floor, positioning the toy box close to you, between you and your dog. Place a treat in it and encourage him to get it. As he puts his head in the box to investigate, click (or verbally cue with "Yes!") before he gets the treat. Let him eat the treat.
- Repeat several times to build his confidence.
- Now place his toy in the box. When he investigates, click as soon as he nudges or touches the toy.
- Repeat this step a few times to build confidence.
- Put his toy in the box again, but this time don't click (or verbally reward) when he nudges it. By withholding the click and treat, he's likely to try to mouth or pick up the toy, which is what you want.
- When he mouths or picks up the toy, click and treat. Try to click while his head is still over the box. This way, when he drops the toy to get his treat, the toy will fall into the box.
- Advance to putting the toy beside the box, and give your dog time to figure out what you want. Click and treat when he nudges or picks up the toy—or any action that will help shape the final behavior, such as nudging the toy or even putting his head back in the box. You may need to help him a bit with "Get it" or whatever word or phrase you are using for a *retrieve* command.
- Eventually, your dog will make the connection between the click and treat for putting his head or nose in the bucket and for picking up the toy. When he drops the toy in the bucket, click and reward with a jackpot of cookies.
- Practice several times and put a command to the behavior, such as "In the bucket."

This is a fun but quite challenging trick; it may be too advanced for very young puppies. Sporting dogs who like to retrieve will probably find it a snap to learn.

"Name That Toy"

Challenge your dog mentally and increase his vocabulary by teaching him the names of different toys and showing him how to distinguish among them. For instance, teach him which toy is his Frisbee, ball, tuggie, squeaky, and so forth, and then teach him to pick up that toy.

- Start by putting names to each of his toys.
- If he picks up a tug toy ask him "Is that your tuggie?" If he picks up his ball, ask "Do you have your ball?" Throw his purple stuffed toy, and when he brings it back, ask him "Is that purple man?" or whatever silly names you want to name his toys. The point is to build his vocabulary by naming his toys.
- Eventually, when he can distinguish among them, tell him "Get your ball" or "Get your tuggie."
- Have him redeem the toy for a yummy cookie by bringing it back to you or dropping it in the toy box.

Again, start slowly with one toy at a time, and progress at a speed within your puppy's physical and mental capabilities.

Tugging

As previously mentioned, tug-of-war has fallen out of favor with some trainers because it is a test of strength. The theory is that puppies who win strength games often assume that they are stronger than their owners, both physically and mentally, and being stronger, they naturally assume that they are more suited to be pack leader. Some dogs may see this as an opportunity to exploit the situation and take over as top dog.

More importantly, tugging stimulates or creates arousal in some dogs, especially high-octane dogs. When a puppy or adult dog gets too wound up, too over the top with excitement, owners usually lose

Jumping and Puppies

control of the game, thereby losing control of their dog.

However, by setting the ground rules from day one, tugging games need not be eliminated from your repertoire of training tools. First, you must win as often as your puppy or adult dog wins. If you win all the time, your dog will get bored and lose interest. If your dog wins all the time, he may think that he is stronger than you. Ideally, as trainer Sylvia Bishop likes to say, "You win, he wins, you both win." This way, your dog will enjoy playing with you, and you will be giving him the right message regarding his status in the pack.

Second, you must control all of the games, including tugging. You should determine when the two of you will tug, how hard and how long each of you will tug, when your dog is to release the toy, and when the game is over. If your puppy or adult dog becomes too stimulated or out of control or begins barking or nipping at your hands or snatching the toy from your hand, stop the game immediately. Resume the game once he has calmed down and you have regained control of the situation.

Using "Tug" for Obedience Commands

"Tug" is an excellent interactive game that allows you to instill specific obedience commands. For example, when your puppy is tugging, tugging, tugging, gently release the pressure and watch him fold into the *down* position. (This might take a bit of coordination and practice on your part.) When he does so, tell him "Good *down*!" While he is in the *down* position, let him tug for five or ten seconds. While he is tugging, gently use the toy to pop him into a *sit* position: "What a good *sit*!"

Another game is to have him tug, tug, tug, and then pop him through your legs with the command "Go through." Spin around and tug some more! Or while he is tugging, pivot yourself into the *heel* position and take two or three steps while he is still tugging. While tugging, do a spin or a twist and tug some more.

Use your imagination to come up with fun and creative games that will help instill confidence, expend mental and physical energy, and build a strong human–canine relationship.

Tug and *Release* Commands

Early on, you should teach your dog a *tug* and a *release* command. For example, when he is tugging, tell him "Good tug!" or "Tug" or "Get it" or "Pull." This will teach him to associate the behavior with the command. By teaching him to tug, you can teach him to

This owner is using a fun game of tug to teach her puppy the *heel* position.

stop tugging with "Give" or "Out" or "Drop it" or whatever command you choose. Some dogs are more reluctant to give up a toy, and getting them to release it may take a bit of finesse on your part. If this is the case, do not continue tugging. This will only encourage more tugging on the dog's part.

- Until he understands the *release* command, simply show him a different toy and encourage him to get it.
- To do so, he must let go of the first toy.
- When he lets go of the first toy, put your command—"Give," "Out," "Drop it," etc.—to the behavior of releasing the toy.

Teaching a *release* command will help you remain in control of the situation. If you cannot get him to give up the toy on command when he is playing, he is controlling the situation.

Trick and Treat

Tricks are a great way to stimulate your puppy's mind, as well as burn off some physical and mental energy, which is essential for high-drive, high-energy dogs who are naturally clever and who have abundant reserves of energy. Rewarding and entertaining, trick training helps build a stronger human–canine relationship. It's also a fun way to show off how clever your canine really is. Plus, you get to spend quality time with your dog, and when you and your dog do fun things together, you will enjoy each other's company a lot more.

Tricks are an extension of basic obedience training; they increase and challenge your dog mentally and physically. Dogs—especially high-drive and high-energy dogs—are very intelligent and tend to become bored quite quickly. Without adequate physical and mental exercise, they will become frustrated and destructive, which will lead to all sorts of behavioral problems. Someone once said, "Dog is a man's best friend—but if he's taught some basic skills and tricks, he will become an even better friend."

Natural Tricks

Good trainers know how to utilize a dog's natural behaviors to teach fun tricks, as well as basic obedience commands. For example, learn to put a command to every behavior

your dog performs. If your dog jumps up, tell him "Good jump!" If he rolls over, say "Good roll over!" If he hops on his hind legs, say "Good hop!" While the words themselves don't mean anything right now, it won't be long before your puppy or adult dog begins associating the words with the command.

It's worth reiterating that these are fun tricks. You should never correct or punish your dog or use harsh training methods for teaching tricks or basic obedience. What is the point of learning tricks if there is no fun in it?

Finally, while you can teach an old dog new tricks, some young puppies may not be physically or mentally mature enough for some, especially those that involve jumping. A good rule of thumb is to never jump dogs under the age of six months (some experts recommend two years of age), and never allow them to jump anything higher than their elbows.

"Nose Touch"

Used frequently by agility trainers, the "Nose Touch" or "Hand Target" is a fun trick to teach your puppy to think and stimulate his mind—not to mention impress your family and friends. Plus, as your puppy grows and matures, it can be used to get him to come to you by encouraging him to "touch" your hand.

This trick is easily taught with a clicker. Absent a clicker, use a crisp "Yes!"

- For young or very small puppies, start by kneeling on the ground with your puppy standing or sitting in front of you. For older or bigger puppies or adult dogs, you can try this exercise while you are standing up—just be sure that your dog's nose can reach your hand without jumping up (that's a separate trick).
- Hold the clicker and a treat in your right hand.
- When your puppy looks at you, hold your left hand (the one not holding the clicker and treat) palm open at your side. (Depending on your puppy, you may need to hold it closer to him rather than at your side.)

Right- or Left-Pawed?

Like humans, dogs tend to be right- or left-handed—or pawed. Therefore, some tricks may be easier than others. Some dogs, for instance, naturally favor one side or the other—such as turning to the right or left. Pay attention to your dog and see if he is right- or left-footed. Start with his natural side and then progress to teaching him to use both his left and right side. This will challenge him physically and mentally and help him become more balanced.

You can take any of your dog's natural behaviors and turn them into a fun trick just by consistently rewarding the behavior. (1) Hold your hand up. (2) Click and reward when your dog touches your hand.

- Most puppies, being the curious creatures that they are, will come over and sniff your hand.
- As soon as your puppy touches the palm of your hand, click (or say "Yes" if you don't have a clicker).
- Then bring your right hand with the treat to your left hand.
- Feed him from your left hand—the one your puppy touched.
- You can also add a command when he touches the palm of your hand, such as "Touch."
- Alternate between hands so that your puppy learns to touch both your right and left hand.

Some puppies and adult dogs aren't as inquisitive (or inclined toward operant conditioning). If this is the case, hold a tidbit of food between your index and middle finger. Hold your hand out, palm side down, with the treat between your fingers. Most dogs, with their exceptional noses, will be able to smell the treat. When they touch it with their nose to investigate, click (or verbally praise Yes!") and reward with the treat by letting your dog get the food while it is between your fingers.

"Twist" and "Spin"

The "Twist" and "Spin" tricks are fun, simple to teach, and help increase a dog's vocabulary and stimulate his mind. They can also be incorporated into basic obedience commands.

For "Twist":

- Start with a tasty tidbit of food; hold it close to your dog's nose.
- Keeping the treat at nose level, encourage him to turn his head to the right (clockwise) by slowly moving the treat backward, past his shoulder and toward his tail.
- Continue luring his head toward his tail until he moves his front or rear feet.
- Once his feet move, continue luring his head past his tail.
- As soon as he passes the halfway mark, chances are high that he will complete the circle on his own and end up with his head facing you.
- As he completes the circle, add the command "Twist."
- Repeat this exercise several times until your dog is doing a complete circle— or twist—in one flowing movement.
- Eventually, with plenty of practice and encouragement, he will learn to twist on command rather than being lured.

"Spin" is the same game, only circling in a counterclockwise position:

- Follow the previous instructions, but rather than lure your dog's head clockwise, lure it to the left in a counterclockwise movement.
- When the circle is completed, reward him with plenty of praise: "Good spin!"

For many agile, high-drive breeds, learning to twist or spin comes quite easily.

Most puppies and adult dogs learn quite quickly when lured with food. A tug toy or ball can also be used if your dog is crazy about toys. Use the toy to lure him into a spin or twist, and then reward him by playing a quick game of tug.

As he becomes more proficient, begin challenging him by asking him to spin and then walk back (see next trick) into the *down* position. Or ask him to twist and then sit. (See Chapter 10 for teaching the *sit* and *down*.) Once he has mastered the commands and is spinning and twisting on his own, begin adding some distance and then have him spin then down or twist and then sit. Or have him walk back, then spin, then walk back some more. Use your imagination to come up with fun ways to incorporate the twist and spin into other games and /or basic obedience commands.

Avoid doing multiple twists or spins at a time as your dog is likely to become dizzy and may even get sick to his stomach.

"Walk-Back"

Teaching the walk-back is relatively easy and well within the capabilities of most owners. An equally impressive way to build your dog's vocabulary and stimulate his mind—not

Using play as a basis for training is great for high-drive dogs.

to mention impressing your family and friends—this trick teaches a dog to walk straight backward, away from his owner, on command. Not only is it fun and impressive, but it's also useful because you can teach your dog to easily maneuver out of your path by backing up. It's also a great rear end-strengthening exercise.

A couple of methods exist for teaching this trick. Both are relatively easy, so pick the one that works best for you. Train between two barriers, such as between a couch and coffee table, between a wall and a couch, or between two exercise pens, which will keep your puppy moving in a straight line backward.

- Start with your puppy between the two barriers and facing you.
- Take a step toward him, which should cause him to take a step backward.
- Praise (or click) "Yes!" or "Good walk back!" or whatever verbal cue you choose.
- Quickly reward with a yummy treat at knee level (your knee, not the puppy's) or under your puppy's chin. (If the cookie is too high, it will cause him to sit.)
- Repeat this process several times.
- The goal is to have your puppy walk back on his own rather than you luring him backward.
- After multiple repetitions, wait and see if your puppy will move backward on his own.
- If so, praise (or click) and reward.
- If your puppy just stands and stares at you, take another tiny step toward him to get him moving backward.
- Praise (or click) and reward any movement of his back feet.
- Once you have your puppy walking backward, you can continue taking steps

toward him to get him to walk backward, or you can progress to where you stand still and give him the verbal cue to walk back—and continue walking backward as far as you want.

If you hold the treat too high, your dog is likely to sit rather than walk back.

Here is an alternative method if you choose not to use barriers. (If necessary, to maintain control, teach this exercise on leash.)

- Start with your dog standing directly in front of you and facing you.
- With a tasty tidbit of food between the index finger and thumb of each hand, hold the food about knee high (your knees, not the dog's knees) and directly in front of the dog's nose. (Good hand position is important. If your hand is too high, he will sit. If your hand is too low, he will down.)
- Make a small chute by bending your knees slightly.
- As your puppy nibbles on the food, take a small step toward him.
- Your body movement should encourage him to walk backward.
- As soon as he takes a step backward, praise with "Yes!" (or click) and reward.

In the learning stages, you are luring and maneuvering your dog to walk backward with the food. Eventually, with plenty of repetition and consistency, he will learn to walk backward on command. That said, most puppies figure out quite quickly what behaviors get them a treat, and he may begin offering this behavior as a way to get a treat. If so, offer plenty of praise and encouragement.

This trick can also be taught using a tug toy. While your puppy is tugging, tugging, tugging, simply take one step toward him. The law of physics—and the lack of resistance on the tug toy—will cause him to take one or two steps backward. As he walks backward, offer plenty of praise and a yummy reward.

When play is used as a basis for training and bonding, your high-drive dog is sure to respond.

3

Part III

Living With Your
High-Energy Dog

10

Practical Exercises and Basic Manners

All puppies, especially high-drive, high-energy puppies, should learn early in life some practical exercises, such as riding in the car, walking on a loose leash, door manners (not bolting out doors), grooming, and exercise pen and crate training.

They should also learn some basic obedience skills, including *sit*, *down*, and *come*, which was discussed in Chapter 9. High-drive or high-energy dogs operate in blast mode a great deal of their lives. Therefore, to make your life and your dog's life more enjoyable—and to have some semblance of order at home and in public—these dogs need to learn early that there are rules that must be followed, which include basic obedience commands and manners. If your adult dog's early education was a bit neglected or received a failing grade, don't despair. It's never too late to begin working on and reinforcing basic commands and manners. The job might be a bit more challenging, especially if your dog has already developed a few naughty behaviors, but it's a task that's well within the capabilities of most owners.

If you teach your dog basic manners, activities like going to the vet will become a breeze.

Ideally, you should start instilling these behaviors right away. They should be priority one for any dog, but especially puppies because puppies grow quickly, both physically and mentally, and this valuable time can never be recaptured. Time is of the essence. Conditioning a young puppy to accept and enjoy these behaviors and activities will make your life—and his—much easier as he grows into an adult dog.

Practical Exercises

Both puppies and adult dogs will benefit from learning these practical exercises.

Car Rides

Most dogs love to ride in the car, which means that they can be included in a lot of family outings, whether it's a quick trip to the grocery store or a longer trip across the state or country. While some dogs seem to take to car rides naturally, others need a bit of coaxing and conditioning. Teaching a dog to enjoy riding in the car should start early in his life, which means taking him for lots of positive rides while he is young, impressionable, and receptive to learning new things. Ideally, the best thing is to put your puppy in a comfy crate with a Nylabone or chewy toy and drive him

Motion Sickness, Carsickness, and Phobias

Young puppies or adult dogs who have never been in a car or who have developed phobias are often anxious or apprehensive about car rides. Some dogs drool, shake, and even vomit. For dogs who have true motion sickness, which is normally associated with an inner ear problem, medications are available and can be used under the supervision of a veterinarian. Carsickness, on the other hand, is usually associated with fear or an apprehension of the car's noise and movement, a response to the dog's inability to control his circumstances, or a traumatic experience in a car or at the journey's end, such as an unpleasant experience at the veterinarian's office, groomer, obedience class, or animal shelter.

around town. Take him to the bank, post office, veterinarian, and groomer for cookies and kisses. When done in a fun and positive manner, puppies will quickly learn that fun things always happen when car rides are involved. It won't be long before your puppy goes into thrill mode as soon as you reach for the car keys.

If your puppy has problems riding in the car, begin reconditioning him by simply sitting in the car without the motor running while you verbally praise him for being brave, and reward him with tasty treats. Progress to sitting in the car with the motor running. Again, verbally praise and reward with yummy treats. The next step is short, fun trips around the block, to the post office, bank, and so forth. Each time, gradually increase the distance, always making the experience fun and positive. Put a favorite blanket, toy, or treat in his crate to keep him comfy and occupied.

Although it is tempting to allow your precious pooch to ride loose, or heaven forbid, in your lap, the safest place for a turbo-charged puppy or adult dog is in a crate. Dogs—especially young dogs and puppies—are inquisitive, curious, busy creatures. Putting them in a car doesn't change that behavior. Crating them keeps them safe and prevents them from engaging in naughty and destructive behaviors, such as chewing armrests, munching leather seats, or ransacking grocery bags. Plus, a crated dog allows you to focus on your driving and not on your dog.

Door Manners

Puppies and adult dogs should learn early on not to barge out doors or gateways. The goal is for your puppy to sit and wait—or at the very least simply wait—while you open the door and go through first. Only then can he follow. When you stop at the door, your

If your dog barges out the door and you can't control him, it could be potentially dangerous.

puppy should stop, too. For better control, it is helpful if you keep your puppy or adult dog on leash.

To start:

- Praise (or click) and reward any tendencies not to lunge or bolt at the door.
- Reward and feed him with the treat over his head but close to his nose so that he is encouraged to drop his rear into a *sit*.
- Praise (or click) and reward for sitting; be generous so that your puppy understands that you pay well for desired behaviors.
- Release him as you back away from the door, and then practice the door approach several times.
- As he becomes more proficient at sitting and waiting, practice reaching for the door and praising (or clicking) and rewarding for maintaining a *sit*.
- Progress to opening the door, then stepping through the door, and then calling your puppy through the door.
- To cement this behavior, put a command to it, such as his name coupled with "Okay" so that he understands that he must be released to go through the door—this will prevent him from bolting out the door as soon as you are through it.

Teach your puppy or adult dog that being released to come through the doorway does not mean that he gets to tear off down the driveway or across the yard, chasing birds or squirrels and acting recklessly. Practicing these exercises on leash will teach him that he must pass through the door and stay close to you.

Grooming and Handling

Grooming is an essential and necessary task when you own a dog. Rather than consider it a chore, think of it as a pleasant way to keep your dog's skin and coat in tip-top condition, as well as an ideal and fun way to spend quality time with your dog while simultaneously building a strong human–canine bond. A puppy who is exposed to positive and delightful grooming experiences will grow into an adult dog who takes pleasure in the regular and requisite routine.

If your puppy came from a reputable breeder, he is probably used to being handled, examined, and gently stroked. Hopefully he has had every toe and tooth counted and his ears and tail area examined many, many times. Most likely he's had at least one bath and may already be accustomed to and tolerate being brushed and examined.

If not, don't despair—it's never too late to begin. If grooming is unfamiliar to your puppy, chances are he may be frightened, nervous, or unsure. Patience, gentle handling, calm words, and plenty of hugs, kisses, and yummy rewards will help build his confidence and teach him to accept and enjoy the handling and grooming process.

Remember, most high-drive, high-energy dogs live their entire lives in blast-off mode, so it's highly beneficial to teach them to accept these practices as soon as possible. Also, most high-drive, high-energy dogs like a job, be it field work, herding, swimming, etc., which means that they can get pretty dirty on a regular basis. Teaching them to accept grooming— especially standing still while you wipe their feet before going indoors or jumping in the car—will make your life and his much more enjoyable.

Your dog should be comfortable being handled and groomed.

Grooming Table

Teach your puppy or adult dog to stand and lie down on a grooming table, and your life will be much easier when it comes to brushing, trimming nails, and examining his body for stickers, burrs, cuts, hot spots, and such. Although they are an investment, grooming tables are well worth the money if you plan to groom your dog, as opposed to having him professionally groomed. Puppies who grow into adult dogs who learn to relax on a grooming table are more likely to relax on a veterinarian's examination table, making a trip to the vet's office less stressful for all involved.

To get your dog used to the grooming table:

- Place him on the grooming table.
- Have your puppy stand or lie still for a few seconds while you praise (or click) and reward.
- Puppies have limited attention spans, so do not expect him to remain still for extended periods. In the beginning, you want progress—not perfection
- Progress to the point where your puppy will accept having his body stroked with your hand, then gently, slowly, and calmly brush him all over.

Harsh handling during these learning stages will come back to haunt you when your puppy begins to resent this necessary chore.

Teach your pup to accept having his teeth brushed.

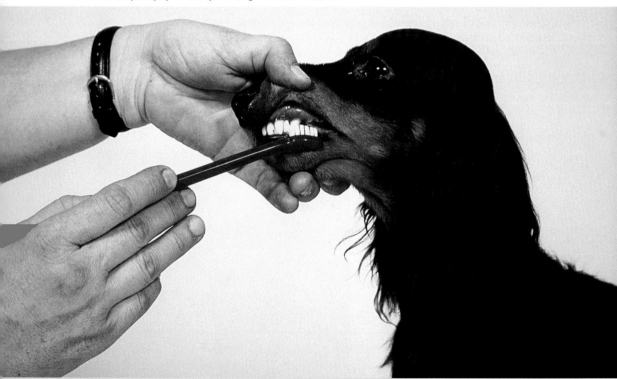

Training Collars and Devices

Young puppies and adult dogs should wear a flat nylon or leather buckle collar with identification at all times. If you teach your puppy manners from the beginning, a flat buckle collar will hopefully be sufficient for all his training. However, if you have a physically strong puppy, such as an American Pit Bull Terrier, Rottweiler, or German Shepherd Dog; a very strong-willed puppy who is difficult to control; or you are physically challenged, you may need to consider a training collar other than a buckle collar. Here are a few options to consider:

- A training harness, which is different than a tracking or weight-pull harness, tightens when the dog pulls. When you apply pressure, it forces the dog to turn toward you if you are beside or behind him.

- Head halters go around the dog's nose and cause pressure when he pulls. When you apply pressure, it forces the dog to turn his head toward you if you are beside or behind him.

What not to use:

- Choke chains and prong collars, also known as pinch collars, put pressure on your dog's neck and throat. While it may be tempting to use these devices on an energetic, intense, or powerful dog, these collars are best left to the professionals. In the hands of an inexperienced person, these types of collars can cause serious damage to a dog's neck and throat. Taking the time to train your puppy to walk properly and not pull without these devices will be much more rewarding to you both.

- Electronic collars are never necessary when training obedience or household manners. And do not allow anyone—trainers, behaviorists, or in-laws—to convince you otherwise. Highly controversial, electronic collars, which are used by some trainers, can cause untold and irreparable damage to a dog.

Brushing

Brush your puppy daily using a soft brush—even if you have a smooth-coated breed—and use plenty of tasty tidbits to reward good behavior. Regular brushings are essential for removing dead hair, promoting and distributing natural oils, and bringing out the shine and luster in a dog's coat. A puppy who is conditioned to enjoy regular brushings will grow into an adult dog who takes pleasure in this daily chore.

Dental Care

Teach your pup to accept having his teeth brushed. Good dental hygiene is essential, and conditioning a young puppy to regular brushings and examinations will make your life—and his—much easier as he grows into an adult dog. If left unattended, your dog can develop periodontal disease, a progressive disease that can, in advanced cases, lead to decayed gums, infection, and liver, kidney, and heart damage. An estimated 80 percent of dogs over the age three years have some stage of periodontal disease. And like humans, dogs experience painful toothaches, although some dogs—especially stoic breeds—may not physically exhibit signs of pain, or the signs may be subtle and overlooked by some owners.

To condition your puppy to accept teeth brushing:

- Massage his gums with your index finger and toothpaste made specifically for dogs (never toothpaste made for humans).
- Praise (or click) and treat for any behavior that indicates he is not resisting.
- Progress to massaging top and bottom and the front gums, too.
- Avoid wrestling with your puppy or restraining him too tightly, which will only hamper the process and make him resistant to this necessary chore.

After a few days—depending on your puppy—you can advance to the following:

- Use a toothbrush or finger brush suitable for the size of your puppy's mouth.

Get your puppy used to nail trimming early on.

- Start with the canine teeth—the large ones in the front of the mouth, which are easiest to reach. You should be able to brush them with little interference or objection from your puppy.
- Progress to a few more until you have brushed all 28 teeth (or 42 teeth, if you have an adult dog).

Watch out for those sharp baby teeth, and remember to keep a positive attitude, praising and reassuring your puppy throughout the process.

Nails

Conditioning your puppy to having his feet and toes touched and examined will make regular nail trimmings much easier as he grows into an adult dog. Plan to clip them at least once a week for life or every other week, depending on how fast your puppy's nails grow. Nothing is more frustrating than trying to wrestle down a dog who hates his nails trimmed. You don't want your puppy growing into an adult dog who must be sedated every time his nails need trimming.

Some puppies and adult dogs, depending on their individual temperament, do not object to having their feet handled. Others, however, must be conditioned to the practice. Practicing the game "No Wiggling" (see Chapter 9) will help condition him to stand still, which will make nail trimming a lot easier. Follow these quick tips to condition your puppy or adult dog to having his nails trimmed:

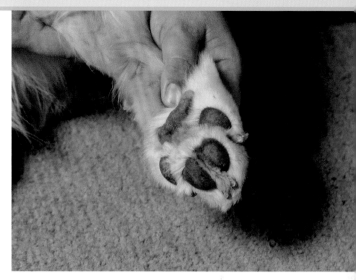

Many dogs object to having their feet handled, so get your dog used to it early on.

- Start by conditioning him to accept (and hopefully enjoy!) having his feet touched and handled. Most puppies and untrained adult dogs will instinctively pull their paws away when they feel them being held. Don't be bossy or argumentative if he pulls away. Take a deep breath, smile, and start again. Wrestling or trying to restrain your puppy or adult dog will only make the situation worse.
- Absent a professional or makeshift grooming table, get on the ground with your puppy.
- Pick up each paw, then praise (or click) and reward for being brave. In the beginning, it's beneficial to have a helper, someone who can distract, "bribe," and praise your puppy with treats while you touch his feet and toes.
- Progress to touching the clippers to his nails. Praise and reward with a tasty tidbit.
- Clip one nail. Praise and reward.
- If your dog doesn't object, progress to clipping several nails. Praise and reward.
- Some puppies and adult dogs find this process highly stressful. If that's the case, try breaking the process into several sessions.

Remember to keep the process positive. If you are stressed, your puppy or adult dog will be stressed, too, which is counterproductive.

If you choose to do so, accustom your puppy to a small, battery-operated nail grinder:

- Turn the motor on.
- Hold it close to your puppy's foot.
- Generously feed him treats.
- As he becomes comfortable with the noise, progress to touching one toe with the nail grinder and rewarding lavishly.

- It won't take long before you are able to use the nail grinder on all of his nails.

Nail grinders are excellent grooming tools, but they can hurt a dog's feet if not used correctly. When in doubt, have a breeder, groomer, or veterinarian show you how to do it properly.

Work on grooming and handling routines daily, and it won't be long before your puppy accepts and enjoys being groomed. With all aspects of grooming and handling, always start slowly and progress at a rate that is suitable for the age and mental maturity of your puppy.

Basic Obedience

A key element of living harmoniously with a turbo-charged dog is obedience training. As previously mentioned, all dogs need boundaries. Obedience need not be a daunting task, however. Make it fun. Use the games in Chapter 9 to instill fun and make obedience training something you and your dog really enjoy and look forward to doing together.

Name Recognition

To teach your puppy his name:
- Say it in a fun, enticing tone of voice: "Fido!"
- When he turns his head in acknowledgement, praise with "Yes!" (or click) and reward with plenty of yummy treats.

Teach your puppy to stay near your side by rewarding him when he's close.

- Do this five or six times in succession, three or four times a day.

    It won't take long before your puppy learns his name.

"Follow You"

Teach your young puppy or adult dog to follow you everywhere you go by rewarding him for staying close to your side.

    To start:

- Get and keep your puppy's attention by using tasty tidbits, such as chicken, steak, or cheese.
- In the beginning, lure and reward your puppy by holding the treat near your side. (An alternative to luring is to click and treat each time your puppy is close to you.)
- Be generous with the treats and your praise so that he learns that being close to you is a fun and rewarding place to be.
- If your puppy is toy crazy, reward him with a fun tug game while he is close to you.

    Do this multiple times throughout the day in as many different places as you can, such as in your house and yard, and it won't be long before your puppy wants to be by your side all the time.

Walk Nicely on Leash

Ideally, your puppy should be wearing a buckle collar and dragging a leash around the house and yard. (Note: Never allow your puppy to drag a leash around while unattended. He may catch it on a table leg, tree stump, etc., and panic or injure himself.) This serves two purposes. First, if your puppy begins to wander off, you can simply step on the leash and reel him in—"There you are, my silly boy!" Second, it helps with the walking on leash part of training, and here is how: If he is accustomed to dragging a leash around and following and being close to you, it won't take

Praise and reward sensible walking, and soon your puppy will be walking nicely on his leash.

Don't Pull!

Did you know that owners inadvertently create leash aggression by automatically pulling back on the leash when another dog or person approaches? A tight leash/collar signals to the dog "Yes, be careful. There is danger out there!"

Not So Fast!

Some dogs, especially turbo-charged dogs, seem to be on a hectic timetable and need to get to places fast. Sometimes it's because they are going somewhere exciting, such as the park to swim or play fun retrieve games; sometimes they just can't wait to get to the corner lamppost. Generally speaking, these dogs aren't being willfully disobedient—they're just excited and eager to go someplace interesting. However, if you let your puppy or adult dog drag you down the street so that he can get to the park as fast as he can, which is obviously faster than you had intended, he is controlling the situation. You are inadvertently rewarding him by giving him want he wants, which is to get wherever he's going as fast as possible. You are also allowing him to practice unwanted behaviors, behaviors you don't want—not necessarily behaviors he doesn't want. In these instances, stop and stand still. When your puppy stops pulling on the leash, calmly praise him, then continue walking. He should quickly learn that walking at your side is more rewarding than pulling you down the street.

more than a few sessions to teach him to stay close to you while attached to his leash and to walk nicely on leash close to your side. Walking nicely on leash is no big deal for the puppy because he has learned that following and being close to you is fun and rewarding.

To get started:

- Once your puppy is happily following you around and keeping up with your pace, try the "Follow You" game (see previous) with you holding the leash while walking around your living room or fenced yard.
- Avoid pulling or jerking the leash to get him to follow. Remember, his reward for doing his job (i.e., following closely and staying by your side) is yummy treats or his favorite toy.
- Remember to praise (or click) and reward only sensible walking, and reward while your puppy is close to your side. (Otherwise, your puppy is likely to associate lunging and jumping with leash training, and you will never progress if you reward your puppy for pulling and tugging on leash.)
- Progress a few steps at a time, gradually increasing the distance that your puppy can walk nicely by your side on leash.

Another technique is to tether your puppy to you while you're in the house or yard.

- Attach one end of a 6-foot (1.8 m) leash or long line to your puppy and the other end to your waist.
- Praise and reward your puppy when he is close to you (as opposed to straining at the end of his leash).

Practice these "games" four or five times a day, first around the house and yard and then eventually up and down quiet, nondistracting sidewalks or safe streets.

Sit

Sit is a must-know command for every dog. A dog who understands the *sit* command provides you with an avenue of control. Think of the situations in which your puppy or adult dog will need to know how to sit—at the vet's office, waiting to be fed, waiting to cross the street, or sitting and waiting while you open the door. He will need to sit when you put on his collar on or take it off, when you want to check his coat for stickers or burrs, or when you want to brush him or trim his nails. The *sit* command increases his vocabulary and instills order in both of your lives.

Many of the games discussed in Chapter 9 began instilling the *sit* command. To work on a more formal technique, try these steps:

A treat held close to and slightly over a puppy's nose is used for teaching the *sit* command.

- Begin with your puppy on leash. This is especially helpful if your dog, like most puppies, has his own agenda, tends to wander off, or is easily distracted.
- Start with your leash in one hand, a tasty tidbit in the other hand, and your puppy standing in front of you.
- Hold the tidbit firmly between your thumb and index finger so that your puppy cannot get it until he is in the correct position.
- Show your puppy the tidbit by holding it close to and slightly above his nose.
- As he raises his nose to take the food, slowly move the treat in a slightly upward and backward direction toward his tail, keeping the treat directly above his nose. (If your puppy jumps up or brings his front feet off the ground, the cookie is too high. If he walks backward, the cookie is too far back or too low.)
- At this point, your puppy's hips should automatically sink toward the ground—as they do, give the *sit* command.
- Make sure that you give the *sit* command as your puppy's rear end hits the ground. (Saying it too soon will teach the wrong association.)
- While your puppy is sitting, praise him with "Good sit!" and reward him with the treat.
- Release your puppy with a release word, such as "Okay" or "Free," and play with him for a few seconds.
- Repeat the exercise three or four times in succession, three or four times a day.

Use a treat to lure your dog into the *down* position.

Tips for Training Success

Follow these guidelines and your puppy will quickly learn that training and playing means a good time with you.

- Teach your puppy every day. Handle him. Socialize him. Groom him. Play train him. Crate and ex-pen train him. There is plenty to accomplish in a very small window of opportunity.

- Keep sessions short. Puppies have limited attention spans—about ten seconds— and they can sit still for only a few seconds. Train three or four times a day, three or four minutes each session.

- Make training fun. Fun maximizes your puppy's propensity to learn.

- Choose the right time to train. Train when your puppy is awake and eager to play. Don't wake him up to train him, and don't train him on a full tummy.

- Train within your puppy's mental and physical capabilities. Puppies and adult dogs learn at different rates. Progress at a speed within your puppy's ability to learn— just below his threshold where he might become bored or frustrated. If he starts wiggling or struggling or mouthing you, you likely have expected too much.

- Always set your puppy up to succeed. Achievable goals will keep both of you motivated. Progress in baby steps, always praising and rewarding him every time he does a baby step right.

Down

Teaching the *down* command can be a bit more challenging than the *sit* because it is considered a submissive position for some dogs. If your puppy has an independent personality, this exercise will take a bit more patience and persistence on your part. Do not give up! Remember, puppies learn through repetition and consistency. Again, many of the games in Chapter 9 begin instilling the *down* command. For a more formal technique, try these steps:

- Begin by kneeling on the floor so that you are at eye level with your puppy.
- With your puppy standing in front of you, hold a tasty tidbit of food in one hand.
- Let him sniff the treat.
- Move the treat toward the floor between his front feet.
- When done correctly, your puppy will plant his front feet and fold his body into the *down* position as he follows the treat to the ground.
- When his elbows and tummy are on the ground, give the command "Down."
- While your puppy is in the *down* position, calmly praise him with "Good down" and reward with the treat.

Tips for Treats, Chews, and Food Toys

Treats and food toys are great training tools, especially for crate and ex-pen training, when your puppy is teething, and to keep him occupied while riding in the car. Chews are available in a wide variety of shapes, sizes, and products, including beef, muscle, pig ears, smoked hog hide, rolled rawhide, dehydrated pig snouts, and even dehydrated bull parts. (Yes, dog love them!)

To keep your puppy safe, buy size-appropriate bones and food toys for his body type and chewing power. Hard nylon and rubber toys, like the ones Nylabone makes, are made for real gnawing and gnashing. Marrow bones or hard rubber toys, which can be stuffed with cheese or meat, are great for chewing and keeping a puppy occupied. A word of caution: Do not give your puppy bones that he could swallow whole or get caught in his mouth. Always pick up and toss bones and chew toys when they are gnawed down to small pieces.

- Be sure that your puppy is still in the *down* position when you praise and reward, or you will be teaching the wrong association.
- Release your puppy with a release word, such as "Okay" or "Free."
- Repeat the exercise three or four times in succession, three or four times a day.

Stay

The *stay* command can be a bit tricky to teach because most puppies aren't emotionally prepared to handle it—especially in a formal environment—until they are about five, six, or seven months old. Plus, a *sit-stay* or *down-stay* command can be a very stressful task for some high-drive, high-energy dogs, depending on their individual temperament and personality. Additionally, owners can inadvertently create lifelong *stay* problems by putting too much pressure or stress on a dog by rushing the process or overcorrecting. Instead, begin playing a fun version of the *stay*, which is the *wait* command. This is a great command to teach untrained adult dogs or puppies who are about four months old.

This "game" was adapted from an exercise used by trainer and author Bobbie Anderson. To start:

- In the beginning, play in an enclosed area, such as your living room or small fenced yard or patio.
- Stand next to your dog (he should be standing, too) and hold his leash in either your left or right hand. (Always use a buckle collar, never a pinch or choke chain.) Have a pocketful of tasty tidbits or his favorite toy.
- Tell your dog in a nice, fun voice "Wait."
- With your free hand, toss his toy (or a treat) about 5 or 6 feet (1.5 or 1.8 m) in front of him.

- If he strains or jumps at the end of his leash, remind him in a nice, fun voice "You have to wait! Don't you cheat." Be proactive and try to remind him before he starts pulling or straining on the leash (or at least pulling and straining uncontrollably).
- When he's been standing (i.e., "waiting") nicely for a few seconds, tell him "Get it" and give him some slack in the leash. Go with him. Once he gets it, back up so you encourage him to bring it back. Holding on to the leash prevents him from wandering off.
- To encourage him to bring the toy back so that you can repeat the game, put a command to it, such as "Bring it here," and tap your legs or chest to encourage him to come back.
- It won't take long before he realizes that bringing the toy back means that he gets to continue playing.

    When done properly, it won't be long before your dog thinks that waiting is a fun game. Eventually, this command will morph into a *stay* as your dog matures and is increasingly able to handle it.

Exercise Pen and Crate Training

Ex-pens and crates are indispensable for raising a well-behaved puppy or adult dog. Ideal for placing anywhere you need a temporary kennel, such as a kitchen or family room, crates and ex-pens are first-rate ways to ensure that your puppy is safe and secure when you cannot give him your undivided attention. Placing the ex-pen or crate in the kitchen area—or wherever your family tends to congregate—will allow your puppy to get used to the many sights, sounds, and smells from the safety of his personal den.

Ex-pens can be used as temporary kennels.

Ex-Pens

For ex-pen training:
- Place a comfy blanket or dog mat in the pen, along with plenty of toys to keep him entertained.
- Make it a fun, positive place to be, and provide him with plenty of praise (or clicks if you're using a clicker) and treats for being in the pen.
- Make sure to also reward him anytime he is not jumping on the sides or for offering to lie down.

    In the beginning, supervise your puppy closely so that he does not become overwhelmed, frightened, or attempt to jump out. For instance, have him spend at least an hour or so each day in his ex-pen when you are watching television or cooking dinner or anytime you are in the room to monitor him. Increase your

Crates Are Great!

When used properly by responsible dog owners, a crate is an excellent training tool. Although many owners look upon a crate as cruel or inhumane, it really should be viewed from a dog's perspective. Before dogs became domesticated pets, they tended to seek safe, enclosed areas for security and protection. A crate mimics that safe, enclosed environment. Puppies, especially very young puppies, tire quickly and need a lot of sleep during the day. A crate placed in a quiet corner of the kitchen or family room will satisfy their natural instinct to seek a safe and secure environment. When properly introduced, a crate will become a safe zone for your puppy—a quiet place all his own to sleep, eat, and retreat from the demands of being a puppy.

success rate by doing this when he is tired after playing or going for a long walk and when he is more likely to lie down and chew a Nylabone rather than when he is revved up and full of energy.

Crates

Your puppy's crate should be a fun, positive, and inviting place. Most puppies quickly learn to love their crate when it is associated with good things, such as feeding, yummy treats, security, and sleep.

To get started:

- Teach your puppy to love his crate and to willingly run into it by rewarding him every time he chooses to get in it.
- Leave the door open and allow him to explore in and around his crate.
- Praise "Good boy!" or "Aren't you clever" (or click) and reward with yummy treats while he is inside his crate.
- Place a comfy blanket or crate pad and a few of his favorite indestructible chew toys inside the crate to encourage him to go inside.

If your puppy is hesitant about the crate:

- Let him see you toss a yummy tidbit of food toward the back of the crate.
- Praise him for going inside the crate to get it.
- Feed your him meals inside the crate, luring him inside with his food bowl.

If your puppy whines or cries:

- Avoid reinforcing the behavior by letting him out of the crate or coddling him, such as saying "What's the matter, honey?"
- Wait for him to be quiet for a minute or two before opening the door (provided you are certain that he does not need to relieve himself).

Reward him for coming out of his crate, too, but only on your command. This will teach him not to barge out of the crate when you open the door and will keep him safe while traveling. (A dog who bolts out of his crate and out of the car and into traffic risks getting lost or suffering serious and life-threatening injuries.)

Add a command, such as "Kennel up" or "Get in your crate" when you want him to go inside the crate, and say "Okay, out" when you want him to come out of the crate. Reward each behavior (going in and coming out) multiple times daily. Make going in and coming out of his crate a game so that it will be a fun place for him to be. It won't be long before your puppy is dashing in and out of his crate on command.

Most puppies learn to love their crates when they are associated with good, fun things.

Chapter 11

Common Problems of High-Energy Dogs

In a perfect world, your precious pooch would never get into trouble. Unfortunately, that's a reality that exists only in your mind. In the real world, it is silly and unrealistic to expect a turbo-charged dog (or any dog for that matter) to go through his entire life without getting into some sort of mischief or developing an annoying habit or two. After all, these dogs were bred for a particular task, be it ratting, hunting, retrieving, guarding or controlling livestock.

They might be unemployed and living in the city, but they still retain their natural instincts, as well as all the energy that is required to perform those tasks. Add to the equation a dog's natural behaviors, which include digging, chewing, barking, and ransacking and scavenging the trash, and you have a potential recipe for disaster. While these are natural behaviors for dogs, they aren't necessarily acceptable to owners, and therein lies an enormous problem. These misbehaviors can drive even the most fanatic canine lover nuts—and they are the primary reason most dogs and owners clash. In fact, studies indicate that behavioral problems are one of the top reasons dogs are released to humane societies. Each year, thousands of great dogs are euthanized for doing what comes naturally or for breaking rules they didn't even know existed. That's a sobering fact.

If your dog's type-A personality and extracurricular activities are causing him to wear out his welcome, don't despair. Nearly all dog behaviors—even the most exasperating ones—are quite predictable and easily remedied.

How Your Dog Sees the World

A key component to preventing behavioral problems is seeing the world through the eyes of your dog. It's really that simple. When you discover and understand the root cause

of the problem—why your dog does what he does—you can reliably and accurately correct the problem.

As previously mentioned in Chapter 2, dogs and humans view the world differently. Dogs have different priorities. They like to sniff bums, lick unmentionable body parts, eat poop, roll in stinky stuff, drink toilet water, and ransack trashcans. Their brains aren't hardwired to be vindictive. Dogs don't lie around conjuring up ways to make our lives more difficult. They don't think *If I shred the couch today, that'll show my owner who wears the pants in this family!* Dogs live in the moment. When left to their own devices, they will do exactly what they feel like at that given moment, which isn't always compatible with their owner's expectations. By

He may look "guilty," but he's just reacting to your body language.

learning to think like a dog and by learning to see the world through his eyes, you can let go of that silly idea that your dog is misbehaving out of spite.

That Guilty Look

Ahhhh, you say, but my dog *does* know when he's done something wrong—he even looks guilty! If, for example, your dog slinks away when you arrive home to find your kitchen looking like the county landfill, it's not due to any feeling of "guilt," but rather it's your dog reacting to your body language. Perhaps you pursed your lips or cursed under your breath when you walked in. Maybe you sighed or made a groaning noise. Either way, a dog—even the smartest high-drive, high-energy dog—does not have the mental wherewithal to make the connection between ransacking the trash two hours or ten minutes earlier and you arriving home. Dogs do, however, have the innate ability to zero in on minute shifts in body language, be they ever so slight. Your dog doesn't know he did anything wrong. He's merely reacting to your body language that no doubt he decodes as *You'd better run for the hills 'cause you're in big trouble now, buster!*

It's much easier to prevent problem behaviors from developing by managing your dog's environment. This way, he is not put in a position where he can get himself into trouble. That said, if your dog has already developed an annoying habit or two, this chapter will help get the broken owner–dog relationship back in sync.

Why They Do It

In the simplest of terms, most dog actions, big or small, can be grouped into two categories—behavioral or medical.

Medical

Medical problems can include painful urinary tract infections, diabetes, or renal disease, which can make getting outside to potty a problem for some dogs, making accidents on your carpet common. Any number of health issues, from allergies to hormonal imbalances to life-threatening diseases, could also be to blame for housetraining issues. Pain, such as a broken tooth, broken bone, torn ligament, pinched nerve, sore muscles, etc., can cause a dog of sound temperament to growl, bite, or snap. Teething, while not a medical problem per se, causes puppies and junior dogs to chew and chew and chew (oftentimes on inappropriate items) to relieve the discomfort associated with teething. If your dog is showing signs of any behavior problems, first have him checked out by his veterinarian.

High-drive, high-energy dogs need huge amounts of exercise.

Boredom Busters

Young dogs of working breeds—shepherds, collies, retrievers, pointers, and terriers, to name a few—require exercise in units of hours, not minutes. A 10-minute stroll around the block does not come close to meeting the exercise requirements of a turbo-charged dog. Your dog's age, breed, and individual personality will dictate exactly how much exercise he requires. A puppy, for example, will tire more quickly than an adult dog. Therefore, he will require short but multiple exercise periods spaced throughout the day. Generally speaking, though, most adult dogs of working breeds will require a minimum of two to three hours or more of physical exercise each day, such as running, jogging, walking, hiking, swimming, retrieving, and so forth—yes, *each day!*

Mental exercise is as important as physical exercise, so try to come up with fun games that can stimulate your dog's brain. For example, in addition to obedience exercises, teach him to wave, walk backward, spin, twist, speak, jump through a hoop, or find a ball hidden in a box or bucket. Interactive exercise—meaning that you and your dog play together—is vital. However, for those times when you can't interact, chew toys will exercise your dog's teeth and gums, while food-dispensing and interactive toys will provide an hour or two of mental stimulation.

It's worth noting that mental stimulation can be as exhausting as physical exercise. Perhaps you've been mentally exhausted after learning something new or engaging in a particularly trying task, such as balancing your checkbook or mastering the computer. Dogs are no different. Learning a fun trick or a new obedience command can tax their brains. That's why it's important to always teach your dog new exercises in a fun, stress-free environment. Use plenty of positive reinforcement, and try to motivate your dog to want to learn. To ensure that he wants to continue learning, always stop before he runs out of mental steam and becomes frustrated.

There are medical problems that can cause behavioral issues.

Behavioral

If your dog receives a clean bill of health from his veterinarian, the problem may be behavioral. This means that it's time for a bit of detective work because the root cause of naughty canine behaviors can be caused by one or more factors—some of which you could inadvertently be causing.

Boredom

High-drive, high-energy dogs need huge amounts of physical and mental exercise to burn off excess amounts of energy. Take the Border Collie, for example. If you own one, you know that his intense desire to work supersedes all else. Given a choice between a juicy steak and a field full of sheep, 99.9 percent of them will opt for the cantankerous ewes. These high-drive dogs have hardy, intense, type-A personalities and get-it-done-right-now attitudes. They can cover long distances, work in all weather conditions, and do it for hours on end.

So it's easy to see why herding dogs, as well as hounds, terriers, and sporting dogs, require more daily physical and mental stimulation to burn off excess energy than, say, a Bulldog. These turbo-charged dogs are not happy sitting around the house all day. They quickly become bored, which leads to undesired behaviors, including munching couches, shredding patio furniture, digging, barking excessively, ransacking trashcans, obsessive-compulsive behaviors, and so forth. Many of these unwanted behaviors could be avoided if dogs received more physical and mental exercise. A tired dog is a good dog!

Lack of Training

Dogs are clever, but they do not come preprogrammed knowing how to understand our language or how to sit, down, come when called, or chew their own toys (as opposed to your expensive leather shoes). Surprisingly, it is not uncommon for owners to expect their dogs to do whatever is asked of them, regardless of whether or not the dogs have had any training. Lack of training is a top reason that many dogs develop unwanted behaviors, thereby getting into trouble for breaking rules they didn't even know existed.

Also, owners sometimes expect dogs to read minds. A dog won't learn to come when called, potty outdoors, or stop barking unless he is trained to do so. You can't wish or chant away undesired behaviors. Your dog will not magically stop peeing from one end of the house to the other unless you instill good housetraining practices from day one. Nor will he miraculously start coming when called just because you holler the command louder and more frantically each time. As a responsible owner, it is your job to teach your dog in a fun and humane manner which behaviors are acceptable and which should be dropped, immediately.

Training is a two-way street. Granted, dog training isn't rocket science, but dog-training techniques continue to improve regularly, and keeping up to date on positive training methods and canine behaviors will make you a better owner. Most day-to-day dog behavior issues can be managed with a combination of common sense, canine know-how, and of course, educational books like this one. But both you and your dog will no doubt benefit if you also sign up for group or private obedience lessons with an experienced professional—preferably one who has experience dealing with the quirks and idiosyncrasies of high-drive, high-energy breeds. Training classes will also allow your dog to socialize, learn, and practice obedience commands around other dogs.

Stress

Like humans, dogs become stressed for a variety of reasons, including boredom, lack of socialization, unfamiliar surroundings, isolation, strange or loud noises, other dogs and animals, unfamiliar people, and rambunctious toddlers running about. The constant stimulation of being in a crowd of people can stress even the sweetest, most lovable dog, provoking him to bolt, growl, or snap.

Improper living environments, such as a Vizsla (a high-energy sporting breed) confined to a small yard or apartment with

Boredom can often cause stress in dogs.

inadequate physical and mental stimulation, can stress a dog, which will eventually lead to neurotic and destructive behaviors.

Learning a new task or making a mistake while training can cause some dogs stress, depending on their temperament. Pushing a puppy or adult dog beyond his mental or physical capabilities can trigger stress, impeding a dog's ability to learn. *Down* is a vulnerable position for dogs; therefore, dogs who are asked to lie down during stressful situations can become even more stressed and worried. Many seemingly innocuous events, such as another dog approaching or passing by too closely, tension among canine siblings, a change in schedule, or a change in your work schedule can stress some dogs. Injured dogs frequently become fearful and highly stressed, which can lead to aggression. Perhaps you've experienced similar emotions—crabby, cranky, grouchy—when you've been injured. Dysfunctional households can cause many dogs stress, too, including hyperactive children who can't sit still or families who frequently fight or yell.

These are only a few of the situations that can trigger stress, which can lead to a multitude of unwanted behaviors, including aggression, submissive urination, digging, chewing, barking, and general unruliness.

It's normal for dogs to bark, so you need to find out why your dog is barking before you can take steps to minimize it.

Common Canine (Mis)Behaviors

You may be dealing with one or more undesired behaviors from your dog. Depending on how long the problem (or problems) has been allowed to go on, it may take a while to restore order, but in most cases, problem behaviors are entirely fixable. It goes without saying that any dog can engage in naughty or obnoxious behaviors. However, as previously mentioned, most high-drive, high-energy breeds are incredibly bright, and they also tend to become bored quite quickly. Therefore, it stands to reason that a Border Collie or Jack Russell Terrier is more likely to get himself into trouble than, say, a Bulldog or a sedate, calm Pekingese. Let's take a look at the more common canine behaviors that annoy and frustrate owners.

Barking (Excessive)

Defining excessive or problem barking is often problematic in itself. Your neighbors, for example, may not consider their dog's barking a problem if he barks all day while they're at work. After all, it's not a problem for them because they're not home to listen to it. But no doubt it's a problem for you if you're home all day. If you live in an apartment and your dog barks incessantly all night, animal control is likely to pay you a visit and possibly issue a fine. If you live on a farm with no close neighbors, and your dog's barking doesn't bother you, it probably isn't a problem for anyone else. Likewise, if your dog barks at the occasional squirrel or bird in the yard or only when the mail carrier shows up, you probably don't have much to worry about.

Excessive barking can also be more of a problem in certain breeds. Some high-drive, high-energy dogs are noisier than others. Shelties are notorious for barking. Originally bred an as all-purpose dog who would alert farmers to intruders, their barking is part and parcel of their breeding. Many of the northern breeds—Siberian Huskies, Alaskan Malamutes—love to bark or howl. Most terriers love to voice their opinion, too. Australian Shepherds and Border Collies, on the other hand, are for the most part not noisy breeds, and excessive or chronic barking is generally not a problem. (That said, when taken on an individual basis, there are still a number of Aussies and Border Collies who love to vocalize and backchat.)

Barking Body Language

Paying attention to your dog's body language, as well as the sound of the bark, will give you a good indication of what he may be thinking. For example, raised hackles and a stiff, on-the-toes stance or pacing stiffly while barking generally indicates arousal. Sights and sounds that are often unnoticeable to humans are keenly perceptible to dogs. On the other hand, dogs who bark because they are happy or excited will twirl, hop on their hind legs, or spin in circles.

Why Is He Barking?

Every dog is different. However, it is natural for dogs to bark or otherwise vocalize, and they do so for a variety of reasons. It's highly unlikely that your dog is barking for no reason. Understanding *why* your dog is barking is key. You may not always be able to identify the trigger that starts the barking, but you can learn why your dog does it. For instance, dogs bark when they get excited, when they are playing with their canine buddies, when the doorbell rings, and to greet you when you arrive home. Dogs frequently bark out of boredom, lack of confidence, or because of anxiety issues. If you have done enough proper socialization, your dog should not regard every little noise as an endless opportunity to bark.

Many dogs also have an innate instinct to protect their territory and will alert bark without being taught to do so. Your dog's barking is reasonable and appropriate if he is alerting you to suspicious intruders or unexpected visitors. If you can quiet him with a single command (or two!), you probably do not have much to worry about—assuming you want to stop the barking. A dog barking at suspicious activity outside the house is generally considered a good thing by most owners.

Don't Encourage Him

Problems usually arise when a dog is too hyped up to stop barking. For this reason, it is best to curtail any problems immediately. This includes never encouraging your dog to bark. For instance, when the doorbell rings, avoid asking your dog "Who's there?" or "Let's go see!" This can excite him and encourage him to bark. It may seem like a fun game when he is 10 or 12 weeks old, but it is a difficult and annoying behavior to stop once it becomes ingrained.

Reward your dog when he's quiet.

If your puppy is barking as an attention-seeking behavior, it is best to ignore him until he quiets. Then calmly praise with "Good quiet!" or "Good boy!" Resist the urge to verbally or physically acknowledge your dog's barking by shouting "NO!" or "SHUT UP!" This will only encourage the unwanted behavior because in a dog's mind, negative attention is better than no attention at all. By verbally responding to your dog, you are inadvertently giving him what he wants, which is attention.

Avoid soothing or otherwise coddling your dog when he is barking. This too will inadvertently encourage the unwanted behavior. If your dog is barking and you are telling him "It's okay, honey, Mommy loves you," the dog will think that he is being rewarded for barking. In the his mind, he is thinking *When I bark, my mom tells me it's okay. So I should keep barking.*

Most barking problems can be prevented if you plan ahead and have a clear picture of

Tips for Problem Barkers

These tips will help enhance your chances of success:

- Consistency and timing are the keys to success. Be consistent each time your dog barks until you can train him to respond to your "Quiet" or "No bark" command.

- Positive reinforcement is much more productive than punishment.

- Verbally praise and reward the behavior you want, which is your dog *not* barking.

- Dogs learn an appropriate alternative to barking when you are there to teach them. If you are seldom home, you cannot expect them to learn on their own.

- Dogs are individuals. They learn at different rates. You may see improvement within a few days, or it may take many weeks. Remember, Rome wasn't built in a day.

the behaviors you will and will not accept. However, if your dog has already developed a barking problem and is well on his way to wearing out his welcome, you can try a shaker can as a training aid, coupled with positive reinforcement.

Using a Shaker Can

Shaker cans make a lot of noise—and that's what you want! The concept is that the noise from the shaker can interrupts your dog's barking, and once the barking behavior is interrupted, you can praise and reward him for not engaging in that behavior.

Shaker cans are easy to make—simply fill an empty soda can with a dozen or so coins or small pebbles, and tape the opening closed. As soon as your dog begins to bark—for instance, when the doorbell rings—immediately shake the can, and then give a command, such as "Quiet," "Enough," or "No bark." If done correctly, the noise should be loud enough to startle the dog and interrupt his barking. When he stops barking, immediately praise with "Good quiet!" or "Good boy!" Reinforce the behavior with a tidbit of food, but be sure to do so when your dog is *not* barking. Otherwise, you will be teaching the wrong association and inadvertently reinforcing the barking.

Keep multiple shaker cans strategically placed around the house—near the telephone, front door, bedroom, living, room, etc.—for convenience and accessibility. Have shaker cans strategically located outdoors as well.

A word of caution: Be sure to place the shaker cans out of your dog's reach. Aluminum cans are sharp and dangerous when punctured or torn. Dogs, curious creatures that they are, can cause serious damage to their teeth, tongues, mouths, and stomachs if they

Why Not Use a Crate?

Some owners will crate their dog during the day to try to prevent him from barking at outside stimuli. But it's not wise to put a high-drive, high-energy dog in a crate for six, eight, or ten hours while you are at work. It might be okay for an hour or so while you run to the store, but crating a high-drive dog for long periods is likely to create even more problems!

chew on the can. Once a dog gets the can open, he may try to swallow the coins, which presents a potential choking hazard. Most importantly, never throw the can—or any other objects—at your puppy or adult dog. You may injure or frighten him, and he will most likely learn to fear you.

Prevention

The best prevention against future barking problems is smart dog management.

Never allow your puppy or adult dog to be put in a situation where he is allowed to develop bad habits. For example, leaving him in the backyard unsupervised all day where he is inspired to bark at constant stimuli (other dogs barking, a cat on a fence, a bird overhead, leaves falling, neighbors coming and going, life in general) is just asking for trouble. Barking at environmental stimuli is often self-rewarding for the dog. A dog barks at the mail carrier, and when she leaves, the dog thinks *Look how clever I am! My barking made her leave!*

A dog housed indoors can also develop barking habits. If he sits on the furniture and stares out the living room window, he may be encouraged to bark at stimuli, such as neighbors, other dogs going for a walk, kids on bicycles, or the UPS delivery person. In these instances, you may need to keep the blinds or curtains closed so that he is not encouraged to gaze out the window in anticipation. Or consider using baby gates to corral him in the kitchen or laundry room—away from the windows—while you are gone. Provide him with a meaty bone or chew toy, such as those made by Nylabone, to take his attention off any excitement that might be going on outdoors. Teaching him to stay off the furniture is also a good idea but difficult to reinforce if you're not home or if you have already allowed the behavior to develop.

If your dog barks while in the excitement of play, stop the game immediately. When he stops barking, praise with "Good quiet!" or "Good boy!" Once you have regained control of the situation, begin playing again.

Chewing

It is hard to imagine an adorable eight-week-old Norwich Terrier, Shetland Sheepdog, Pharaoh Hound, or any puppy for that matter as a one-dog demolition team. However, do not let their cute looks deceive you. Most puppies, especially high-drive, high-energy breeds, can be incredibly aggressive chewers who can wreak havoc in your household.

Many puppies teethe until they are nine to twelve months old.

They can destroy drywall, carpet, drapes, and linoleum. They can turn your favorite pillows into confetti, shred your bedspread, and destroy electrical cords and potted plants. They will gleefully shred magazines and books and anything else they can get their teeth on—and that's in the 15 minutes it takes you to drive to the post office and back!

If you must leave—even for two minutes—take your puppy or untrained adult dog with you, or confine him in a crate, exercise pen, or kennel. Do not put your pet in a position where he can develop bad habits. This point cannot be emphasized enough. Puppies chew, especially when they are teething. If you leave your puppy unattended or unconfined while you run to the mailbox or take a quick shower, don't be surprised when you find the heel missing off your favorite pair of leather shoes.

Prevention

Few owners escape canine ownership without losing a slipper, a pair of rubber galoshes, or a potted plant. Puppies are going to chew—it is a fact of life. However, the key to minimizing destruction and preventing bad habits is management. Never allow your puppy (or untrained adult dog) to be put in a position where he can get himself into

Teething

Around four weeks of age, puppies begin to develop their baby teeth—also known as deciduous teeth or milk teeth. Teething is the process of growing baby teeth. The process ends when a dog's permanent teeth are in place. Teething varies from puppy to puppy, with most puppies undergoing some form of continuous teething until they are about six to nine months of age. This causes an uncontrollable urge to chew as a means of relieving some of the discomfort and as a way to facilitate the removal of their baby teeth.

trouble or develop bad habits. Any puppy left unsupervised is trouble in the making.

If you allow your puppy free run of the house, don't be surprised when you come home to find epic amounts of destruction. It is unfair to scold or otherwise punish a puppy for your temporary lapse of good judgment. Therefore, to foster good habits and minimize destructive behaviors, follow these simple guidelines:

- Before bringing your new puppy home, plan ahead. Have an exercise pen or playpen and a crate ready. Do not wait until you decide that you need them. If you have a puppy (or untrained adult dog), you *will* need them.
- When you cannot constantly watch your puppy, keep him confined in an exercise pen, playpen, crate, or puppy-proofed area with his favorite chew toy. This includes when you need to jump in the shower for five minutes, while you are making dinner, or when you dash outside for two seconds to move the sprinkler.
- Once your puppy arrives at your home, know where he is and what he is doing at all times. You would not dream of taking your eyes off a toddler, and you should never take your eyes off a puppy when he is not safely confined.
- Puppy-proof your home. Puppies are ingenious when it comes to finding items to chew. Pick up anything and everything he is likely to put in his mouth, including shoes, purses, jackets, schoolbooks, candles, rugs, electrical cords, dolls, and so forth.
- Make sure that your puppy receives plenty of exercise each day. Both puppies and adult dogs require daily physical and mental stimulation. Lacking appropriate and adequate exercise, they will release pent-up energy through chewing, digging, or barking.

The Importance of Chew Toys

There are a variety of chew toys available in all sizes and shapes that will entertain your puppy or adult dog for an hour or two. Chew toys will satisfy your dog's need to gnaw on something while diverting him from chewing on inappropriate items. While some chew toys are better than others, there is no scientific formula for finding the right chew toy. Most times it is a matter of trial and error. Avoid toys or bones that are too hard and

Teach Your Puppy Right From Wrong

When you supervise your puppy in the house, you are able to monitor his whereabouts, and in the process, provide him with appropriate chew toys. If, for instance, you are watching television, have one or two chew toys available for your puppy. You may need to encourage him by showing him the toy. When you see him settle down to chew on it, calmly praise him. Then allow him to chew without interruption. You can try tethering him to the leg of the couch or coffee table with a lightweight leash to prevent him from wandering off. Of course, supervision at all times is essential. Otherwise, he's likely to chew the table or couch leg.

Until your puppy is reliable, it is never wise to give him free run of the house. Remember, puppies are individuals. It is impossible to arbitrarily put an age on when a puppy is reliably trained. Some puppies have a stronger desire to chew than others; a general guideline is about one year of age. Much will depend on how conscientious and committed you are to managing your puppy's environment, instilling good behaviors, and discouraging unwanted behaviors.

As your puppy grows and matures, his desire to chew will diminish. It is important, however, to continue giving him bones and chew toys throughout his life to exercise his jaws, keep his teeth clean, and entertain him for a few hours.

that may crack your dog's teeth, as well as ones that are too small or that break apart and present choking hazards.

Chews are available in a wide variety of shapes, sizes, and products, including beef muscle, pig ears, smoked hog hide, dehydrated pig snouts, and tightly rolled rawhide. (Some colored rawhide chews can stain carpets and furnishings.) Cow hooves, while a popular canine favorite, are hard and can chip or break your dog's teeth. You might want to try specially designed nylon and rubber bones, like the ones Nylabone makes, which are safe and excellent for satisfying a puppy's need to chew.

Rope toys and tugs are often made of 100-percent cotton and frequently flavored to make them more attractive to your puppy or adult dog. Some have plaque-fighting fluoride floss woven into the rope to deep clean your dog's teeth and gums. Be careful that your puppy cannot shred the cotton ropes, which may be a potential choking hazard.

Plush toys vary in their durability. Some are easily shredded by tenacious, seek-and-destroy dogs who can chew out the squeaky part in record time, while other dogs like to carry them around or snuggle with them. When choosing these toys, opt for the durable models if your puppy is likely to shred and disembowel them and then attempt to consume the innards.

A super-sized carrot is often a good chew toy for young puppies. They are tasty, durable, easily digestible, and puppies seem to love them. Stay away from raisins and grapes, which can be toxic in certain quantities.

Digging

Dogs love to dig—yet another fact of dog ownership. Some breeds, such as terriers, dig more so than others. Their idea of fun can cause you a significant amount of frustration and heartache, especially when your precious pooch digs his way to China right under your newly planted roses. However, most dogs, regardless of their breed, are quite capable of wreaking havoc in your garden or yard given the right incentive, such as gophers or a stinky manure pile.

If your dog digs and you don't care that his full-time job is excavating your yard, you have nothing to worry about. Let him dig away, provided, of course, it is safe for him to do so. However, if you prefer not to have potholes in your garden and lawn, prevention is the best solution.

Terriers love to dig!

Is He Bored?

Some dogs dig holes to bury their favorite toys or bones. Others will dig to find a cool spot to escape the heat. Most dogs dig out of frustration or boredom. Remember, turbo-charged dogs were bred for a specific job that requires an abundance of energy. Absent adequate physical and mental stimulation, these dogs are likely to dig as a means of coping with their excess energy and/or boredom. If your puppy or adult dog is digging out of boredom or to release excess energy, do something that will stimulate his mind, burn energy, and tire him out. Use your imagination to come up with fun games. For example, purchase a food-dispensing puzzle that allows him to exercise his brain as he tries to outsmart the toy. There are chew toys that can be stuffed with squeeze cheese or peanut butter, and they will provide your dog with hours of entertainment. Or play fun find it games where you hide a tasty tidbit of food under a small box or bucket and encourage him to find it. Play hide-and-seek games where you encourage him to find you.

Is He Hot?

If your dog is digging to find a cool spot to escape the heat, his digging may be the least of your problems. Most dogs, especially heavily coated breeds, black dogs, and brachycephalic (flat face, short muzzle) breeds, do not tolerate hot weather. You need to get him out of the heat and provide him with a cool spot, such as an air-conditioned room or a cool grassy area with plenty of shade.

Prevention

Many dogs are attracted to the smell of chicken and steer manure and love to dig and roll in fresh soil and newly fertilized gardens. The best solution for digging in gardens is prevention. Try the following:

- Do not allow your dog free access to the garden areas where he can dig and wreak havoc.
- As an alternative, install a small fence around the garden, or put chicken wire under the soil so that digging becomes less productive and rewarding for the dog.
- If digging is in his blood, set your dog up with his own piece of heaven. Try fencing off a section of the yard just for him where he can dig and dig to his heart's content.

Jumping Up

Dogs greet their doggy buddies by mouthing and jumping on each other. They paw and wrestle and bark and body slam each other. For dogs, this is great fun and perfectly acceptable doggy manners. So it should come as no surprise when dogs try to greet humans by jumping on them. It's their way of getting close to your face and saying "Hi!" Dogs don't

Born to Jump?

For the most part, jumping up does not appear to be a trait specific to high-drive, high-energy dogs. (However, more than a few breeders and owners jokingly comment that Australian Shepherds are genetically programmed to jump on people—it's in their DNA, they say.) Lacking any scientific data on the topic, it stands to reason that a strong-willed, confident and/or overexuberant, rambunctious, untrained dog would be more inclined to jump on someone when greeting them than, say, a highly submissive dog, who is more likely to pee submissively.

understand that humans frequently take offense to this type of behavior. Of course, if you don't mind your dog jumping on you—and some owners don't—then you have nothing to worry about. However, what you think is cute, harmless puppy behavior will be far from amusing when your dog weighs 50 pounds (22.5 kg) and has four muddy feet.

If you don't want your adult dog to jump on you, don't allow the behavior when he is a puppy.

Prevention

The key is to discourage all occasions of jumping up. If you do not want your adult dog to jump on you, do not allow the behavior when he is puppy. It is also unfair to allow him to jump on you but correct him for jumping on visitors, or to allow him to jump on you today but not tomorrow when you are wearing white pants.

Try these steps to prevent jumping up:

- For young puppies, try crouching down as he comes to greet you. As you do this, slip your thumb in his collar under his chin (your thumb should be pointing down toward the ground) so that he cannot jump up. Give him praise only when all four feet are on the ground. Your praise should be sincere but not overly enthusiastic. Otherwise, you are likely to wind him up even more.

- Teach him not to jump by teaching him to sit for a kiss or cookie. High-breed, high-energy dogs are smart, but even the smartest one hasn't figured out how to simultaneously jump on someone and sit for a cookie at the same time.

- To prevent your puppy or adult dog from jumping on visitors, put his leash on before you open the door. This will allow you to control his behavior without grabbing at his fur or collar. When he sits nicely without pawing or mauling your guests, calmly praise and reward him with a tasty tidbit. Say "That's my good boy!" or "What a good *sit*!"

Lack of Focus

If you do not have a dog's attention, you cannot teach him anything. Unfortunately, one characteristic of high-drive, high-energy dogs is that they can quickly become bored. That means that your job will be more challenging but certainly not impossible. Have you ever seen a distracted Border Collie when he's working sheep? What about a retriever who is focused on a downed bird—does he get distracted by a cat in the field or a strange noise? Probably not. Few terriers are distracted when they are unearthing a rat or any other vermin. These animals are focused and attentive to their job, be it herding, retrieving, ratting, or whatever they were bred to do.

Jumping on Kids

Small children like to run, flail their arms, and make loud squealing noises. This type of behavior is attractive to young puppies and adult dogs, especially dogs from the herding group. Most young children cannot control a jumping puppy, let alone a 50- or 100-pound (22.5- or 45.5-kg) adult dog. Therefore, always supervise children and manage your dog so that he is not put in a position where he can develop bad habits or inadvertently get himself into trouble.

Ideally, you should be as interesting to your dog as any sheep or downed bird or rat in a hole. Most puppies grow into adult dogs who ignore their owners because they have been allowed to develop the habit of ignoring them. And some owners are, well, boring. When it comes to owning a turbo-charged dog, you must be more interesting than anything and everything in his environment, be it sheep, other dogs, cats, clouds passing by, dirt, rocks, strange noises, intriguing smells, kids running around, and so forth. Oftentimes this requires being silly, rolling around on the ground, hopping on one leg, making funny noises, or whatever else it takes to get your dog's attention back on you in a fun and humane manner. The fun attention games discussed in Chapter 9 will help instill these behaviors in young puppies or untrained adult dogs.

Obsessive-Compulsive Behaviors

Although any breed can develop obsessive-compulsive behaviors, the Border Collie, more so than any other breed, is most closely associated with neurotic or fanatical behaviors. A byproduct of their herding instinct is their penchant for attacking moving objects, including lawn mowers, weed whackers, and vacuum cleaners. Others have been known to attack wheelbarrow tires, puncturing them with a single bite. Rakes, brooms,

Many sighthounds won't have a reliable *recall* because their prey drive is so high.

and snow shovels are equally stimulating to them. Some will gleefully shake cherished rugs, pillows, shoes, and carelessly discarded undergarments into oblivion.

Because these dogs are highly intelligent, highly complex creatures, it is not unusual for their obsessions to develop into obsessive-compulsive behaviors. Stories have been told of Border Collies who become mesmerized by reflective surfaces, such as mirrors, glass, or the stainless steel on refrigerators and dishwashers. Others go berserk at the sight of a fly. Some snap at the rain. More than a few Border Collies are mesmerized by the television or obsessed with sidewalk cracks. Others spin in endless circles. More than a few Border Collies have been surrendered to humane societies, abandoned, or given away to rescue organizations as a result of their neurotic behaviors.

Some experts believe that certain dogs are predisposed to obsessive-compulsive behaviors, and then their environment triggers the behavior, such as living in a kennel or crate during their formative years. Other dogs can live in kennels or crates and don't develop these behaviors.

Prevention

Understanding a breed's unique physical and mental requirements and making sure that the dog has a job are key components to help preventing obsessive-compulsive behaviors. The job need not be indigenous to the breed, such as herding or retrieving, but it must be something that provides appropriate and adequate physical and mental stimulation. (See Chapter 12 for some fun ideas.) Preventing or managing neurotic behaviors requires that owners spend a significant portion of their day exercising, training, and interacting with their dog. By doing so, you can end up with a wonderful pet and cherished companion.

When dealing with obsessive-compulsive behaviors, don't hesitate to call a professional trainer or behaviorist.

Running Off or Not Coming When Called

Any dog, if left to his own devices, can develop the annoying and dangerous habit of running away from his owner or refusing to come when called. Some breeds, such the Siberian Husky, can never be completely trusted off leash—even the well-trained ones.

Their inherent desire to run makes controlling or confining them at all times a necessity.

Prevention

The good news is that it is one of the easiest problems to solve. The key is to never allow your puppy to be put in a situation where he is allowed to develop the bad habit of running off. (Do you see a pattern of preventive behavior developing?) Each and every time you go outside, your puppy (or adult dog) should be on leash. If you want your puppy to run around and explore his surroundings, he should be dragging his leash or a lightweight long line. If your puppy starts to wander off, simply step on the long line and reel him back in.

If your adult dog has already developed the annoying habit of running off or ignoring your *come* command, a leash or long line will prevent him from continuing to do so. Then, go back and reteach him to come when called. (See Chapter 10.) You should never get in the habit of chasing your puppy or allowing your kids to chase your puppy. Dogs think that this is a fun game, but it teaches a dog to run away from you, which is not only annoying but also dangerous. A puppy or adult dog who runs away from his owner can easily dart into traffic and cause serious injury to himself.

Separation Anxiety Issues

Separation anxiety can be a real problem for owners because these dogs can become extremely anxious and destructive when left alone. They can chew furniture, drywall, carpeting, rugs, and linoleum. They can urinate and defecate from one end of the house to the other. They frequently pace, drool, whine, howl, or bark. In severe cases, they may even injure themselves.

It's important to understand that these dogs are not intentionally being bad or destructive. Like most canine-related issues, the causes of separation anxiety can vary from dog to dog. Most often, these dogs have anxious-type personalities and are bonded to one person in particular. They become extremely upset when separated from that person and become so stressed that they vent their anxiety by chewing, barking, or soiling the house. Some dogs who are highly insecure and fearful in

Destructive chewing can be a sign of separation anxiety.

general can display similar behaviors, which can be a lesser yet equally frustrating degree of separation anxiety. As previously mentioned, the root of some behaviors, including separation anxiety, may have physical causes, such as allergies, hormonal imbalances, or pain. So it's important to have your dog checked by a veterinarian.

Stress may also trigger separation anxiety or similar behaviors. A dramatic change, such as the death of someone in the family, moving, a change in your work schedule, or a new person in the household may trigger a problem.

True Separation Anxiety or Boredom?

It's worth mentioning that true separation anxiety differs from dogs who don't fall apart when you're gone but rather get into mischief when left alone. The root cause is frequently excess energy coupled with boredom. Many high-drive, high-energy dogs fall into this category. Because they have so much mental and physical energy, they are easily stimulated, and any unannounced visitor, delivery person, or even the mail carrier arriving may excite him, which can then trigger unwanted behaviors. These dogs require

Behavior issues can arise in high-drive dogs who have too little exercise.

Drug Sensitivities

Some serious problem behaviors are managed by drugs. But did you know that some breeds of dogs are more sensitive to certain drugs and can have adverse reactions, including life-threatening complications? The problem is caused by a mutation in the multi-drug resistance (MDR-1) gene. The gene encodes a protein, P-glycoprotein, that is responsible for pumping many drugs and toxins out of the brain. Unlike "normal" dogs, dogs with the mutant gene cannot pump some drugs out of the brain, which may result in abnormal neurologic signs.

The MDR-1 mutation has been found in Collies, Shetland Sheepdogs, Australian Shepherds, Old English Sheepdogs, German Shepherd Dogs, longhaired Whippets, Silken Windhounds, and a variety of mixed-breed dogs.

Researchers have identified more than 20 therapeutic drugs that have been reported to cause problems in some dogs. A few of the more common drugs include:

- ivermectin (antiparasitic agent)
- Imodium® (over-the-counter antidiarrheal agent)
- acepromazine (tranquilizer)
- butorphanol (pain control)

The only way to know if your dog has the mutant MDR-1 gene is to have him tested. For additional information, contact Washington State University College of Veterinary Medicine, Veterinary Clinical Pharmacology Laboratory. www.vetmed.wsu.edu/depts-vcpl/

a multifaceted program, including management, physical and mental stimulation, training, and confinement to keep them happy, safe, and out of trouble while alone.

Professional Help

If any canine issue begs for professional intervention, it is true separation anxiety issues. Depending on the severity of the problem, it can be a difficult and complicated behavior to manage. Novice, inexperienced, or well-intended owners can exacerbate the problem if they over- or underreact to the situation. A professional trainer can help you discover the root cause of the problem, as well as develop a training program to help you teach your dog in a humane and safe manner how to learn to accept being alone for short periods. If you go this route, look for trainers or behaviorists who focus on positive motivation and humane training methods. Harsh training methods will only exacerbate the problem.

Seeking Professional Help

Despite your best efforts to raise a well-behaved dog, undoubtedly times will arise when things go terribly, terribly wrong, and you may need to call in an expert. Some ingrained habits may require Dr. Dolittle to put the damaged dog–human relationship back in sync. Some problems, such as aggression, are difficult and complicated areas of canine behavior that require expert guidance. These behaviors are multifaceted and often have overlapping causes. For instance, genetics, lack of socialization, sexual maturity/frustration, lack of obedience training, inappropriate corrections, and pain are a few of the reasons why dogs might display aggression. If you feel that you and your dog need expert advice, don't hesitate to seek it. There is no shame in asking someone whose bread and butter is training dogs for guidance. Before you can say "Pass the doggy biscuits," your precious pooch's reform school behaviors will be a thing of the past, and you and your dog will be much happier in the long run!

Remedies

Countless over-the-counter remedies, such as pills, herbal concoctions, and flower essences, are available. Although many owners have had good luck with these, you'll want to do your research so that you are not giving your dog anything that might cause an allergic or life-threatening reaction. Acupuncture, aromatherapy, and touch therapy, when coupled with positive training, may also provide some relief. Nutritional therapies and homeopathic remedies, which are frequently recommended by experts, may provide some benefits. Some veterinarians prescribe anti-anxiety medications, which are identical to those taken by humans. Again, you'll want to do your research. Some of these drugs may have significant side effects, so consider using them only as a last resort.

Prevention

How your dog reacts to being left alone will depend on his personality and temperament, how strongly he is bonded to you, and whether or not you've conditioned him to being by himself. Some dogs are okay with being left alone, especially if they have a yummy bone or interactive toy to entertain them. If your dog appears relatively nonchalant about you leaving, count your lucky stars! You probably don't have much to worry about. However, you'll still want to take steps to reinforce his good behavior so that he is comfortable and capable of adapting to other stressors he might encounter later in life. And of course, you'll want to prevent any future problems from developing because prevention is a lot easier than having to retrain a dog who develops issues as he grows and matures.

When you first get a puppy or adult dog, spend as much time with him as possible—training, socializing, building a solid foundation, loving him, kissing him, snuggling with him, and bonding. Part of the bonding process also includes teaching your puppy in a fun, humane, positive, and consistent manner to accept being alone for short periods.

- Start slowly by creating times when your puppy will be alone for a few seconds or minutes, such as when you go to the bathroom, wash dishes, run outside to move the sprinkler, or when he is eating his breakfast or dinner. During these times, your puppy should be crated or safely corralled behind baby gates or in an exercise pen so that he does not get himself into trouble chewing, pottying, and so forth.

- Help your puppy or adult dog adjust to times alone by giving him a yummy chew toy or an interactive food-dispensing toy. While he's busy chewing or playing with his toy, go into another room for a few minutes and then come back. Do this nonchalantly. Don't make a big fuss or announce your departure or arrival. It will also help if your puppy is tired, such as just after a play session or long walk. If he is tired, he will be less likely to care that you aren't right there. (This generally works for puppies or adult dogs who are not overly anxious or who do not have true separation anxiety issues.)

- Exercise your dog physically and mentally with long walks, rides in the car, and retrieve and tug games.

- Obedience train your dog so that he builds confidence and coping skills.

Training will help give your dog the confidence he needs.

- Enrich his environment and alleviate boredom (which can lead to separation anxiety issues) by giving him a job, be it herding, retrieving, agility, swimming, or any other multitude of canine activities.

- Groom him. Kiss him. Talk to him. Love him.

- Finally, provide him with the education he needs to develop into a well-behaved, treasured, and loving companion who can cope with being left alone for short periods.

12

Activities for Your High-Energy Dog

High-drive, high-energy dogs love to learn. In addition to fun tricks, games, and basic obedience commands, they also need a job, be it herding, obedience, hunting, Schutzhund, agility, flyball, jogging, hiking, swimming, skijoring, dock diving, or whatever. In the absence of adequate physical and mental exercise, high-drive and high-energy dogs quickly become bored and destructive.

Any safe and fun interactive sport or activity between you and your dog will help burn off pent-up energy and build a strong human–canine relationship. A high-energy dog's "Send me in, Coach!" attitude makes training and showing these dogs a great deal of fun. Regardless of whether you choose to compete or do canine sports just for fun, don't think that you must limit yourself to your dog's natural instincts. A truly versatile group, high-octane dogs are capable of competing in multiple venues and canine activities. Some dogs do extremely well in a particular sporting event or activity because of their breed, while others excel because of their individual personality and temperament. You may have to try a few different activities, but chances are there is a canine sport—or two!—with your dog's name written all over it.

Let the Games Begin!

Conformation is the cornerstone of the American Kennel Club (AKC), United Kennel Club (UKC), and Kennel Club (KC) shows, but if your dog is not breed quality, don't worry; there are lots of activities you can enter that will stimulate your dog's mind and allow him to strut his agility, athleticism, and intelligence. Through American Kennel Club-sanctioned events alone, you and your dog can participate in agility, Canine Good Citizen, conformation, herding, obedience, rally obedience, and tracking. Only AKC-registered purebred dogs are permitted to compete in AKC-sanctioned events. However, there are plenty of sports and canine activities in which a mixed-breed dog can strut his stuff.

Agility

Agility is one of the fastest-growing sports for dogs and one of the most exciting, fast-paced canine sports for spectators. Similar to equestrian Grand Prix courses, canine agility courses include assorted jumps and hurdles. Dogs demonstrate their agile nature and versatility by maneuvering through a timed obstacle course of jumps, tunnels, A-frames, weave poles, ramps, a teeter-totter, and a pause box.

As an agility handler, the goal is to navigate your dog through successive obstacles while trying to regulate his speed and precision, and of course, trying to stay the heck out of the way of a fast-moving dog. A perfect score in any class is 100, and competitors are faulted if they go over the allotted course time or receive a penalty, such as taking an obstacle out of sequence, missing a contact zone, touching the dog, and so forth.

All-breed agility trials are the most common type of trial, and they are open to all AKC breeds and varieties of dogs. Specialty trials are restricted to dogs of a specific breed or varieties of one breed. Because dogs compete in height divisions, nearly any dog can excel, from Papillons to Giant Schnauzers. However, some breeds are seen more often in the ring, with Border Collies, Australian Shepherds, Labrador Retrievers, Golden Retrievers, Belgian Tervurens, and Belgian Malinois being some of the more

Navigating weave poles is one of the obstacles in agility.

popular medium- to large-sized breeds. Don't discount the small breeds, as Papillons, Pomeranians, and most terriers are popular in the 8-inch (20-cm) height division.

Classes and Titles

AKC trials offer two types of title classes: Standard and Jumpers With Weaves. The Standard class has a pause box and contact obstacles—those yellow contact zones at each end of the obstacle. The dog must place at least one paw in the contact zone—otherwise, he receives a fault. The goal is to encourage safety in training and in running the course. The Jumpers With Weaves class also has a variety of obstacles but does not have contact obstacles or a pause box that slows the competitor's forward momentum. Within each agility class there are different levels of competition:

- **Novice:** For the dog who is just starting in agility. There are 13 to 15 obstacles on the course, and the focus is on completing each obstacle with a minimum of handling skill required.
- **Open:** For the dog who has completed the Novice level. There are 16 to 18 obstacles on the course, and the degree of difficulty increases. The Open class also requires significantly more handling skills than the Novice class.

- **Excellent:** For the dog who has completed the Open level. There are 18 to 20 obstacles, the degree of difficulty increases significantly, and the focus is to provide competitors with the opportunity to demonstrate their superior training, communication, and handling skills.

For the diehard agility competitor, the Master Agility Champion Title (MACH) is the pinnacle of agility competition. It's challenging but not impossible for the high-octane dog and owner team.

The only drawback with agility is that it requires a lot of equipment, which can be pretty expensive to purchase. If you are handy with a hammer and saw, you can build a lot of the equipment yourself.

Getting Started

Most organizations (see sidebar "Top Agility Organizations") have age limits in place to prevent dogs from competing in sanctioned events before they are physically and mentally mature. This is vitally important to owners of high-drive, high-energy dogs because these dogs are confident and willing to do anything and everything that is asked of them. The AKC and KC do not allow dogs to enter an agility ring until they are 15 months old. The United States Dog Agility Association (USDAA) requires dogs to be 18 months old before competing. Dogs vary in their training and growth characteristics

Agility is a great sport for many high-drive dogs because it is physically and mentally challenging.

Top Agility Organizations for Purebred and Mixed-Breed Dogs

American Kennel Club (AKC)
- trials open to AKC-registered purebred dogs only
- dogs must be registered with the AKC or have AKC limited registration, Purebred Alternative Listing or Indefinite Listing Privileges (PAL/ ILP), or be an approved Foundation Stock Service (FSS) breed
- minimum age for competition: 15 months

Australian Shepherd Club of America (ASCA)
- trials open to purebred and mixed-breed dogs
- ASCA tracking number may be required for nonASCA-registered dogs
- minimum age for competition: 18 months

Canine Performance Events (CPE)
- trials open to purebred and mixed-breed dogs
- CPE registration is required
- minimum age for competition: 15 months

Kennel Club (KC)
- trials open to purebreds, nonpedigreed, and nonpurebred dogs
- dogs must be registered with the Kennel Club's Breed Register or Activity Register
- minimum age for competition: 18 months

United Kennel Club (UKC)
- trials open to purebred dogs recognized and registered with the UKC and mixed-breed dogs registered with the UKC
- minimum age for competition: 6 months

United States Dog Agility Association (USDAA)
- trials open to purebred and mixed-breed dogs
- USDAA registration is required
- minimum age for competition: 18 months

depending on their breed and size. Consult your veterinarian and carefully consider at what age it is safe for your puppy to begin training—especially jumping, weave poles, A-frames, and so forth.

To successfully compete in agility, your dog will need basic obedience skills, and it is never too early to begin instilling those behaviors. Many handling skills and behaviors are specific to agility, such as teaching your puppy to take direction from both your right and left side and while running away from you; turning left and right after a jump; targeting for contact training; and so forth. Ideally, you should spend your puppy's formative first year teaching the groundwork. If you have all of that in place at one year of age, the equipment training will go very quickly. That said, it behooves you to train with someone who is experienced in teaching and competing in agility. Otherwise, handling and training problems are likely to develop, and these are often difficult to backtrack and correct.

Canine Freestyle

Canine freestyle is an engaging canine sport that allows you and your dog to kick up your heels, so to speak. In the simplest terms, canine freestyle is a choreographed performance between a dog and handler, set to music, which usually has a catchy melody and a good dance beat. Dog and owner wear matching costumes or accessories that also complement the performance.

Canine freestyle is a choreographed dance sequence.

Don't let the catchy name fool you, though—canine freestyle is more than dogs heeling to music. The sport is patterned after Olympic skating, with dogs and handlers performing twists, turns, leg kicks, pivots, and other cool and creative maneuvers. These maneuvers are entwined with basic obedience commands, such as heeling, *sits*, *downs*, and *fronts*. Many advanced competitors teach their dogs to crawl, back up, wave, bow, sidestep, bounce, roll over, spin, and play dead. Freestyle routines vary dramatically and are creatively choreographed, with an emphasis on the human–canine bond.

Although you see a number of Border Collies and Golden Retrievers participating in freestyle, most high-drive, high-energy dogs do very well in this sport because of their natural athleticism, trainability, and instinct for performing and hamming it up. As with other canine sports, canine freestyle offers a number of divisions and categories to suit a dog and handler's varying levels of experience.

Getting Started

Several organizations promote canine freestyle, with styles varying among the organizations, including the Canine Freestyle Federation, Inc. (CFF), or the World Canine Freestyle Organization, Inc. (WCFO).

Dogs must be six months of age to compete in competitions. As with most canine events, canine freestyle requires a strong bond between dog and owner. Therefore, you will want to start right away instilling basic obedience commands, such as *sit*, *down*, *stand*, and *come*, and teaching fun tricks and moves, such as spins, pivots, jumps, and so forth. This is a lot for dogs to learn, and most are 12 to 18 months old before they can physically and mentally perform many of the maneuvers in a competitive environment. Look for obedience trainers who compete in canine freestyle and can guide you through the rules and regulations as well.

Canine Good Citizen® Program

Canine good citizen promotes good pet manners.

Training and competing with your dog is always fun, but if organized competitions are not your cup of tea, the American Kennel Club's Canine Good Citizen® (CGC) Program might be the perfect alternative. Implemented in 1989, the CGC Program is a public education and certification program designed to promote good dogs and good owners and demonstrate that the dog, as a companion to humans, can be a respected member of the community. The CGC Program encourages owners to develop a positive and worthwhile relationship with their dogs by rewarding responsible dog ownership and good pet manners. It is designed to encourage owners to get involved with and obedience train their dogs.

The program does not involve the formality or precision of competitive obedience, but it does lay the foundation for good pet manners and is often used as a stepping-stone for other canine activities, such as obedience, rally obedience, and agility.

The CGC Program is a noncompetitive, ten-part test that evaluates a dog's behavior in practical situations at home, in public, and in the presence of unfamiliar people and other

In dog shows, dogs are judged against a breed standard.

dogs. The pass or fail test is designed to test a dog's reaction to distractions, friendly strangers, and supervised isolation. Additionally, a dog must sit politely while being petted, walk on a loose leash, walk through a crowd, and respond to basic obedience commands, including *sit*, *down*, *stay*, and *come*. The evaluator also inspects the dog to determine if he is clean and groomed. A dog who successfully completes the test receives a certificate stating that he is a Canine Good Citizen and is entitled to use the initials "CGC" after his name.

Getting Started

CGC tests are offered by local dog-training clubs and are often given in conjunction with dog shows or matches. Humane societies occasionally sponsor CGC tests, too. Both purebred and mixed-breed dogs are eligible to participate. Although there is no age limit, dogs must be old enough to have received their immunizations.

Conformation (Showing)

Conformation shows (dog shows) are the signature events of the competitive dog world. The conformation ring, commonly referred to as the breed ring, provides a forum for breeders and handlers to showcase the best in breeding stock. These animals are evaluated as potential breeding stock and are usually incorporated into future breeding programs in an effort to improve the breed. For this reason, dogs competing in conformation may not be spayed or neutered.

How Dog Shows Work

The best way to understand the conformation ring is to think of it in terms of an elimination process. Each breed recognized by the American Kennel Club competes in a regular class against dogs of the same breed. Doberman Pinschers compete against other Doberman Pinschers, Golden Retrievers compete against other Golden Retrievers, and so on. For the newcomer, it often appears as if the dogs are competing against one another, and in a sense they are. However, the judge is not comparing the quality of one Golden Retriever against the quality of another Golden Retriever. She is evaluating each Golden Retriever against that breed's breed standard and seeing how closely each dog measures up to the ideal dog as outlined in the standard. The regular classes are divided by sex, with the male and female dogs being judged separately. The male dogs are always judged first, and after being examined by the judge, they are placed first through fourth according to how well they measure up to that breed's breed standard in the judge's opinion. After the males have been judged, the females go through the same judging process.

After the regular classes have been judged, the first-place winners of each class are brought back to the ring to compete against one another in the Winners Class. The dog selected is the Winners Dog and is awarded championship points. A Reserve Winners Dog is also chosen but does not receive points unless the Winners Dog, for any reason, is disallowed or disqualified. The same process is then repeated with the female dogs, resulting in a Winners Bitch and Reserve Winners Bitch.

The Winners Dog and Winners Bitch go back into the ring with any Champions entered to compete for the Best of Breed award. If either the Winners Dog or Winners Bitch wins Best of Breed or Best of Winners, they may also win more points. The Best of Breed dog or bitch then goes on to the Group. The Group winners are then judged, with

All-Breed, Specialty, and Group Shows

There are three types of American Kennel Club (AKC) conformation shows.

- All-breed shows are exactly what the name implies. Open to more than 150 breeds and varieties of dogs recognized by the AKC, these shows include the prestigious Westminster Kennel Club and are the types of conformation shows you are most likely to see on television.
- Specialty shows are for one specific breed, such as the Australian Shepherd. Most often, local, regional, or national breed-specific clubs sponsor these shows.
- Group shows are shows that are limited to dogs belonging to one of the seven groups. For example, a herding group show would feature only breeds belonging to the herding group.

Benched Shows

Conformation shows are either benched or unbenched. At a benched show, dogs are grouped together by breed in a central area and are on display during the entire show, except for grooming, exercising, and showing. A benched show is an educational venue that allows spectators to view, admire, and learn about dog breeds in an up-close and controlled surrounding. While a few shows remain benched—including the prestigious Westminster Kennel Club show and the UK's prestigious Crufts Dog Show—the majority of shows today are unbenched. At unbenched shows, dogs may be kept anywhere when not showing, and you are not required to stay on the grounds after you show your dog.

Group placements—first through fourth place—being awarded in each of the seven groups. The first-place Group winners compete for the most coveted and most prestigious award: Best in Show.

Earning a Championship

To attain an AKC Championship title, each dog must win a total of 15 points. Only the Winners Dog and Winners Bitch receive points. The number of points earned at each show is predetermined by a point schedule that varies from region to region.

The number of points awarded at each show depends on the breed, the number of dogs entered in the competition, and the location of the show. For example, points awarded to a Labrador Retriever in New York will differ from the number of points awarded in California. The number of points that can be won at a show is between one and five. Three-, four-, and five-point wins are considered *majors*. One- and two-point wins are considered *minors*. Of the 15 points required for a Championship title, six or more of the points must be majors. The remaining points may be attained in any combination, including major or minor wins, but must be won under different judges than the two major wins. Thus, you need to win points under at least three different judges. A dog can add to the number of points he won in the Winners Class if he also wins Best of Breed, Best of Opposite Sex, or Best of Winners. Once the requirements are met and officially confirmed, a championship certificate is issued for the individual dog.

Getting Started

The AKC and KC require dogs to be six months of age at the time of competition. However, before mailing your entry forms, your dog should be well versed in breed-ring etiquette—meaning that he should accept being examined head to toe, gait on leash (move at a trot), and stack (stand or pose) freely. He should be well socialized with other dogs and people, of sound temperament, physically fit and conditioned, bathed, and groomed according to the breed's standard. Don't be afraid to ask your dog's breeder, or any breeder knowledgeable about your specific breed, for help evaluating his strengths and weaknesses. (All dogs have them!) Many trainers and breeders offer handling classes that can help you and your dog prepare for a successful career in the show ring.

Dog showing is a gratifying and rewarding way to meet new people who share your love of dogs, spend countless hours with your dog, and build a strong human–canine bond. However, dog showing, like most sports, is an art that must be learned and practiced regularly. If you are interested in conformation shows, you will need to learn to groom, condition, and present your dog in the best possible light. You must learn about the structure and movement of your breed. You will need to dress appropriately—not so flashy that you detract from your dog but not so casual that you look like you came straight from mucking stalls. You should get proper shoes that provide comfort and are suitable for running. There are so many things of which you will have no control—the weather, judging schedules, bitches who come into season, schedules that move slower than you'd like—but you can control how you and your dog are represented and presented in the ring.

Regardless of the event, you must have a thorough understanding and comprehension of the rules and regulations governing the show. You should obtain a copy of the rules and regulations for the governing organization, such as the AKC, KC, or UKC, and read them thoroughly. Most importantly, you must learn the art of winning and losing. Showing dogs requires a great deal of patience and objectivity. There will always be differences of opinion, shows you thought you should have won, and shows you won that you never should have. You must learn to be humble in your wins and gracious in your defeats.

The best way to get involved in showing dogs is to attend shows and ask a lot of questions. Most dog people are more than willing to help a newcomer. If possible, join a local dog club, and find a mentor, breeder, or professional handler who is familiar with your breed and who is willing to help you maneuver the ins and outs of dog shows.

Dock Diving

What could be more fun for high-octane water-loving dogs than running full speed ahead and hurling themselves into a giant pool of water? Owners and spectators alike have taken to this high-flying canine sport, and for good reason. It's all about speed and how far or how high a dog can jump, and both experienced and amateur dogs can make a big splash.

Dock diving is a perfect sport for a high-energy, water-loving dog.

The concept of dock diving originated when men working on the docks waged bets with each other to see how far their dogs would jump into the water. Safety is, of course, paramount, and rules and regulations are in place to help prevent injuries. However, compared to some canine events, the rules are pretty simple.

Big Air is basically a long jump competition where dogs run down a 40-foot (12-m) dock, get airborne, and land in a specially constructed pool of water. Owners can throw a "chase" object as long as it is throwable, floatable, and retrievable, such as a bumper, ball, dead fowl trainer, or Frisbee. The official jump distance is measured from the end of the dock to the point at which the base of the dog's tail breaks the water's surface. (The base is where the dog's tail meets the body.) There are five divisions for dogs, from novice (beginner) to super elite (pro). Novice dogs jump under 10 feet (3 m), while elite dogs must jump 25 feet (7.6 m) and above.

Extreme Vertical is a high jump competition for dogs. Dogs jump from the end of the dock and grab a bumper that is suspended over the water before splashing into the water. The height of the jump is measured from the surface of the dock to where the dog grabs the target hanging in the air.

Although water-loving retrievers—Golden Retrievers, Labrador Retrievers, Chesapeake Bay Retrievers, Flat-Coated Retrievers, and Curly Coated Retrievers—tend to dominate the sport, don't discount your nonretriever breed. Some Belgian Tervurens, Belgian Malinois, and even Great Danes are having a great deal of fun competing.

Many high-energy dogs love flying disc competitions.

Getting Started

DockDogs® is the organization that sponsors regional, national, and international Big Air and Extreme Vertical events. Practices and competitions are open to all breeds, including mixed breeds. Dogs must be at least six months old. Dogs eight years and older are eligible to compete in a veteran's class.

Earthdog Tests

Terriers are feisty, energetic dogs whose ancestors were bred to hunt and kill vermin by tracking game above and below ground, barking at their quarry in the den, and then bolting or drawing it for the hunter. Many of today's terriers are pets, and few are regularly hunted to ground in natural hunts. However, noncompetitive AKC earthdog tests offer these "game little dogs" an outlet for their excess energy and instincts while providing owners a standardized gauge to measure their dogs' natural aptitude and trained hunting and working behaviors.

AKC earthdog tests are divided into three levels—Junior, Master, and Senior Earthdog—with each level becoming progressively more difficult.

Getting Started

AKC tests are limited to small terriers and Dachshunds, and dogs must be six months of age to compete. For a list of terriers approved to compete in AKC-sanctioned earthdog tests, visit www.akc.org. The American Working Terrier Association (AWTA) also holds field trials and issues certificates of gameness (CG), hunting certificates (HC), and working certificates (WC).

Flyball

Invented in the late 1970s, flyball is yet another exhilarating choice in the list of entertaining sports you can do with your high-octane dog. It's the perfect "game" for all tennis ball-loving dogs. To say that flyball is fast paced is an understatement. It is a high-octane relay race that showcases your dog's speed and agility. Don't worry—your dog does all of the running in this game. It is team sport rather than an individual competition and an equally thrilling and entertaining spectator sport.

The course consists of four hurdles (small jumps) spaced approximately 10 feet (3 m) apart. Fifteen feet (4.6 m) beyond the last hurdle is a spring-loaded box that contains a tennis ball. Just as in any relay race, the fastest team to successfully complete the game wins. The goal is for each dog to take a turn running the relay by leaping each of the four hurdles and then hitting a pedal or lever with his paw to trigger the box, which shoots a tennis ball up in the air. Once the dog catches the ball in his mouth, he races back over the four hurdles to the finish line, where the next dog is anxiously awaiting his turn.

Catch a Flying Disc!

Most high-drive, high-energy dogs are wonderful athletes with speed, trainability, and a natural desire to retrieve fast-moving objects, which make them the perfect Frisbee or flying disc competitor. No doubt you have seen these high-flying, talented dogs competing on televised programs, such as Animal Planet or ESPN's Great Outdoor Games.

Several organizations sponsor flying disc competitions, including Skyhoundz, Unified Frisbee Dog Operations (UFO), and the International Disc Dog Handlers' Association (IDDHA).

The first team to have all four dogs run without errors wins the heat. If a dog misses a hurdle or fails to retrieve the ball, he must repeat his turn.

While Border Collies tend to dominate the sport, more than a few Parson and Jack Russell Terriers, Australian Shepherds, Shetland Sheepdogs, and Golden Retrievers are giving them a run for their money. Other breeds not normally associated with flyball who are successfully competing include American Cocker Spaniels, American Pit Bull Terriers, German Shorthaired Pointers, and Pembroke Welsh Corgis.

Getting Started

For information, contact the North American Flyball Association (NAFA) or the British Flyball Association (BFA).

Herding

For hundreds of years, herding dogs have been selectively bred for improved herding ability. Many were also developed as farm and ranch dogs, as well as companions and guardians of the family and the family's possessions. A lot of breeds are still utilized in a working environment by farmers and ranches around the country. However, a good number of herding breeds are full-time pets and live in the city and suburbs—far removed from the sights, smells, and activities of livestock or a working environment. The good news is that you and your herding dog—even if he is a city slicker—can still get involved and compete in recreational or competitive herding.

Herding trials give many breeds a chance to use their natural herding instincts.

Sheepdog trials in the United States are fashioned after the British trials and are considered to be the true test of sheepdogs. They are designed to parallel the everyday work of a sheepdog in a working environment, and while each trial is a bit different, they normally consist of an outrun, lift, fetch, drive, pen, and shed. Sheepdog trials welcome any herding breed, but they are more closely associated with Border Collies, who dominate the trials. Other herding breeds can and do occasionally compete in them, but you are more likely to find nonBorder Collie breeds strutting their stuff at Australian Shepherd Club of America–sanctioned (ASCA) stockdog trials or AKC herding trials.

AKC Herding Tests and Trials

As herding dogs become increasingly popular as pets, many owners are dabbling in AKC-sponsored events that are designed to test their dog's herding instinct. These tests and trials are artificial simulations of working pastoral or farm conditions, but they are not always reflective of true farm work. However, they do provide a standardized test by which owners can measure their dogs' inherent herding abilities and training.

The AKC herding program has two major divisions: Herding Tests and Herding Trials.

Herding Tests are noncompetitive tests and are intended for dogs with minimal herding experience. Dogs must, however, show a sustained interest in herding livestock. Within this division, owners can earn two certifications: HT (Herding Tested), which indicates that a dog has shown herding instinct and is under basic control, and a PT (Pre-Trial Tested), which indicates that a dog and handler worked together as a team. Dogs must possess a modest amount of training but are not yet skilled enough to compete in the lowest-level trial. A pre-trial test helps novice handlers develop the skills necessary to compete successfully at trial level.

Herding Trials are competitive trials intended for dogs with substantial training. Dogs must demonstrate the ability to move and control livestock. The titles awarded in each division are: Herding Started (HS), Herding Intermediate (HI), and Herding Advanced (HX).

AKC titles need not be earned in order; however, once your dog earns a qualifying score in an upper class, he can't go back to a lower class on that course/stock.

When a dog has completed his HX title, he is eligible to compete for a Herding Champion Certificate (HC). A Herding Champion dog must have earned an HX and at least 15 championship points in the advanced classes.

Getting Started

Dogs must be nine months of age to compete in AKC-sanctioned herding events. All dogs classified as herding breeds, as well as Rottweilers and Samoyeds who are registered with the AKC, are eligible. Other organizations, such as the ASCA, require dogs to be six months old on the day of competition. The ASCA, in addition to its stock dog program that certifies a number of nonAustralian Shepherd breeds, offers a Ranch Dog program that is open to multiple herding breeds and crossbreds. For additional information, visit www.asca.com.

Despite a dog's innate herding skills, he will also need to know basic obedience commands. At the very least, he should know *down* and *come* and should be under the verbal control of his owner. This is, of course, easier said than done when a hard-driving herding dog is focused on livestock. Ideally, look for obedience trainers who can instill basic commands in a fun and humane manner, as well as for stock dog trainers who are knowledgeable about herding and your breed's herding style. Look for stock dog trainers who use their dogs in a working or competitive environment.

Obedience

Every aspect of dog ownership involves some form of obedience training, yet the obedience ring seldom, if ever, receives the PR and media attention of other canine events. An obedience competition goes well beyond the CGC Program and tests a dog's ability to perform a prescribed set of exercises in a formal environment. Some compare it to ballroom dancing because both dog and owner are extensions of each other—both working in sync. Others compare it to the formal and elegant equine dressage tests with owners achieving a harmonious relationship with their dogs, all the while paying meticulous attention to minute details.

Obedience tests a dog's ability to perform a prescribed set of exercises in a formal environment.

In addition to enriching the bond and relationship between a dog and handler, obedience training is designed to emphasize the usefulness of purebred dogs as the ultimate companion and helpmate to man, and as a means of recognizing that dogs have been trained to behave in the home, in public places, and in the presence of other dogs.

Levels

There are three levels of AKC competitive obedience:

- **The Novice Level:** The dog is required to heel on and off leash at a normal, fast, and slow pace; come when called; stand for a physical examination by the judge; and do a *sit-stay* and a *down-stay* with other dogs. Other than giving commands, handlers are not allowed to talk to their dog during the exercise, nor are they allowed to use toys, treats, or other training aids in the ring. Dogs who complete this level receive a Companion Dog (CD) title.

- **The Open Level:** The Open class is quite a bit more difficult than the Novice class because all exercises are performed off leash. A dog will be required to do similar heelwork exercises as in the Novice class, as well as a retrieve exercise, a drop on recall, a high jump, broad jump, and a *sit-stay* and a *down-stay* with other dogs while the handlers are out of sight. Dogs who complete this level receive a Companion Dog Excellent (CDX) title.

- **The Utility Level:** Utility is the final and most difficult and challenging level of training. The exercises include scent discrimination, directed jumping, retrieving, hand signals, and a moving stand and examination. Completing this level awards your dog a Utility Dog (UD) title.

If you've gotten this far, you are seriously committed to the sport of obedience, and you may decide to work toward a Utility Dog Excellent (UDX) or Obedience Trial Championship title (OTCH)—the crème de la crème of obedience competition. While it is considered the most prestigious title, it has also proven to be the most elusive crown since the title's inception in 1977.

Getting Started

Dogs must be six months old before entering an AKC-sanctioned obedience trial. That said, dogs are not physically or mentally mature enough to compete at six months. Lots and lots of work goes into training an obedience dog to perform specific commands in a stressful, distractive, and competitive environment. Entering a dog before he is physically and mentally ready can do untold damage to his confidence and eagerness to perform in the future. Generally speaking, most dogs are not ready for the novice ring until they are 18 to 24 months of age or older.

The best way to get involved in obedience is to sign up for a dog obedience class or join a local dog obedience club. Look for trainers who teach and compete in obedience competitions because many of the methods for teaching competition obedience differ from basic pet obedience.

Rally Obedience

Rally obedience is the newest AKC event. It is a combination of agility (sort of) and obedience. However, the emphasis is less on speed and precision and more on how well dogs and handlers perform together as a team. It was created with the average dog owner in mind and as a means to help promote a positive human–canine relationship with an emphasis on fun and excitement. It also takes the pressure off of competing while still allowing owners to showcase their dogs' obedience skills.

In rally obedience, the dog and handler move through a course that has been designed by the rally judge. The dog and handler proceed at their own pace through a course of designated stations—between 10 and 20 stations, depending on the level. Each of these stations has a sign providing instructions regarding the skill that is to be performed, such as Halt & Sit; Halt, Sit, & Down; Right Turn; About Right Turn; or while heeling perform a 270-degree left turn.

Unlike traditional obedience competitions, handlers are permitted to talk to their dogs, use praise, clap their hands, pat their legs, or use any verbal means of communication and body language throughout the performance. Handlers may not touch their dogs or make physical corrections.

Getting Started

Any dog who is eligible for AKC registration can enter rally obedience. Dogs must be six months of age before competing. Like regular obedience training, your dog has a lot to learn before he can compete in a rally event, which generally takes 18 to 24 months. That's why you should get started as soon as possible while your puppy is young and receptive to learning. Look for a trainer who trains and competes in rally or obedience competitions.

Schutzhund

The word *Schutzhund* is German and means "protection dog." The sport is perhaps the most misunderstood canine sport, and contrary to public opinion, Schutzhund is not about attack training or teaching a dog to be vicious—quite the opposite. Its purpose is to demonstrate a dog's intelligence and to measure his mental stability, endurance, structural efficiencies, ability to scent, willingness to work, courage, and trainability. Schutzhund has become an increasingly popular sport in the United States and Britain, and many breeds respond well to this type of discipline. The sport requires a great deal of intensive training and control, and dogs must excel in tracking, obedience, and protection work.

Schutzhund is a three-phase, three-level dog sport. The three levels of titles are Schutzhund I, II, and III

Schutzhund means "protection dog."

Before beginning any physically challenging activity with your dog, take him to the veterinarian for a thorough checkup and examination. Joint problems, such as hip and elbow dysplasia, show up in some breeds and should be of paramount importance and concern for owners. They may preclude your dog from some of the more physically demanding activities. (But there are plenty of low-stress activities that are wonderful for puppies and older dogs, too.)

Great care must be taken when jumping young dogs (generally under the age of two years) because too much pressure on developing joints and limbs can injure your puppy and lead to lifelong problems, and no one wants that. Ideally, puppies and young dogs should never jump anything higher than the height of their elbows. Always consult your veterinarian before beginning any jumping activities with your dog.

(also known as VPG 1, VPG 2, and VPG 3). To earn a Schutzhund I, II, or III title, a dog must pass all three test phases—tracking, obedience, and protection work—at the same trial. This is what makes Schutzhund a difficult yet challenging sport.

Before being allowed to compete on the Schutzhund field, a dog must first pass a preliminary temperament test. The test, given by the overseeing judge at the beginning of the trial, is to evaluate the dog's basic character and mental soundness. Additionally, the dog's temperament is observed during the entire course of the trial, and the dog can be failed at any time if the judge feels that he has an unstable temperament.

Getting Started

Only confident dogs with a stable temperament should undertake protection training. Inappropriately aggressive dogs or nervous, shy dogs are totally unsuitable for this type of work. The protection phase is intended to ensure that dogs possess the collection of traits and characteristics required for working guard dogs, as well as the proper temperament for breeding. Control and discipline are paramount in protection training. Look for experienced Schutzhund trainers who understand the essence of Schutzhund training.

For information on trials and titles in the United States, contact the United Schutzhund Clubs of America (USA) or the American Landesverband of the Deutscher Verband der Gebrauchshundsportvereine (LV/DVG). In the United Kingdom, contact the British Schutzhund Association.

German Shepherd Dogs, Rottweilers, and Belgian Malinois are breeds most closely associated with Schutzhund. However, a number of nonSchutzhund breeds have proved their mettle by successfully competing in this fascinating sport.

Skijoring

In its simplest terms, skijoring is being pulled on skis by one or more dogs while in a harness. The great thing about skijoring is that almost any dog (over 30 pounds [13.6 kg]) can participate, which makes it ideal for sporty, athletic, high-octane dogs. With a minimum amount of equipment, an eager dog, and a pair of cross-country skis, you and your dog can burn off excess energy (and calories!), build a strong bond, develop a trusting relationship, and do it all in the great outdoors.

Getting Started

Skijoring is fairly easy to learn, but it does require some basic skills. You should be somewhat proficient on cross-country skis, your dog must be accustomed to wearing a harness, and he must know how to pull, which usually isn't a problem for most high-drive, high-energy dogs. Your dog should know some basic obedience skills as well. Skijoring is fun, exhilarating, and the perfect canine activity if you and your dog enjoy winter sports and the great outdoors.

Swimming

Swimming is the perfect prescription for cooling off, burning calories, and sharing quality time with your dog. Believe it or not, not all dogs will take to the water like, well, a fish to water. You may need to take it slowly and introduce your dog to water playfully and gradually. Never toss your dog in the water—this is neither fair nor humane. Doing so will no doubt frighten him, not to mention possibly injure him and turn him off to swimming and water activities for the rest of his life.

For the reluctant dog, try to find a swimming pool, lake, or shallow pond that has a gentle sloping bank. Kiddie pools or wading pools are also excellent for the hesitant swimmer. Encourage your dog to wade in with you, or throw a floatable toy for him to retrieve, being careful in the beginning to toss it close to the bank of the pond or edge of the pool. If you toss it too far, he will likely find the task of retrieving too daunting.

Swimming burns calories and cools off your dog.

Nothing beats an invigorating walk on the beach with your dog. He may be content to dip his feet in the foam, or he may be more adventurous and take a full-body plunge. It is important to keep him close to shore, regardless of his superior athleticism and swimming capabilities. Riptides and undercurrents are unpredictable, and your dog can quickly wade into trouble.

Equally important, swimming is fairly strenuous—even for physically fit canines—and should be gradually introduced into your dog's regimen. Most high-energy dogs will play until they exhaust themselves, collapsing into a heap of sleep. Therefore, always watch for signs that your dog is getting tired, such as panting, slowing down, or slapping the water with his front feet. A life jacket designed specifically for dogs may provide a safety net for your water-loving companion.

Most dogs love to use their nose, so tracking can be a fun sport to learn.

Tracking

Tracking is a popular sport that tests a dog's ability to recognize and track a human scent over varying terrains and climatic changes. It is designed to showcase a dog's intelligence and extremely high level of scent capability, which should be pretty easy for most hunting, herding, and retrieving breeds.

Teach your dog to track for fun, such as finding his toys or a treat you've hidden in the house or around the yard. Teach him to "Go find the kids" or find a wayward senior dog. Or teach him to track as a sport, where the primary goal is for the dog to follow a scented track and locate an article left at the end of the trail by a tracklayer.

Titles

The AKC offers three tracking titles: Tracking Dog (TD), Tracking Dog Excellent (TDX), and Variable Surface Tracking (VST). If a dog successfully completes all three tracking titles, he earns the prestigious title of Champion Tracker (CT).

For a dog to earn an AKC TD title, he must follow a track laid by a human tracklayer. The track must be 440 to 500 yards (402 to 457 m) with three to five changes of direction, and the track must be aged at least 30 minutes but not more than 2 hours before the dog can begin scenting (following the track).

A TDX title is the next level and slightly more difficult than a TD. It is earned when a dog follows a track that is between 800 and 1,000 yards (731 and 914 m) and between three and five hours old. The TDX track must have five to seven directional changes and must also include the additional challenge of human cross tracks, which as the name implies, is a human track that crosses the primary track. A dog must also locate four articles rather than the one article required for a TD.

TD and TDX tracks are laid through open fields and wilderness areas and include varying terrain conditions, such as gullies, plowed land, woods, and vegetation. However, urban sprawl has severely limited those spaces in some parts of the country. As a result, the VST title was designed to utilize industrial and office parks, college campuses, and so forth. To earn a VST title, dogs must first have a TD title, and they must follow a track that is 600 to 800 yards (548 to 731 m) in length and between three to five hours old. The track may take them down a street; between buildings; across a college campus, asphalt parking lot, or concrete sidewalk; and the like.

Unlike obedience and agility titles, which require a dog and handler to qualify three times, a dog only needs to complete one track successfully to earn each title.

Getting Started

If you and your dog love the great outdoors, tracking might be the sport for you. The best way to get involved in tracking is to contact a local dog obedience club or a national organization, such as the AKC, KC, or Canadian Kennel Club (CKC).

Dogs must be six months of age to enter an AKC tracking event. Chances are, however, that a dog will be 18 months or older before he is physically and mentally capable of successfully competing. But do start teaching your puppy right away in a fun and humane manner how to track. Fun puppy games can teach him how to use his innate scenting skills. He should also know basic obedience commands, such as *sit*, *down*, and *come*. Look for trainers who teach and compete in tracking events.

Walking, Jogging, Hiking

When built correctly and conditioned properly, most breeds can trot for long distances. As a result, high-energy dogs make excellent exercise companions, and no doubt you and your dog will benefit from the cardiovascular workout and companionship. It is worth reiterating that most breeds can and do suffer from heat-induced illnesses. Therefore, if you plan to include your dog in your daily walks or jogs, it is advisable to limit these activities to cooler parts of the day, such as the early morning or evening. Hot sidewalks and roads can burn a dog's feet, causing an enormous amount of pain and discomfort. If the sidewalks and roadways are too hot for your bare feet, chances are they will be too hot for your dog's feet. How far your dog can walk, jog, or hike will depend on his age, physical condition, the terrain covered, and the weather. An extended hike through rough terrain and rocky surfaces may be a piece of cake for the conditioned dog but too

Walking or jogging with your dog is a great way to burn off excess energy.

taxing for some canine couch potatoes. It is always a good idea to carry plenty of fluids for both you and your dog.

Weight Pull

Canine weight-pull competitions are not unlike tractor-pull competitions, except your dog is (thankfully!) doing all of the work. Dogs compete within their individual weight class to see which one can pull the most weight over 16 feet (4.8 m). A dog can pull a weighted sled on snow or a wheeled cart on a natural surface, and the weight is gradually increased until one dog remains.

Dogs wear specially designed harnesses that disperse tension and reduce the possibility of injury. It's worth mentioning that dogs excel at this venue because they love to work—not because they are being forced to pull. As with all canine activities, start slowly and progress at a rate suitable for the mental and physical capabilities of your dog.

While northern breeds, such as Alaskan Malamutes, and strong-bodied breeds, such as American Pit Bull Terriers, American Bulldogs, and Rottweilers, are popular breeds for weight pulls, never underestimate those do-it-all Border Collies. A 34-pound (15.4-kg) Border Collie from LaPine, Oregon, pulled 1,650 pounds (748.4 kg) on snow. Some unlikely candidates in the 20-pound (9-kg) weight class include a Boston Terrier, Parson Russell Terrier, and a West Highland White Terrier.

The specially designed harness for weight-pulling competition prevents injury.

Getting Started

Although the AKC does not sanction weight-pulling competitions, titles are available through a number of dog clubs and organizations, including the UKC and the International Weight Pull Association (IWPA).

Dogs must be two years old to compete in weight pulls sanctioned by the IWPA, but they can begin light training around 18 months of age.

Canine Careers

Your dog's ancestry may be herding, hunting, guarding, or ratting, but that doesn't mean that he can't excel in assistance and therapy work, too.

Assistance Dogs/Service Dogs

The terms *therapy dogs* and *service dogs* are often used interchangeably. However, there is a significant difference. The Americans with Disabilities Act (ADA) uses the term "service dog" to define a dog who has been "individually trained to work or perform tasks for the benefit of a person with a disability." Professionals within the industry often refer to them as assistance dogs rather than service dogs. Therapy dogs provide companionship and emotional support but do not perform tasks, and federal law does not legally define them.

Under the umbrella of assistance dogs, there are four categories: therapy dogs, guide dogs, service dogs, and hearing dogs. Although many breeds do serve quite respectfully as guide dogs for the blind, hearing alert dogs for the hearing impaired, and service dogs for the disabled, organizations tend to employ Golden Retrievers, Labrador Retrievers, and German Shepherd Dogs for those jobs.

Therapy Dogs

Therapy is an important area in which you and your dog can help enhance the humane–canine bond by providing unconditional love, companionship, and emotional support to nursing home, hospital, assisted living, and mental health residents. Owners volunteering with their dogs make regularly scheduled visits and brighten the lives of residents by providing stimulation, companionship, and a vehicle for conversation and interaction.

Only dogs who are well mannered and have a sound temperament should undertake this work. While it is personally satisfying to see how your dog can brighten the lives of residents, 90 percent of the work is done by your dog, and he must have the physical and mental fortitude to cope with strange noises and smells, distractions, and oftentimes erratic behaviors. Additionally, your dog must be willing to accept a considerable amount of attention, petting, and touching from strangers. It helps if your dog has a foundation of basic obedience training or his Canine Good Citizen certificate. Although the AKC does offer Canine Good Citizen certifications, they do not certify therapy dogs. There are independent organizations that certify therapy dogs.

Getting Started

For additional information, contact therapy dog clubs in your area or these national organizations that perform a number of functions, including evaluating, educating, training, registering, and/or certifying therapy dogs:

- Delta Society
- Therapy Dogs Inc.
- Therapy Dogs International (TDI)
- Love on a Leash

Therapy dogs brighten the lives of everyone they meet!

Your high-octane dog wants nothing more than to be with you, but he also wants and needs physical and mental stimulation. As you can see, these canine activities fit the bill. Regardless of which activity (or activities!) you choose, positive interaction with your dog on a daily basis will help build a strong human–canine relationship, and that's what living with a high-drive dog is all about.

Resources

Index

Acknowledgements

Photo Credits

Bibliography

Anderson, Bobbie, *Building Blocks for Performance*. Crawford: Alpine Publications, 2002.

Bishop, Sylvia, *It's Magic. Training Your Dog With Sylvia Bishop*. Canine Press, 1994.

Grandin, Temple, *Animals in Translation: Using the Mysteries of Autism to Decode Animal Behavior*. New York: Scribner, 2004.

Grandin, Temple, *Animals Make Us Human: Creating the Best Life for Animals*. New York: Houghton Mifflin Harcourt, 2009.

Rugaas, Turid, *On Talking Terms With Dogs: Calming Signals*. Dogwise, 2005.

Scott, John Paul and John L. Fuller, *Genetics and the Social Behavior of the Dog*. Chicago: University of Chicago Press, 1998.

Resources
Clubs and Registries

American Kennel Club (AKC)
5580 Centerview Drive
Raleigh, NC 27606
Telephone: (919) 233-9767
Fax: (919) 233-3627
E-mail: info@akc.org
www.akc.org

American Mixed Breed Obedience
Registration (AMBOR)
PO Box 223
Anoka, MN 55303
E-mail: ambor@ambor.us
www.ambor.us

Canadian Kennel Club (CKC)
89 Skyway Avenue, Suite 100
Etobicoke, Ontario M9W 6R4
Telephone: (416) 675-5511
Fax: (416) 675-6506
E-mail: information@ckc.ca
www.ckc.ca

North American Mixed Breed Registry
(NAMBR)
RR#2 - 8649 Appleby Line
Campbellville, Ontario
Canada L0P 1B0
E-mail: info@nambr.ca
www.nambr.ca

The Kennel Club
1 Clarges Street
London
W1J 8AB
Telephone: 0870 606 6750
Fax: 0207 518 1058
www.the-kennel-club.org.uk

United Kennel Club (UKC)
100 E. Kilgore Road
Kalamazoo, MI 49002-5584
Telephone: (269) 343-9020
Fax: (269) 343-7037
E-mail: pbickell@ukcdogs.com
www.ukcdogs.com

Sports and Activities
Agility

Canine Performance Event
www.cpe.com

International Agility Link (IAL)
www.agilityclick.com/~ial

North American Dog Agility Council
(NADAC)
www.nadac.com

United States Dog Agility Association
(USDAA)
www.usdaa.com

Canine Freestyle

Canine Freestyle Federation, Inc.
(CFF)
www.canine-freestyle.org

World Canine Freestyle Organization, Inc. (WCFO)
www.worldcaninefreestyle.org

Dock Diving

DockDogs
www.dockdogs.com

Earthdog

American Working Terrier Association
(AWTA)
www.dirt-dog.com

Flyball

British Flyball Association (BFA)
www.flyball.org.uk

North American Flyball Association
(NAFA)
www.flyball.org

Flying Disc

Skyhoundz
www.skyhoundz.com

International Disc Dog Handlers'
Association (IDDHA)
www.iddha.com

Unified Frisbee Dog Operations
(UFO)
www.ufoworldcup.org

Herding

American Herding Breeds Association
(AHBA)
www.ahba-herding.org

Australian Shepherd Club of America
(ASCA)
www.asca.org

Obedience

American Mixed Breed Obedience
Registry (AMBOR)
www.amborusa.com

Schutzhund

Deutscher Verband der Gebrauchshundsportvereine (DVG)
www.dvgamerica.com

British Schutzhund Association
www.schutzhund.ukk9.com

United Schutzhund Clubs of America
(USA)
www.germanshepherddog.com

Weight Pulling

International Weight Pull Association
(IWPA)
www.iwpa.net

Therapy

Delta Society
www.deltasociety.org

Love on a Leash
www.loveonaleash.org

Therapy Dogs Inc.
www.therapydogs.com

Therapy Dogs International (TDI)
www.tdi-dog.com

Training and Behavior Resources

Animal Behavior Society (ABS)
Certified Applied Animal Behaviorist Directory: www.animalbehavior.org/ABSAppliedBehavior/caab-directory

Association of Pet Dog Trainers
(APDT)
150 Executive Center Drive Box 35
Greenville, SC 29615
Telephone: (800) PET-DOGS
Fax: (864) 331-0767
E-mail: information@apdt.com
www.apdt.com

About the Author

Tracy Libby is an award-winning freelance writer and co-author of *Building Blocks for Performance* (Alpine 2002), *The Australian Shepherd* and *The Border Collie* (Terra-Nova® series) and *Staffordshire Bull Terriers* (Animal Planet® series). Her articles have appeared in numerous publications, including the *AKC Gazette*, *Puppies USA*, *You and Your Dog*, and Dog Fancy's *Popular Dogs* series. She is a member of the Dog Writers Association of America and a recipient of the Ellsworth S. Howell award for distinguished dog writing. She lives in Oregon and has been involved in the sport of dogs for 20 years, exhibiting in conformation, obedience, and agility.

Acknowledgements

My most grateful thanks to my husband, Paul, whose love and encouragement have been the constant in my life, enabling me the opportunity to write and train dogs every day.

To my parents who have loved me through all of my endeavors—canine or otherwise. Thanks for never saying no when I brought home another dog.

Special thanks to Bobbie Anderson and Sylvia Bishop. Without their insight, patience, friendship, and words of wisdom through the years this book would not have been possible. Most of the ideas and training techniques given here are theirs, and I am indebted to them for their kindness and for willingly sharing their expertise.

Thanks are also due to C.A. Sharp for her expertise and never ending thoughts and contributions regarding genetics. And to all of the interesting and remarkable breeders, trainers, handlers, and competitors I have had the good fortune to meet the last twenty-three years. There have been so many that to mention them all would fill an entire book.

Thanks to Heather Russell-Revesz at TFH Publications, Inc., for expertly steering this book through all the necessary stages and with good humor.

Finally, to all my dogs, past and present, who have touched my life and who are the source and inspiration for this book. I have learned so much from them, and I live in gratitude to each and every one.